SOUTHERN LITERARY STUDIES

LOUIS D. RUBIN, JR., EDITOR

THE CAVALIER IN VIRGINIA FICTION

THE
Cavalier
IN VIRGINIA FICTION

RITCHIE DEVON WATSON, JR.

LOUISIANA STATE UNIVERSITY PRESS

BATON ROUGE AND LONDON

Copyright © 1985 by Louisiana State University Press
All rights reserved
Manufactured in the United States of America
Designer: Barbara Werden
Typeface: Linotron Monticello
Typesetter: G&S Typesetters, Inc.
Printer and binder: Edwards Brothers, Inc.

Library of Congress Cataloging in Publication Data

Watson, Ritchie Devon.
The cavalier in Virginia fiction.

(Southern literary studies)
Bibliography: p.
Includes index.
1. American fiction—Virginia—History and criticism.
2. Virginia in literature.   3. Aristocracy in literature.
4. Men in literature.   5. Social ethics in literature.
6. Historical fiction, American—Virginia.   7. Plantation life in literature.   I. Title. II. Series.
PS266.V5W3   1985   831'.009'3520621   84-21306
ISBN 0-8071-1212-7

Publication of this book has been assisted by
a grant from the Andrew W. Mellon Foundation.

CONTENTS

Contents

PREFACE

A S THOSE who have studied the South's history and its culture have often observed, southerners are drawn, not to meticulous historical reconstructions of their past, but to idealistic visions of what that past might have been or ought to have been. The South's writers can legitimately claim a substantial degree of credit for the preference of their fellow southerners for historical romance. They have concocted, generation after generation, the most flattering accounts of their native region, and they have inevitably placed at the center of these idealized fictional landscapes the larger-than-life figure of the southern aristocrat, or Cavalier.

The most interesting and exhaustive analysis of the rise of the Cavalier character ideal in the United States is William R. Taylor's *Cavalier and Yankee: The Old South and American National Character* (1961). As the title indicates, however, Taylor's study focuses on the development of both the Cavalier figure and its opposing character type, the Yankee. In addition, the book concentrates exclusively on the decades which precede the Civil War. Taylor's concern is to examine the ways in which the development of Cavalier and Yankee stereotypes contributed to sectional tensions which ultimately could be resolved only by civil war. His interest, in his own words, is "primarily with the dynamics of the legends rather than with their literary origins or the degree of their historical authenticity."[1] Room exists for a broader examination of the Cavalier ideal, and further questions about the Cavalier tradition remain to be addressed. How far does the legendary Cavalier of southern literature depart from the lives of the real men who inspired the ideal in America? What are the literary origins of this southern aristocratic figure? How has the Cavalier myth fared since the Civil War in a nation historically devoted to the ideals of democratic egalitarianism, and how

---

1. William R. Taylor, *Cavalier and Yankee: The Old South and American National Character* (New York, 1961), 21.

has the South reconciled its visions of a Cavalier-dominated past with the social, political, and economic exigencies of the present?

A convenient and contained way of examining a subject as broad as the growth of the Cavalier ideal in southern literature is to focus on the development of the aristocratic tradition in a single southern state, a microcosm which epitomizes the evolution of the concept in the entire region. Of all southern states Virginia is most naturally adapted to the role of microcosm. For over a span of nearly two centuries the most potent and evocative projection of the mythical southern aristocrat has been the Virginia Cavalier.

There are clear reasons for the special emotive power of the Virginia Cavalier. The Cavalier ideal was first nurtured and expressed in America in the colony of Virginia, and the aristocratic ethos was more firmly established in the Old Dominion at the time of the Revolution than in any other colony. Virginia was the first of the southern states to develop a distinct literary tradition. Indeed, it would not be a great exaggeration to claim that until after the Civil War Virginia was the *only* southern state to develop one. As Henry Nash Smith has observed, southern writers of the antebellum period held up the Cavalier ideal as a justification for the South's peculiar institution of slavery, but no southern writer created Cavaliers more colorfully than did the Virginia school of romantic historians, men such as John Pendleton Kennedy, William Alexander Caruthers, and John Esten Cooke. The Old Dominion thus furnished the region's original literary plantations. Those of the newer southern states were, in the words of Smith, "depicted as duplicates" of the Virginia model.[2]

Even after the Civil War, Virginia might be fairly described as occupying the dominant position in southern regional literature, and writers such as Thomas Nelson Page and Mary Johnston, through their presentations of the Virginia Cavalier, helped to rehabilitate the southern gentleman in northern eyes. Not until the 1920s with the flowering of the southern literary renascence, which Virginians James

---

2. Henry Nash Smith, "The South and the Myth of the Garden," in Patrick Gerster and Nicholas Cords (eds.), *Myth and Southern History* (Chicago, 1974), 128.

Branch Cabell and Ellen Glasgow had anticipated, did the Old Dominion surrender its role as the major literary spokesman for the South, a distinction it had held for roughly 120 years. This long period of dominance explains why, as late as 1935, Edwin Mims could write to Ellen Glasgow that with the publication of *Vein of Iron* she had completed "the Virginia—and therefore Southern—Saga."[3]

Virginia thus gave birth to and nourished the Cavalier ideal, an ideal which eventually took root in the hearts and minds of nearly all southerners. Southerners in turn have long acknowledged their indebtedness to Virginia as the source of their most precious myth. In the words of Clarence Cason, the Old Dominion "is the concentrated quintessence of what is to be cherished and revered in the life of the Southern squirearchy. It is the Castile and Aragon of American Bourbonism."[4]

Virginia serves as an ideal microcosm not only because it has been the primary source of the myth of southern aristocracy and the inspiration for the South's romantic writers but also because its own novelists have formed such a remarkably tight-knit group. Perhaps no other state in the Union has developed a stronger feeling of social and cultural entity, and this feeling has produced a correspondent bonding among the state's writers. Jay B. Hubbell has noted that until the beginning of this century the Old Dominion "felt so strongly her entity as a state—a nation, one might almost say—that it has been possible to study her literature without paying much attention to the literature of the rest of the country."[5] Even in the twentieth century, writers as diverse as Ellen Glasgow and William Styron continue to share attitudes and concerns which are uniquely Virginian, and they continue to utilize the Cavalier figure in their fiction, though they work with the figure in the analytical fashion of the twentieth century rather than in the rhetorical fashion of their nineteenth-century predecessors.

Before proceeding to an analysis of the way Virginia's writers from

3. Quoted in Michael O'Brien, *The Idea of the American South* (Baltimore, 1979), 231.

4. Clarence E. Cason, "Middle Class and Bourbon," in W. T. Couch (ed.), *Culture in the South* (Chapel Hill, 1935), 491.

5. Jay Broadus Hubbell, *Virginia Life in Fiction* (Dallas, 1922), 40.

the Federal to the contemporary period have used the Cavalier concept in their fiction, I have attempted to provide a context for understanding the evolution of the mythical figure. I have tried to establish the primary tenets of the code of the gentleman on which the aristocratic ideal in Virginia was based and to investigate the extent to which the Cavalier ideal has spread beyond Virginia and insinuated itself into the fiction of both southern and northern writers since the beginning of our nation's literature, a phenomenon which attests to the remarkable hardiness of a myth which continues to survive in a culture that ostensibly repudiates its most basic values. Next I have sought to provide a historical context within which the Cavalier ideal may better be understood, to determine through reference to contemporary historical scholarship exactly what sort of men the early Virginia planters were. I have attempted to measure with some degree of accuracy the discrepancy between the Virginia planters who lived in the colonial period and the fictional Virginia Cavaliers whose way of life was celebrated by the Old Dominion's writers during the nineteenth century.

If the fiction that will be examined in subsequent chapters were of only local interest, there would be little use in reading or writing about it. But as I hope these introductory pages have suggested, Virginia's novelists offer important insights both to southerners and to all Americans. The curious, even preposterous manner in which her nineteenth-century writers interpret and vindicate their state through the Cavalier figure tells us much about the defensive and uncritical attitude that nearly all southerners have adopted on occasion toward their region, and the more realistic and introspective approaches of her modern writers toward the Cavalier concept reflect the attempts of many southerners in this century to come to more suitable terms with a past that now seems as dark, bloody, and tragic as it is glorious. The Virginia novelists offer insights to all Americans as well, for the Cavalier figure is as much a part of our national mythology as are Paul Bunyan and Natty Bumppo. Like these figures, he offers us a key—a key which can help us better understand our collective aspirations as well as our collective fears and neuroses.

THE CAVALIER IN VIRGINIA FICTION

ONE

The Cavalier Myth

THE PERSISTENCE OF THE LEGEND

ONE is likely to feel a sense of incongruity about "The Virginians Are Coming Again," for its creator, Vachel Lindsay, a self-proclaimed tramp and poetic vagabond, is not ordinarily associated with aristocratic attitudes. Yet in this poem the chanter of frontier democracy and Johnny Appleseed celebrates an unlikely subject, the aristocratic Virginia Cavalier.

> Babbitt, your tribe is passing away.
> This is the end of your infamous day.
> The Virginians are coming again.
>
> With your neat little safety-vault boxes,
> With your faces like geese and foxes,
> You
> Short-legged, short-armed, short-minded men,
> Your short-sighted days are over—

Your habits of strutting through clover,
Your movie-thugs killing off souls and dreams
Your magazines drying up healing streams,
Your newspapers blasting truth and splendor.
Your shysters ruining progress and glory.
Babbitt, your story is passing away—
The Virginians are coming again.

All set for victory, calling the raid,
I see them, the next generation,
Gentlemen, hard-riding, long-legged men,
With horse-whip, dog-whip, gauntlet and braid,
Mutineers, musketeers,
In command
Unafraid:
Great-grandsons of tidewater, and the bark cabins,
Bards of the Blue-ridge, in buckskin and boots,
Up from the proudest war-path we have known
The Virginians are coming again.[1]

Of course Lindsay has given his subject a twist; these are not ghosts of the past but a new generation of Cavaliers. This new generation, however, is endowed with the perceived virtues of its ancestors—heroism, unselfishness, and nobility of character. And it will use these virtues to repudiate the encroaching commercial values of a modern "Babbitt" culture. Lindsay's poem is a particularly appropriate introduction to a study of the Cavalier figure in Virginia fiction because it suggests this figure's enduring strength and his tenacious hold on the imaginations of generations of Americans, a hold that has transcended sectional differences.

There is general agreement among contemporary historians and literary critics that the Cavalier, as he is projected in American poetry and fiction and as he is defined by popular culture, is more an embodiment

---

1. Vachel Lindsay, "The Virginians Are Coming Again," in Harriet Monroe and Alice Corbin (eds.), *The New Poetry* (2nd ed.; New York, 1932), 310–11.

of certain ideals of character and conduct than an objective historical representative of an actual class of men. Like most mythical figures, however, his origin is rooted in history. There existed in Virginia during the seventeenth and eighteenth centuries a class of wealthy planters who provided the broad outlines for the Cavalier myth. Many of these planters were in fact gentlemen of distinction, and they aspired to follow a distinctive code of conduct.

As Louis Wright has explained, the seventeenth-century Virginian's ambition was to re-create in the new colony the country life of the English gentry as well as its conception of gentility and refinement.[2] The code of the New World Virginia gentleman was thus copied from an Old World Elizabethan pattern. Wright also points out that the precise definition of *gentleman* is difficult to establish and that the qualities which went into the making of such a man necessarily shifted from generation to generation. Nevertheless, from the sixteenth to the eighteenth century a loosely defined and flexible social code evolved in England which strongly influenced the social attitudes of the planter class in Virginia. Wright expresses the influence of the English concept of the gentleman this way:

> As social-climbing citizens at home sought to imitate the landed gentry, so Virginia colonists who had the opportunity of acquiring land and accumulating wealth attempted to duplicate the manner of life led by that most envied of mortals at home, the proud and powerful country squire. . . . While they developed an independence of spirit and became Virginians instead of Englishmen in a distant colony, they had a dream of being Virginians like the fine gentlemen of the older civilization. That dream helped to shape the thinking and the cultural ideals of the Virginia ruling class throughout the seventeenth and eighteenth centuries.[3]

2. Louis B. Wright, *The First Gentlemen of Virginia: Intellectual Qualities of the Early Colonial Ruling Class* (San Marino, Calif., 1940), 1–37.

3. *Ibid.*, 37. Wright's conclusions echo those of Philip Alexander Bruce, who, in *Social Life of Virginia in the Seventeenth Century* (1907; rpr. New York, 1964), detailed the close resemblances between English and Virginia social life.

The code's first commandment, as Wright observes, was that a gentleman recognize the inherent inequality of man—that he implicitly accept the idea that certain men were born to lead and that others, the vast majority, were born to follow and serve. The doctrine of aristocracy by birth was of necessity flexible in the developing frontier colony, and certainly not all Virginians accepted the notion uncritically. Yet its widespread acceptance among wealthier planter families explains the tendency towards rigidity of social structure which outsiders, particularly visitors from the Middle Atlantic and New England colonies, frequently criticized.

Assured of his own superiority, a gentleman was expected at all times to be graceful and dignified in his deportment, as well as courteous and thoughtful toward all men, regardless of their social status. In designing a moral code to complement their dignified bearing, Virginia gentlemen, like their English counterparts, followed the advice of Sir Thomas Elyot's *The Book Named the Governor* (1531).[4] They sought to attain qualities of fortitude, temperance, prudence, justice, liberality, and courtesy. Not surprisingly, these Aristotelian virtues tended to supersede strict adherence to the Ten Commandments. Sins of the flesh, for example, might be forgiven if they were not blatant, excessive, or destructive of a gentleman's essential integrity.

Observers of manners and conduct agreed that learning was an essential quality for a gentleman. However, the well-educated social leader scorned crabbed pedantry that delved into esoteric subject matter. He believed the best and most useful knowledge was broad rather than deep. Learning was an adornment worn lightly and gracefully, which—along with dancing, fencing, hunting, riding, and occasionally the playing of a musical instrument—combined to produce a complete and smoothly functioning social creature.

Writers of courtesy books were rather vague about the source of a gentleman's honor. Honor was variously identified with virtue and with

4. In addition to Elyot's work, other important treatises on manners and conduct read both in England and in Virginia during the seventeenth and eighteenth centuries include Henry Peacham's *Compleat Gentleman* (1622) and Richard Brathwaite's *The English Gentleman* (1630).

reputation. But though there was disagreement concerning its precise definition, there was widespread agreement that the gentleman's primary purpose in following his code was to possess and maintain a personal honor which commanded the respect of all. Gentlemen in the seventeenth and eighteenth centuries thus placed primary importance on the preservation of individual honor. Unlike their nineteenth-century successors, however, they did not approve of dueling as an effective means of defending it. The reason for this widespread rejection of dueling is not difficult to discern. The development of the gentlemanly ideal paralleled the rise of the gentry in England and the coming of the Renaissance. The model for this new social concept was certainly not the medieval knight, and the main survivors of the earlier chivalric tradition, the duel and the romance, were rejected by nearly all writers of courtesy books. As Edwin Cady has observed, "The concept of the gentleman left the chivalric influence buried in its past until, glamorized and sentimentalized, it was resurrected by the literary medievalists of the nineteenth century, Scott, Tennyson, and Lanier."[5]

These, then, were some of the ingredients which combined to produce an ideal gentleman. Doubtless, the planters of seventeenth- and eighteenth-century Virginia were at least partially aware of the difference between the ideal conduct prescribed by the code of the gentleman and the reality of their own lives. Yet as the years passed, ideal and reality became more and more blurred. By 1834 the romantic Virginia novelist William Caruthers described eighteenth-century Virginians, not as they had actually lived and acted, but as he imagined their code had exhorted them to live and act. His Virginians became, in short, Cavaliers—a "class of gay birds of aristocratic plumage . . . a generous, fox-hunting, wine-drinking, duelling and reckless race of men, which gives so distinct a character to Virginians wherever they may be found."[6] Caruthers' novels, combined with those of John Pendleton Kennedy

5. Edwin Harrison Cady, *The Gentleman in America: A Literary Study in American Culture* (Syracuse, 1949), 4.

6. William Alexander Caruthers, *The Cavaliers of Virginia; or, The Recluse of Jamestown: An Historical Romance of the Old Dominion* (1834; rpr. Ridgewood, N.J., 1968), I, 4.

and John Esten Cooke, helped to inaugurate the first productive period of southern fiction, which extended from about 1832 to the mid-fifties and which first fully delineated the Cavalier ideal.

It is interesting to note that the plantation system upon which ante-bellum Virginia novelists based their splendid visions was by no means indigenous to the entire colony of Virginia. Jean Gottmann in his study of the Old Dominion describes important topographic and climatic dif-ferences between the hills and valleys west of the Blue Ridge and the gently rolling hills and tidal flatlands of Piedmont and Tidewater Vir-ginia. It is indeed the Blue Ridge which marked the western limits of what Carl Bridenbaugh terms the Chesapeake society, a regional culture dominated in the seventeenth and eighteenth centuries by the planta-tion system devoted to the one-crop tobacco economy and dependent on slave labor. The Chesapeake society developed from the head of the Great Bay in the north, west to the junction of the Monocacy and Poto-mac Rivers in Maryland, south and slightly east of the Blue Ridge through Culpeper and Orange courthouses and Charlottesville across the James to the Roanoke River, and thence east along the Roanoke to the northern shores of the Albemarle Sound in North Carolina.[7]

In spite of relatively wide differences in soil and climate, this region was marked by basic demographic, economic, and cultural similarities. Unlike the Shenandoah Valley and the mountainous regions to the west, which were settled mainly by pioneers of Scotch-Irish and Ger-man stock, Tidewater and Piedmont Virginia was strongly English in character. Uniformly hot summer temperatures allowed the extensive cultivation of tobacco by slave labor. Though the majority of farms in the Chesapeake region were of medium or small size, the large planta-tion was the dominant economic and cultural institution. Pierced by tidal rivers such as the Potomac, the Rappahannock, the York, and the James, the Chesapeake region was accessible to trading ships far inland to the fall line. In contrast to the inhabitants of western Virginia, who concerned themselves with local, internal problems, Chesapeake so-

---

7. Jean Gottmann, *Virginia at Mid-century* (New York, 1955); Carl Bridenbaugh, *Myths and Realities: Societies of the Colonial South* (Baton Rouge, 1952), 1–5.

ciety maintained a brisk trade and strong cultural ties with the mother country. It readily assumed and embraced the ideal of the rural English squirearchy.[8]

In a rather narrowly circumscribed region centering in Tidewater and Piedmont Virginia a society thus developed which was patterned loosely on the English rural model. Here geography and climate combined to produce a region of large manorial estates owned by prominent and wealthy families and operated by large numbers of slaves or indentured servants. In this part of Virginia there was at least a partial correspondence between the structure of Tidewater society and the social code of the English gentleman that was superimposed upon it. With the possible exception of coastal South Carolina and Georgia, no other sections of the South developed a social organization in which either an English gentleman or a Virginia Cavalier would have felt remotely at home. Yet Wilbur J. Cash has astutely observed that the South—that vast territory that extends below the Mason-Dixon Line from the Atlantic seaboard to the Texas plains—arbitrarily appropriated the Virginia Cavalier and renamed him southern aristocrat.[9] During the early nineteenth century the aristocratic ideal was transplanted and nurtured in the remotest parts of Dixie. Thus Henry Stanley, the famous African explorer, was surprised to discover the antebellum farmers of the Arkansas plains and even store clerks strictly upholding the aristocratic code of personal honor. He noted, for example, that a Jew of German extraction, who was the proprietor of a country store in the village of Cypress Bend, owned a fine pair of dueling pistols.[10]

The frontier South embraced the aristocratic ideal for many complex reasons, but Richard Gray isolates one of the most significant. After the Revolution, he notes, the southern states, for primarily economic reasons, slowly lost the cosmopolitan, optimistic outlook which had produced such a large number of revolutionary leaders, especially from Virginia and South Carolina. By the nineteenth century the South

8. Bridenbaugh, *Myths and Realities*, 1–5.
9. Wilbur Joseph Cash, *The Mind of the South* (New York, 1941), 3–5.
10. Quoted in Clement Eaton, *The Growth of Southern Civilization, 1790–1860* (New York, 1961), 2.

had begun to view the North as the enemy and had begun especially to fear its rapidly expanding industrial power. In reaction to this increasing power, the South championed the agrarian ideal and Jefferson's noble yeoman farmer. Yet in order to present a unified front to the North, southerners refused to attack or reject the aristocratic plantation ideal which ran so obviously counter to the yeoman ideal. Instead, they embraced both the yeoman and the planter, blinding themselves to the antinomic relation between the two types.[11] Responding after 1800 to increasingly bitter attacks from the North on Dixie's social institutions, southerners from all areas, from James River plantations to Arkansas shanties, used the aristocratic ideal more and more frequently to justify their way of life, no matter how removed this ideal was from their day-to-day existence.

But though the Virginia Cavalier was transmogrified by the exigencies of history into the southern Cavalier, he remains today the original impression, compared with whom all others are paler copies. To paraphrase Ellen Glasgow, he stands on the summit of the southern Olympus and occupies an especially honored spot in the southern pantheon. William Faulkner acknowledged the veneration with which inhabitants of the Deep South still view the Virginian. "Compared to you," he told faculty and students of the University of Virginia, "my country— Mississippi, Alabama, Arkansas—is still frontier. Yet even in our wilderness we look back to that motherstock. . . . There is no family in our wilderness but has that old aunt or grandmother to tell the children as soon as they can hear and understand: your blood is Virginia blood too . . . so that Virginia is a living place to that child long before he ever hears (or cares) about New York or, for that matter, America." A more humorous instance of the southerner's inclination to venerate his Virginia origins is given by Guy Friddell. When General Douglas MacArthur was described in an introduction as having been born in Arkansas, he quickly inserted this qualification: "It was intended that I be born in Virginia, my mother's home." MacArthur seems to have

11. Richard L. Gray, *The Literature of Memory: Modern Writers of the American South* (Baltimore, 1977), 13–15.

thereby created a new category of Virginian—Virginian by intention.[12]

The migration of the Cavalier ideal far beyond the boundaries of the Chesapeake society is no more astonishing than the persistent appeal of this mythical figure in the twentieth century. Long after the passing away of the plantation system that gave him birth, Virginians continue to venerate their larger-than-life ancestor and the exalted standards that he embodied. Thomas Lomax Hunter's popular "Columns from the Cavalier," published during the 1930s and 1940s in the Richmond *Times-Dispatch*, testify to the continued appeal of the Cavalier in the Old Dominion. Hunter assumes in his columns the stance of a Virginia aristocrat, a preserver and defender of the old social verities. He rejects Jeffersonian political philosophy and extolls the merits of royalty in preserving social order and continuity. "There are times," the crusty Anglophile admits, "when I seriously believe Yorktown was our worst defeat." He frequently expresses a disdain for commercial pursuits and "money changing" and scorns "men who sit behind grilled ironwork and calculate discounts and interests, and look out bleakly at me from amid their frozen assets."[13] Hunter's eighteenth-century Cavalier ancestor might well have had difficulty understanding this prejudice against commerce, for modern historians have demonstrated again and again the business acumen and the sharp eye for profits that characterized the most successful planter aristocrats, such as King Carter and William Byrd. Indeed, the modern Cavalier's rejection of interest and profits shows how far the legendary Virginia aristocrat has become divorced from the historical figure.

Lomax Hunter's essays are wistful eulogies of the past—of country roads, covered bridges, gristmills, and winter ice-cutting. It is interesting to observe that Hunter's golden age of Cavalier grace and felicity is not the colonial Virginia of Byrd and Carter but the bucolic, turn-of-the-century Virginia of his boyhood. This twentieth-century essayist exhibits the Virginia writer's irresistible inclination to view his native

12. Frederick L. Gwynn and Joseph L. Blotner (eds.), *Faulkner in the University: Class Conferences at the University of Virginia, 1957–1958* (Charlottesville, 1959), 212; Guy Friddell, *What Is It About Virginia?* (Richmond, 1966), 2.

13. Thomas Lomax Hunter, *Columns from the Cavalier* (Richmond, 1935), 57, 119.

state's recent past as inevitably superior to its present, an inclination that will be amply demonstrated in subsequent chapters. "It is romance and the memory of romance," Hunter reflects nostalgically, "which makes life livable." [14]

Clearly, the myth of the Cavalier functions like countless other myths created in various periods of history by various people. All myths, as Mark Schorer has noted, "are the instruments by which we continually struggle to make our experience intelligible to ourselves." [15] The myth of the Cavalier has provided a controlling image for both Virginians and other southerners, an organizing set of values around which life may be structured. The Cavalier provides a sort of philosophical justification for life as it was and as it is today in the South. It is not surprising that in a century of rapid and confusing change in which all established social norms are challenged, men like Lomax Hunter should cling tenaciously to the legends and the mythical figures who provide coherence and make experience intelligible.

Yet the South is not alone in venerating the Cavalier ideal. There is ample evidence in American fiction and in popular culture to support the argument that the Cavalier has exerted and continues to exert a strong appeal not merely over Virginians and southerners but over all Americans. Publication of novels presenting a romanticized picture of Virginia's past was and is made possible by a demand for these books in the northern book market. The southern reading public alone has never been able to sustain its native writers, romantic or realistic. On the other hand, as F. P. Gaines has observed and Gunnar Myrdal has confirmed, many northerners have found the myth of the Old South appealing, even though it does not directly correspond to or explain the history and the realities of northern society. One of the reasons for this appeal is that the North, having thoroughly rejected aristocratic ideals in the development of its culture, retains a largely unexpressed fascination with feudalism and social gradations. It has always been drawn to

14. *Ibid.*, 98.
15. Mark Schorer, "The Necessity of Myth," in Henry A. Murray (ed.), *Myth and Mythmaking* (New York, 1960), 355.

the imaginative and romantic side of feudal life which Europe possesses and which America, with the exception of the South of legend, lacks.[16]

William R. Taylor's seminal work links this national nostalgia for the antebellum south with "our collective anxieties about the kind of civilization we have created, and with our reservations concerning the kind of social conformity which, it appears, it has been our destiny to exemplify before the world."[17] It may very well be true, as Taylor suggests, that as this country has moved further away from its frontier heritage toward a dehumanized society of Levittowns and South Bronxes, it has hung on with determination to the arcadian vision of the aristocratic Old South. A romanticized past is thus used to divert us from the seemingly insoluble problems of the present.

Occasionally this American love of aristocracy is frankly expressed, as in Henry Sedgwick's *In Praise of Gentlemen*. Writing during the 1930s in the midst of New Deal progressivism, Sedgwick—a Harvard-educated lawyer, essayist, historian, and biographer—laments the passing of the gentleman. Sedgwick defines a gentleman as a man born to certain social advantages, strong and brave, "truthful, loyal, modest, romantically devoted to one woman, cultivated without pedantry, joyful in the good things of life, magnanimous, generous, not indifferent to dress, and very solicitous for courtesy." He deplores in bewilderment the "rising flood of democracy, political, economic, social, and its great sweep towards an equality of human conditions."[18] Certainly these sentiments are not what one would consider characteristically American. Yet Sedgwick is an American, and the distrust with which he views the present has been shared in this century by a number of Americans who have turned to their vision of the past for solace and relief.

The years following the Great Depression have marked the consolidation of the liberal democracy Sedgwick so deplored—from social security, welfare, and unemployment compensation to the establishment

16. Francis Pendleton Gaines, *The Southern Plantation: A Study in the Development and the Accuracy of a Tradition* (New York, 1924), 2–4; Gunnar Myrdal, *An American Dilemma: The Negro Problem and Modern Democracy* (New York, 1962), 1376.

17. Taylor, *Cavalier and Yankee*, 341.

18. Henry Dwight Sedgwick, *In Praise of Gentlemen* (Boston, 1935), viii, 191.

of multifarious federal regulatory agencies. Yet, interestingly, the hostility toward the technical triumphs of American culture and the suspicion of the ideals of progress and equality have not disappeared. Indeed, conservative critiques of contemporary social values have become, if anything, more acute. One of the more interesting expressions of contemporary conservative thought is the collection of essays, *Did You Ever See a Dream Walking?* In his contributory essay, the editor William F. Buckley laments that America has not acquired the *gravitas* of a great power. Our country has not shown, he observes, "a proper veneration for the values of the Old World, to compare, for instance, with the Roman's humility before the civilization of Greece." In another essay Michael Oakeshott concludes that, in spite of the democratic myth of the nobility of mass man, "he remains an unmistakably derivative character, an emanation of the pursuit of individuality, helpless, parasitic and able to survive only in opposition to individuality." Eric Voegelin reaches perhaps the most negative judgment of the nature of modernism. "The death of the spirit," he believes, "is the price of progress." [19]

A significant degree of doubt and anxiety thus attends the triumphs of democratic egalitarianism in America today, but as William R. Taylor has demonstrated, reservations about the dominant thrust of American culture began to be voiced over 150 years ago, soon after the founding of the Republic. If the stereotyped character of the Yankee came to represent in a positive way that which was quintessentially American, it also suggested the darker aspects of the national character—its greed and materialism. Thus, almost from the beginning of America's literary history many northern writers as well as their southern counterparts admired the grasping Yankee's opposite—the chivalrous and noble Cavalier. James Fenimore Cooper and James Kirke Paulding were two of the most important northern writers of the antebellum period to treat both Virginia aristocrats and southern gentlemen sympathetically. In

19. William F. Buckley, "Introduction: Did You Ever See a Dream Walking?" Michael Oakeshott, "The Masses in Representative Democracy," Eric Voegelin, "Gnosticism: The Nature of Modernity," all in Buckley (ed.), *Did You Ever See a Dream Walking? American Conservative Thought in the Twentieth Century* (Indianapolis, 1970), xxxv, 122, 460.

Notions of the Americans Cooper opined "that in proportion to the population, there are more men who belong to what is termed the class of gentlemen, in the old southern States of America than in any other country of the world."[20]

Although northern approval of the Cavalier character type waned sharply during the years of heated sectional passions immediately before and after the Civil War, southern writers soon set about rehabilitating this representative of a now-destroyed culture. "By the 1880's," Stanley Elkins has observed, "the old time abolitionist who had wept over *Uncle Tom's Cabin* in his youth sat shedding furtive tears over 'Marse Chan.'" As in the antebellum period, southern writers were abetted in their vindication of the planter-aristocrat. Herman Melville's philosophical poem *Clarel*, Henry Adams' *Democracy*, and Henry James's *The Bostonians* all used the Cavalier—in Adams' novel he was a Virginia Cavalier—as a standard of integrity by which the shortcomings of American society in the Gilded Age might be measured.[21]

Romantic and sympathetic portraits of southern gentlemen in general and of Virginia gentlemen in particular continue to appear regularly in twentieth-century American literature, indicating that the passage of time and the domination of a realistic critical spirit have not substantially weakened the evocative appeal of the fictional stereotype. From the South, Stark Young's *So Red the Rose* and Margaret Mitchell's enormously popular *Gone with the Wind* have helped to keep the plantation legend alive. Even the South's greatest novelist, William Faulkner, has upon occasion exploited the heroic and romantic potential of the Cavalier figure. The code of the Cavalier is nowhere given more colorful treatment than in the opening sections of Faulkner's *The Unvanquished*, one of two novels which deals with the aristocratic Sartoris family.

20. For a detailed discussion of Cooper's and Paulding's use of Yankee and Cavalier types, see Taylor, *Cavalier and Yankee*, 95–109, 225–59. Cooper is quoted p. 97.

21. Stanley M. Elkins, *Slavery: A Problem in American Institutional and Intellectual Life* (Chicago, 1959), 5. C. Vann Woodward's *The Burden of Southern History* (Baton Rouge, 1960), 109–40, contains an extended analysis of Melville's, Adams', and James's aristocratic characters.

In *The Unvanquished* both the virtues and the tragic flaws of the southern planter aristocracy are embodied in the character of John Sartoris. Though in the later sections of the novel Faulkner shows his readers the single-minded ambition, the moral abstraction, and the cruelty which eventually destroy Sartoris, in the early Civil War sections a nimbus of courage, gallantry, and honor envelops his character. Sartoris captures a company of Yankees virtually single-handedly and makes a hairbreadth escape from pursuing Union troops by jumping his horse bareback through the lattice half doors of his barn, a Hollywood exit worthy of Douglas Fairbanks or of Errol Flynn. The conflicting perceptions of John Sartoris, seen through the increasingly mature eyes of his son, Bayard, suggest Faulkner's own ambivalence toward the Cavalier myth of his ancestors. Faulkner's imagination, like Bayard's, warms to the memory of impossibly heroic deeds performed by a noble though doomed race of men. Even though he ultimately insists on confronting the profound moral limitations of John Sartoris' aristocratic code, Faulkner, like Bayard, seems also to understand that the heroic vision of the past which is intertwined with that code can never be completely repudiated or escaped. At the end of the novel Bayard realizes that his father and his father's "dream," or code, will always be with him. For the code is "not something which he possessed but something which he had bequeathed us which we could never forget, which would even assume the corporal shape of him whenever any of us, black or white, closed our eyes." [22]

In *Absalom, Absalom!*, one of Faulkner's finest novels, the importance of Virginia in the migration of this Cavalier code to the southwest frontier of Alabama, Mississippi, and Arkansas is vividly and dramatically embodied in the history of the novel's central character, Thomas Sutpen. Sutpen is a product of the western Virginia mountains, where there are no black slaves or large plantations and where "nobody had any more than you did because everybody had just what he was strong enough or energetic enough to take and keep, and only . . . a crazy man would go to the trouble to take or even want more than he could eat or

22. William Faulkner, *The Unvanquished* (New York, 1938), 291.

swap for powder and whiskey." From this archetypically American landscape of rough equality the young Sutpen returns with his family "to the coast from which the first Sutpen had come (when the ship from the Old Bailey reached Jamestown probably), tumbled head over heels back to Tidewater by sheer altitude, elevation and gravity, as if whatever slight hold the family had on the mountain had broken." Here in "the slack lowlands about the mouth of the James River," the young boy encounters a strange and initially perplexing new country, "all divided and fixed and neat with a people living on it all divided and fixed and neat because of what color their skins happened to be and what they happened to own, and where a certain few men not only had the power of life and death and barter and sale over others, but they had living human men to perform the endless repetitive personal offices, such as pouring the very whiskey from the jug and putting the glass into a man's hand." Here in Tidewater Virginia, Sutpen loses his innocence the day he stands before the white door of a plantation mansion and is confronted by a "monkey nigger barring the door and looking down at him in his patched made-over jeans clothes," commanding him never to present himself at the front door again. From that day he understands that the social code embodied by the plantation master is bigger than he, that "to combat them you have got to have what they have that made them do what the man did."[23]

Cleanth Brooks has correctly perceived that Sutpen is not a true representative of the Cavalier tradition. He is, rather, "fixated on the planter as an abstraction . . . not as a role actually lived, savored, and enjoyed. He has pursued an ideal of gracious ease and leisure with an almost breathless ferocity."[24] One of the major ironies of *Absalom, Absalom!* is that a man who embodies many of the character traits of the rapacious Yankee carries a Cavalier vision of Tidewater Virginia to Mississippi, where he wrests a plantation from the wilderness and sets out, calculatingly, ruthlessly, and ultimately unsuccessfully, to establish

23. William Faulkner, *Absalom, Absalom!* (New York, 1951), 221, 222–23, 221–22, 232, 238.
24. Cleanth Brooks, *William Faulkner: Toward Yoknapatawpha and Beyond* (New Haven, 1978), 293.

a Sutpen dynasty like the dynasties of the Virginia aristocracy. In Sutpen, Faulkner brilliantly illustrates the strange process through which the Cavalier ideal was translated from the Old Dominion and successfully imposed on a raw Mississippi society just emerging from the frontier, a society that one would have thought thoroughly impervious to aristocratic ideals.

For Allen Tate, as for William Faulkner, Virginia embodies the essence of the patriarchal plantation South. In *The Fathers* Tate brings his vision of the Old South into conflict with a new and ultimately triumphant northern order by contrasting the Buchans, a planter family of northern Virginia, with the Poseys, a Maryland family that has cut its ties with the land in the process of pursuing business interests in Washington. George Posey, the young and dynamic head of his family, embodies the moral solipsism and social anarchism which Tate ascribes to the laissez-faire mentality of the commercial North. Quite without intending it, Posey, by marrying into the Buchan family, precipitates its destruction—a collapse that coincides with the coming of the Civil War.

What the Buchans carry with them to their ruinous end is an aristocratic code that defines a man, not by the amount of money he possesses, but by his position within a fixed social system. Lacey Buchan, the novel's narrator, who survives the war only to live into a new century dominated by alien values, describes the antebellum code: "The individual quality of a man was bound up with his kin and the 'places' where they lived; thinking of a man we could easily bring before the mind's eye all those subtly interwoven features of his position. 'Class' consisted solely in a certain code of behavior. Even years later I am always a little amazed to hear a man described as the coal man or the steel man or the plate-glass man, descriptions of people after the way they make their money, not after their manner of life."[25] Lacey Buchan describes a system of social values inextricably linked to the Virginia squirearchy, a plantation aristocracy doomed by the forces of history embodied in the character of Marylander George Posey.

As in the nineteenth century, southern writers like Young, Mitchell,

25. Allen Tate, *The Fathers* (Chicago, 1960), 135.

Faulkner, and Tate have not been alone in their sympathetic fictional treatments of the planter aristocrat. Two of America's most popular writers of the 1920s and 1930s, Joseph Hergesheimer and John P. Marquand, drew specifically on Virginia and its romantic Cavaliers for part of their work. Joseph Hergesheimer believed essentially that the North represented the democratic ideal and that the Old South embodied the aristocratic ideal. Though he pledged obligatory allegiance to the principles of American democracy, which he equated with pragmatism, his heart obviously responded to the aristocratic ideal, which he identified with all that was charming and romantic and which he believed had been destroyed by the Civil War. "After eighteen-sixty-five," he wrote, "even in the deep South, society became commercial rather than masculine. The empire of charm largely departed."[26] In *Balisand* Hergesheimer located this "empire of charm" in Virginia of the Federal period, and he crafted a lyrical elegy for a colonial Virginia aristocracy submerged by the rising tide of Jeffersonian democracy.

Virginia's golden age shifts from the colonial to the Civil War period in a series of six short stories which John P. Marquand, America's preeminent twentieth-century novelist of manners, wrote for the *Saturday Evening Post* in 1932. These stories, reminiscent of those of Thomas Nelson Page, feature the exploits of the courageous and noble Scott Mattaye of "Deer Bottom in Virginia." Cavalier Scott loves a beautiful and pure belle of a neighboring plantation, Mary Crease; but as in Page's "Marse Chan," their love is frustrated by a political dispute between their families that centers on the wisdom of Virginia's secession from the Union. A duel of honor between Scott and Mary Crease's brother is eventually made inevitable. Although Scott admires his adversary he understands a gentleman's responsibility. "He could not fight Matt Crease," Marquand observes, "but a gentleman must meet a challenge or leave his honor stained."[27] The duel is averted by the personal intercession of J. E. B. Stuart. Succeeding stories follow Scott's

26. Joseph Hergesheimer, "The Deep South," in his *Swords and Roses* (New York, 1929), 25.

27. John P. Marquand, "Jine the Cavalry," *Saturday Evening Post*, April 16, 1932, p. 114.

heroic exploits under Stuart through Bull Run and Gettysburg to the fall of Richmond.

Though many aspects of Marquand's series hark back to the nineteenth-century plantation fiction, the author also makes a number of perceptive observations about the inevitable destruction of plantation culture. In the first story of the series the reader sees a Mattaye plantation encumbered with wasted land and overgrown fields. Presiding over these poor fields is Scott's father, a man "formed by the gracious living and straitened ideals of a golden age" who rails against "the catch-penny philosophy and the damnable pryin' propensities of an industrious but venal trading race." In spite of his lofty patriarchal and anticapitalistic views, however, the elder Mattaye is forced to secretly sell some of his best slaves to send Scott to the University of Virginia. Scott is the inheritor of a dying tradition. He is, in the words of a northern lawyer he encounters in Richmond on the eve of the war, an "anachronism."[28]

If Marquand clearly understands that his hero is an anachronism, he also displays an equally clear predilection for the chivalric attitudes embodied in Mattaye's code. This sympathy for the Cavalier ideal is most romantically presented in "Far Away," a story which recounts J. E. B. Stuart's daring cavalry ride around McClellan's army. Caught by a Yankee patrol on the Crease plantation, Scott ensures his commander's safe escape by challenging his northern adversary to individual combat on horseback while Stuart slips out the back way and returns with a rescue party. The Yankees are suddenly in the coils of the Rebels, but Stuart allows them to go, "compliments of Miss Mary Crease," observing, "There's such a thing as manners in a war."[29] Marquand's stories illustrate the truism that the South lost the real war but has subsequently triumphed in the fictional contest.

Probably the most illustrious American writer of the period between the world wars to implicitly embrace the chivalric code of the Cavalier is F. Scott Fitzgerald. Andrew Turnbull in his perceptive bi-

28. John P. Marquand, "Solid South," *Saturday Evening Post*, March 12, 1932, pp. 74, 6, 81.
29. John P. Marquand, "Far Away," *Saturday Evening Post*, April 13, 1932, p. 42.

ography describes Fitzgerald's venerable Maryland ancestry, the southern proclivities of his father, and Fitzgerald's ultimate association of his father's gentility and breeding with failure in the practical world. Like Hergesheimer and Marquand, however, though he recognized the non-utilitarian and antique aspects of the southern aristocratic ideal as it was embodied in his father's character, he emotionally identified with the ideal and mourned its passing from the American scene. Fitzgerald's southern sympathies are clear in the "Last of the Belles," in "The Southern Girl," and especially in "The Ice Palace." This last story contains a scene in a Civil War cemetery in Georgia in which the Confederate dead are imaginatively associated with a lost age of "strange courtliness and chivalry." The story's southern heroine appeals to her midwestern fiancé as she stands crying over the graves, "Oh, Harry, there was something, there was something! I couldn't make you understand, but it was there."[30]

The equation of Cavalier gentility with failure is most movingly dramatized in *Tender Is the Night*. Fitzgerald's hero, Dick Diver, is the son of an Episcopal minister, a native Virginian of poor, "tired stock" who nonetheless raises himself to the effort of becoming his son's "moral guide." The lessons that the father inculcates are the simple truths of the code of the gentlemen—"that nothing could be superior to 'good instincts,' honor, courtesy, and courage."[31] The code that Dick's father passes on to him is the old-fashioned code of the southern aristocrat. But as we see in the novel, it is an inadequate guide for success in a modern world dominated by hedonistic and self-indulgent materialism.

The Warrens of Chicago—Devereux, Baby, and Nicole—represent the perversity and moral anarchy that attend the rise of the new American plutocracy. Nicole Warren is the beautiful flower in this plutocracy, feeding, like Flaubert's Madame Bovary, on manure—in this instance the manure of Yankee avidity. Anonymous workers around the world toil to render to her an obscene modern tithe. "As the whole system

---

30. F. Scott Fitzgerald, "The Ice Palace," in Malcolm Cowley (ed.), *The Stories of F. Scott Fitzgerald* (1921; rpr. New York, 1951), 66.

31. F. Scott Fitzgerald, *Tender Is the Night* (New York, 1933), 203–204, hereinafter cited in the text by page number only.

swayed and thundered onward," Fitzgerald observes, "it lent a feverish bloom to such processes of Nicole's as wholesale buying, like the flush of a fireman's face holding his post before a spreading blaze" (55).

The spreading blaze consumes Dick when he decides to marry Nicole. Dick's decision represents, in part, the triumph of Yankee materialism over his father's ideals of honor, courtesy, and courage. The gentlemanly code prizes the acquisition of certain character traits over the accumulation of wealth, but Dick realizes that he cannot disdain the extravagant wealth of the physical world represented by the Warrens and that he cannot have the beautiful things he wants and remain true to his father's code. Dick comes to understand that in choosing Nicole he has cut himself off from his heritage. This is why at his father's grave he utters these enigmatic words: "Good-by, my father—good-by, all my fathers" (205). Forfeiting his past, Dick cannot effectively operate in the present, and thus he eventually destroys himself.

The character of Dick's father is so obviously modeled on that of Fitzgerald's father that one may wonder why the author went to the trouble of making him a Virginian rather than a Marylander and of burying him in Westmoreland County in the Northern Neck of Virginia, rather than in Rockville, Maryland, where both Fitzgerald and his father were buried. The reason, I believe, is more than a simple desire to transform facts into fiction by changing their context. If this desire alone had motivated Fitzgerald he might have made Dick's father a New Yorker and buried him in New York, where he died. Fitzgerald must have understood that Dick's journey South with his father's body to "the low-forested clayland" of Northern Neck Virginia was fictionally and symbolically just. Where better to bury the father and to say goodbye to the code that actuated his life than in the region most deeply associated through our nation's history with that code—Tidewater Virginia. Here by the "sluggish primeval rivers flowing softly under soft Indian names" in a state much more evocative of the aristocratic code than Maryland both Dick Diver and Scott Fitzgerald could stop to say a poignant farewell to the Cavalier idea.

In the years following the Second World War, Virginia has remained a popular locale for historical novels. The most important book in recent years to treat the subject of America's Tidewater tobacco gentry is James Michener's *Chesapeake*. Although this work is set in Eastern Shore Maryland, it describes Carl Bridenbaugh's Chesapeake society, dealing with the social structure that characterized early Virginia as well as colonial Maryland and touching upon Virginia's history as well as Maryland's. *Chesapeake* is vast in its scope. It encompasses economic, political, social, and natural history over a span of five centuries, and its large cast of characters includes Indians and Negroes, as well as white men of varied social backgrounds.

To represent Tidewater's more humble settlers Michener offers the Turlocks, a family whose American branch is established by a runaway indentured servant. The Turlocks inhabit the marshes and over the centuries distinguish themselves as expert watermen and sea captains. The middle class is represented by the Paxmores, Quakers of humble origin who become accomplished and prosperous boat builders. At the top of the social pyramid stands the Steed family. The Steeds typify the aristocracy that ultimately comes to dominate Chesapeake society, and they serve as the primary focus of the action of Michener's sprawling novel.

In *Chesapeake* James Michener achieves both considerable narrative power and notable historical accuracy. His novel makes clear that the bay region was settled by men of diverse backgrounds and that by no means all Tidewater planters could claim a proud English ancestry. The Steeds, however, represent an early Maryland family whose roots run deep in the English gentry. The first American Steed, Edmund, is a son and grandson of knights, and he arrives in the New World in 1607 sure of his social prerogatives and determined to maintain the Catholic faith which has blocked his advancement in England. Succeeding generations of Steeds assume their role as New World inheritors of the rural English gentry, consolidating and expanding their estates, acquiring large numbers of indentured and slave workers, educating their heirs in France and England so they may assume positions of leadership at home, and maintaining their wealth and social precedence through the colonial, revolutionary, and Civil War periods and into the twentieth century. However, Michener emphasizes that it is the

Steeds' industriousness, not their genteel antecedents, that enables the family to survive and to prosper in America. The Steeds are pragmatists. They are willing to trade, to engage in commerce in its most specific sense, as well as to supervise the planting of their fields. Steed ships carry Steed tobacco to England, and Steed shops sell Steed barrels, spars, and cloth to smaller farmers. Thus while many of their fellow planters in Maryland and Virginia ultimately fail, the Steeds, with their sure bourgeois instincts, survive.

Yet, though Michener emphasizes those enterprising aspects of the Steed family temperament which assure their continued social dominance, he also stresses the aristocratic attitude of noblesse oblige which characterizes their dealings with men of all ranks and social classes. The Steeds embrace a middle-class business ethos, but they insist upon defining themselves as gentry, and their personal code is drawn from the English code of the gentleman. This code and its attendant sense of superiority is passed down from generation to generation. When a French official visiting the Steed plantation on the eve of the Civil War asks its master how he can explain the superior strength of the South, his host replies: "The gallantry of its men. . . . You are dining with gentlemen, Captain, and these men abide by their word. If they go to war against the North, it will be to the death." [32] And so the Steeds, a family noted for its pragmatism, romantically enlists its aristocratic code in the defense of a hopelessly antiquated social system.

Chesapeake conveys both an accurate sense of history and a subtle understanding of the myths which contribute profoundly to the molding of events in history. Nothing demonstrates the power of myth to mold reality more than the life of Rosalind Janney, the strong-willed, industrious daughter of a Virginia planter who marries a Steed, manages the plantation after his death, and builds the magnificent house which ever after bears her name. Rosalind possesses a practical nature which blends admirably with that of her husband. She is especially fond of puncturing the Cavalier pretensions of her family, pointedly asking

32. James A. Michener, *Chesapeake* (New York, 1978), 792, hereinafter cited in the text by page number only.

her father: "Why is it, Father, that when we discuss our family you always speak as if we began with Chilton Janney coming to the Rappahannock in the 1650s? Why don't you mention Simon Janney, who started us off on the James in 1610?" (311). Michener goes on to explain why Rosalind's hardheaded question causes the family acute embarrassment:

> It was traditional among the Janneys of the Rappahannock never to mention Simon, who had lived so miserably among the swamps of the James, and certainly not his wife Bess, a convicted fornicatress purchased from a ship captain. Secretly they were aware that aspects of Simon's history existed in court records—his acquisition of land, his purchases of slaves, his argument over the ownership of fields along the Choptank, and the manner in which he purchased from the Fithians the great estate of the Rappahannock—but they preferred to think that these matters would remain hidden. However, against the possibility of discovery, they had manufactured for toothless Bess an acceptable lineage: she was now "Elizabeth Avery, daughter of a prosperous rural family in Hants." (311)

It is ironic that Rosalind's father insists on styling her the granddaughter of a Cavalier "who rode with Prince Rupert," though Rosalind mischievously insists on reminding her family that "our old goat never rode with Rupert, and in no possible way could he consider himself a Cavalier" (310). It is doubly ironic that toward the end of her life clear-eyed Rosalind finds herself held partially in thrall by her family's outrageous genealogy. She grows fond of telling her grandchildren that her grandfather "was a Cavalier and he rode with Rupert at Marston Moor."

> And then one of the children would say, "But you always said he was a dead drunk."
>
> "I never saw him sober," Rosalind would confess.
>
> "And he wasn't a real Cavalier," another child would say, and she would reply, "In his heart he was." (403)

23

James Michener's *Chesapeake* reveals a sensitive understanding of the southerner's proclivity for turning his back on what W. J. Cash has termed "the puny inadequateness of fact." His presentation of characters such as Rosalind Janney lends fictional substance to T. Harry Williams' observation that in many situations a southerner "almost certainly will refuse to recognize reality."[33] The myth of Cavalier aristocracy, no matter how contrary to fact, shapes the lives of all the Steeds and, by extension, of nearly all those living on the Eastern Shore, including watermen and small farmers.

Chesapeake is the most recent novel of critical importance to assess the significance of the myth of the Cavalier. To find the most romantic and the most popular fictional projection of the Cavalier ideal in this century, however, one would need to turn back nearly eighty years to a western novel written by Owen Wister in 1902, *The Virginian*. To epitomize the heroic stature of the cowboy, the Pennsylvania novelist chose as his hero a courtly young cowboy who was born and raised in the Old Dominion. Wister, like many northerners before and after him, responded irresistibly to the appeal of aristocracy incarnated in southern flesh. His Virginia cowpuncher thus becomes a wandering Cavalier of the high plains, expelled from his original habitat but maintaining the essential virtues of his code.

The courtly southern characteristics of Wister's protagonist are emphasized almost immediately in the novel. When the narrator, who has just arrived from the East, meets the man who is to guide him to the ranch of his host he notices that his guide speaks with a "civil Southern voice" which he immediately identifies as coming from "Old Virginia." It is made abundantly clear that the Virginian, though a common ranch hand, is nevertheless a true gentleman. He repels, for example, the narrator's clumsy attempts to establish himself on condescendingly familiar terms. "This handsome, ungrammatical son of the soil had set between us the bar of his cold and perfect civility. No polished person could have done it better." The narrator concludes that the Virginian has proved

---

33. Cash, *The Mind of the South*, 47; T. Harry Williams, "Romance and Realism in Southern Politics," in Gerster and Cords (eds.), *Myth and Southern History*, 111.

himself the better gentleman of the two and that "the creature we call a gentleman lies deep in the hearts of thousands that are born without chance to master the outward graces of the type."[34]

As the narrator's observations indicate, the Virginian is not descended from one of the aristocratic first families of the Tidewater. He is unpretentious, earthy, and indifferently educated; as he writes his prospective mother-in-law later in the novel, his origins are humble: "I am of old stock in Virginia English and one Scotch-Irish grandmother my father's father brought from Kentucky. We have always stayed at the same place farmers and hunters not bettering our lot and very plain" (372). Thus the Virginia Cavalier that Wister creates is one of a new breed which is more naturally equipped to make the transition from South to West and from past to present. He is one of Jefferson's natural aristocrats, a melding of common man with Cavalier. In the frontier West where every man was presumably judged on his merits, Wister seems to have correctly discerned that a rustic Cavalier would function as a much more natural part of the scene than his aristocratic prototype.

Humble though his origins may be, the Virginian nonetheless acts very much like his aristocratic and romantic predecessors. Like every true Cavalier, he must have a lady to love. This lady is Mary Stark Wood, a beautiful girl from Vermont. The ritual of courtship in *The Virginian* is indistinguishable, except in its setting, from the romances of southern plantation fiction. The Virginian performs the obligatory rescue of the lady from a stagecoach foundering in a raging Wyoming river, and he is immediately smitten by the damsel he has saved from distress. True to the Cavalier tradition, he carries away from this encounter a lover's token, a handkerchief embroidered with flowers. Later at a barbecue-dance he defends his lady's honor from the lewd insinuations of the novel's villain, Trampas. Mary also plays her role properly, outwardly spurning her suitor's romantic initiatives, while inwardly and half-consciously giving him her heart. Yet, in spite of remaining Mary's "unrewarded knight," the Virginian does not give vent to his

---

34. Owen Wister, *The Virginian: A Horseman of the Plains* (New York, 1904), 11–12, hereinafter cited in the text by page number only.

misery or falter in his devotion. His attitude is the traditional one of stoic worship, and his stoicism reminds one of other long-suffering Cavalier lovers, such as Thomas Nelson Page's Marse Chan.

Even in the tense and dramatic scene in which Mary discovers and saves the Virginian and is thus forced to recognize her love for him, Wister plays subtly on the idea of his protagonist's innate nobility of character. Gravely wounded by a bullet from a renegade Indian party, he is weak from loss of blood and nearly unconscious when she finds him. In keeping him on his horse and thereby saving his life Mary alertly grasps at a chivalric notion, presumably the only notion capable of impressing itself on the Virginian's fever-ravaged mind. When he cries out to her that he cannot go further, she replies: "You must take me home. . . . a gentleman does not invite a lady to go out riding and leave her" (332). Her lover responds viscerally to this gentlemanly obligation and hangs on in his saddle.

After restoring her cowboy to health Mary understands that she loves him and that she must throw convention to the wind and marry him. But there is one final obstacle—the villain Trampas, who materializes on the wedding day. Determined on revenge, Trampas vilifies the Virginian in a face-to-face confrontation and forces a gunfight. Naturally Mary is horrified by the notion of this sort of killing, and she begs her fiancé to avoid the gunfight if he values her love. But a Cavalier's honor is his most sacred trust. Without this quality, he believes, he would be unworthy of Mary's love. The Virginian explains his position simply but eloquently to the bishop who has come to marry him: "I'd give her twice my life—fifty—a thousand of 'em. But I can't give her—her nor anybody in heaven or earth—I can't give my—my—we'll never get at it, seh!" (470).

Of course the Virginian has gotten at it. The bishop understands the necessity for the gunfight as well as Wister's readers, and he blesses the cowboy as he goes to face and kill Trampas. And though Mary, who is a Yankee, cannot truly understand the code of her cowboy Cavalier, she wrestles and finally subdues her New England scruples and is waiting for her love with open arms when he returns in victory. To paraphrase Wister, she has capitulated to love. The Virginian concludes the romance by sweeping his bride away into his mountain retreat for the idyllic consummation of their love, a scene handled with the properly chaste reverence befitting Cavalier and lady.

In *The Virginian* the Cavalier moved from Civil War battlefields to western plains. The transition was signally successful, for as David B. Davis observes, "When the Southern myth reappeared on the rolling prairies, it was purified and regenerated by the casting off of apologies for slavery. It could focus all energies on its former role of opposing the peculiar social and economic philosophy of the Northeast."[35] Thus, though the plantation gave way to the ranch in Wister's novel, the myth rode on into the twentieth century. So universally popular has the amalgam of Cavalier with cowboy been that *The Virginian* has subsequently been reprinted in more than twenty editions in this country and has been read in translation by millions of readers throughout the world. The durable hero has been resurrected to ride before Hollywood cameras on four different occasions. He has even galloped into the nation's living rooms in a long-running television series of the 1960s.

The emotional appeal of the Cavalier figure in his various forms has not been limited to American audiences, and American authors have not been alone in exploiting his romantic potential. Perhaps the best-known nineteenth-century paean to the Virginia aristocracy was penned by the English novelist William Makepeace Thackeray, whose *The Virginians: A Tale of the Eighteenth Century* was completed in 1859. The fruit of two visits to the United States, the subject matter of Thackeray's novel was also gleaned from conversations with John Esten Cooke and John Pendleton Kennedy. The Cooke-Kennedy influence no doubt explains in part the author's strongly romantic treatment of eighteenth-century Virginia Tidewater society. Jay B. Hubbell has praised the novel's authentic handling of American life, but he seems to overlook the way Thackeray embraces, dramatizes, and celebrates the myth of the Cavalier settlement of the Old Dominion.[36]

The Virginians, sequel to Thackeray's historical romance of early

35. David B. Davis, "Ten-Gallon Hero," *American Quarterly*, VI (1954), 114.
36. Jay Broadus Hubbell, "Thackeray and Virginia," *Virginia Quarterly Review*, III (1927), 76–86.

eighteenth-century England, *Henry Esmond*, follows the adventures of Esmond's twin grandsons, Henry Esmond Warrington and George Warrington, in Virginia and in England. Harry Warrington is none too bright, but he compensates for his lack of intellectual distinction by being handsome, athletic, sporting, generous, brave, and honorable. He is essentially a youthful embodiment of the type of the amiable rural squire. His brother George is more intelligent and more introverted. His strengths are his level-headedness, his sense of responsibility, and his immense erudition. During his early years on his grandfather's Potomac River plantation, George has rather miraculously acquired a fluency in Latin, German, and French and has developed catholic and sophisticated reading tastes. In addition to these prodigious intellectual accomplishments, he plays the violin beautifully.

Thackeray further distinguishes his Virginia heroes by investing them with lofty family trees. The twins' maternal grandfather, Henry Esmond, is an English gentleman and soldier who gives up his rightful title of viscount to his stepson and retires to the family's Virginia lands. Castlewood Plantation in Virginia thus evokes the memory of the ancestral Castlewood estate in England. Harry and George's mother, who prefers to be addressed as Madame Esmond, looks superciliously upon her late husband's lineage, but Thackeray assures the reader that the Warrington branch is also socially solid, Mr. Warrington, Esq., being the younger son of a Norfolk baronet. There can be little question that in assigning his young Virginia gentlemen such august antecedents Thackeray's intention is to reinforce the notion that Virginia's gentry were commonly descended from aristocratic English ancestors.

The Virginians delineates an Anglophile's dream world. Repeatedly Thackeray stresses the veneration with which George and Harry view England. He assures his readers that "all Americans who love the old country—and what gently nurtured man or woman does not?—have ere this rehearsed their English travels and visited in fancy the spots with which their hopes, their parents' fond stories, their friends' descriptions, have rendered them familiar." Thackeray is unequivocal concerning the aristocratic nature of Virginia society. He informs us that "the whole usages of Virginia . . . were fondly modeled after the

English customs," that "the resident gentry were allied to good English families," and that "they dwelled on their great lands after a fashion almost patriarchal." In short the novelist concludes that "ere the establishment of Independence, there was no more aristocratic country in the world than Virginia."[37]

By the end of the novel George lives in England as Sir George Warrington on the inherited estate of his father's brother. Harry serves under his dear friend, George Washington, in the Revolution and after it assumes the family plantations in the Old Dominion. Although George willingly casts his lot with the mother country, even fighting against the Americans in the Revolution, one feels that his brother would have assumed the role of English country gentleman with even greater ease. As George observes: "Had Hal been master of Warrington Manor House, in my place, he would have been beloved through the whole country; he would have been steward at all the races, the gayest of all the jolly huntsmen, the *bien venu* at all the mansions round about" (697). No writer has argued more forcefully for the essential identification of Virginia gentleman with English gentleman, and no writer has presented a more colorful and romantic picture of Virginia's Cavalier heritage than William Makepeace Thackeray in *The Virginians.*

The striking quality of Thackeray's presentation of both Harry and George Warrington is that, though in the external details of their habits and manners they are virtually indistinguishable from their aristocratic English counterparts, they are superior to most of their old world brethren in character and moral refinement. In contrast to the dissolute, scheming, selfish English cousins to whom they are exposed when they arrive in the mother country, the Warrington twins hew religiously to the traditional code of the gentleman. Unlike the innocent and hopelessly naïve Harry, George eventually comprehends the lack of moral fiber of his English relatives. His observations on the relative merits of England and Virginia in forming men of honor seem to reflect Thackeray's own attitude in the novel: "*O beati agricolae!* Our Virginia was

---

37. William Makepeace Thackeray, *The Virginians: A Tale of the Eighteenth Century* (1855–59; rpr. New York, 1923), 21, 24, hereinafter cited in the text by page number only.

dull, but let us thank Heaven we were bred there. We were made little slaves, but not slaves to wickedness, gambling, bad male and female company. It was not until my poor Harry left home that he fell among thieves" (555). The moral superiority of the Virginians is implied in numerous instances. When, for example, Harry is teasingly questioned by a rakish English divine about his female conquests in Virginia, he nobly replies: "It isn't the custom of our country . . . to ruin girls, or frequent the society of low women. We Virginia gentlemen honor women; we don't wish to bring them to shame" (247).

Of course not all of Thackeray's old world characters are reprehensible. Colonel Lambert, the gentleman who eventually becomes George Warrington's father-in-law, represents the best qualities of the English gentry, combining wisdom and kindliness with courage and a sense of duty, good breeding with erudition. In a sense he embodies the best qualities of both Harry and George. He certainly stands in bold contrast to the Virginians' Esmond and Warrington kinsmen. However, in spite of Lambert's presence the overwhelming impression one receives of the English aristocracy in this novel is of shallowness and turpitude.

Thackeray seems to be using his Virginia gentlemen in a way reminiscent of the way American writers utilize the Cavalier. By molding his Virginians into idealized representations of gentility, he is able to measure the imperfections of English society and to dramatize the gap between social ideal and reality. For though *The Virginians* is set one hundred years in the past, Thackeray leaves little doubt that the essential nature of English society remains unchanged. Many American writers, as we have seen, came to understand the usefulness of the Cavalier type in highlighting certain disturbing tendencies of American culture. It would appear that Thackeray arrived at a similar understanding of the Virginia aristocrat and that he used him in a manner similar to that of Cooper, Adams, and James.

The appearance of Yves Berger's *The Garden* over one hundred years after *The Virginians*, in 1962, is an indication that the romance of the Old Dominion has not altogether lost its power over the European imagination. Published in France as *Le Sud, The Garden* sold over 130,000 copies within weeks of its appearance. In this novel, set in

Provence in the 1940s and 1950s, a father and his son retreat from the disgusting spectacle of the present out of linear time and back to antebellum Virginia. Here, during the year 1842, the father believes a perfectly poised golden age was achieved. For the father—and later for the son when he falls under the spell of his father's vision—time should have stopped in 1842. Paradise would then have been "millions of Virginias, that small amount, that adequate amount of civilization which we need, great estates planted here and there in the depths of the forests."[38] Ultimately the father sets out to re-create his vision of Virginia in Provence, attaching porticos and balconies to his country mansion, planting wisteria and magnolias. *The Garden* is, among other things, a testament to the power of myth and of human imagination over reality.

Critics, social scientists, historians, and other intellectuals on both sides of the Atlantic, as well as writers of fiction, still occasionally acknowledge the appeal of the Cavalier idea. Frenchman Jean Gottmann contrasts the serenity of the Old Dominion with the frenetic pace which characterizes life in other parts of the United States. Gottmann labels this American frenzy the "Promethean impulse." It is an attitude, he observes, characterized by incredible drive, titanic endeavor, perpetual dissatisfaction with things as they are, and a constant striving for the biggest and best. Virginia tradition, he concludes, may have a valid mission in national life: "If it came to play a greater part within American civilization it might mellow it somewhat." Gottmann's observations suggest that Virginia continues to represent to both popular and intellectual imaginations a cultural tradition fundamentally removed from those characteristics most commonly and often negatively identified with American culture—ambition, rapid cultural change, and materialism. T. S. Eliot seemed to betray as much an Anglophile's distaste for the forms of a democratic mass culture as an appreciation of the Virginia tradition when he told a Charlottesville audience in 1933: "I think that the chances for the re-establishment of a native culture are perhaps better here than in New England. You are farther from New York; you have been less industrialized and less invaded by foreign

38. Yves Berger, *The Garden* (New York, 1963), 14–15.

races." Louis Wright muses in a similar vein that in the midst of contemporary economic and political confusion "the [Virginia] aristocracy
of the seventeenth and eighteenth centuries may yet teach us important
lessons in leadership."[39] One may be bothered by the reactionary and
elitist sentiments implicit in such statements. They confirm, nevertheless, the survival of the aristocratic ideal as a significant undercurrent in
American thinking, and they suggest that Virginia and her Cavaliers
remain the most magnetic symbol of that ideal.

39. Gottmann, *Virginia at Mid-century*, 561; T. S. Eliot, *After Strange Gods: A Primer of Modern Heresy* (London, 1934), 16; Wright, *First Gentlemen of Virginia*, 353.

TWO

The Historical Context

THE aristocratic ideal embodied in the figure of the Virginia Cavalier continues to exert a strong appeal on the national imagination. Even today the southerner's image of himself, as well as the northerner's image of the southerner, bears a marked resemblance to the gilt-framed portrait of the Virginia aristocrat. A better understanding of the southern mind would seem necessarily to involve a better understanding of the Cavalier figure. Historians and literary scholars agree that he is a myth, the appealing product of human imagination working with the common clay of human history; but this insight invites further questions. What, more precisely, is the mixture of fact and fancy that went into the creation of the Cavalier? What sort of human clay did the mythmakers originally have to work with? What were these early inhabitants of the Old Dominion really like?

The first popular portrait of colonial Virginia society was painted and presented to the American public by nineteenth-century writers of historical romance. Prominent among these novelists were two native Virginians, William Alexander Caruthers and John Esten Cooke. For these writers, of course, there was essentially no disparity between myth and reality. Thus Cooke described his Cavaliers in the Prologue to *Henry St. John, Gentleman,* as "ruffled and powdered" gentlemen, incomparably urbane and cultivated, with polished swords and polished smiles to match. Louis Wright, however, ironically presents in capsule form the best description of this idealized nineteenth-century character:

> Rich and romantic Cavaliers lived in feudal splendor, surrounded by multitudes of retainers. Great houses, filled with furniture and finery brought from England, provided a background for these barons of the Virginia rivers. There the lords and ladies of the new dispensation spent their leisure in cultivating the social graces. With dancing, gaiety, and decorous flirtation they passed the time in Arcadia. Only dueling disturbed the idyllic dream, for in Arcadia gentlemen were touchy about their honor and a duel at dawn under the oaks beside a dark river was the invariable method of settling personal disputes. . . . These silken-coated grandees were all descended from some ancient and distinguished family of England . . . and titles in the family trees of the Colonists were thicker than dogwood blooms in spring.[1]

Twentieth-century historians have examined the records of colonial Virginia with notable objectivity and have found wide discrepancies between the fictional ideal and the realities of Tidewater civilization. Contemporary historians were not the first, however, to throw light on the nature of the Old Dominion's early settlers. One of the earliest descriptions of Virginia and its people was penned by William Bullock and published in London in 1649. In *Virginia Impartially Examined* Bullock complained that the colony's development had been retarded by men who had come to Virginia expecting to strike it rich but who were hindered by insufficient capital and an unwillingness to commit themselves to hard work. He also complained of the "unfitness" of the people transported as indentured servants, characterizing many of them as

1. Wright, *First Gentlemen of Virginia,* 38.

"idle, lazy, simple" people.[2] Certainly the Virginians Bullock describes bear little resemblance to the gay Cavaliers of Caruthers' and Cooke's novels.

John Hammond's *Leah and Rachel*, published in 1656, gave a much more sympathetic portrayal of Virginians. In fact the book was primarily written to counter the viperous attacks of men who contended the colony was merely "a nest of Rogues, whores, desolate and rooking persons." Hammond admitted that in the beginning Virginia had attracted avaricious adventurers, but he insisted that at the present time the honest and industrious were in firm control of the land. "The country," he observed, "is full of sober, modest persons."[3] Yet, though Hammond mounted a spirited defense of Virginians, it is interesting to note that he did not describe them as aristocrats. Indeed, the descriptions of Virginia which followed Bullock's and Hammond's in the eighteenth century are also noteworthy for their lack of attention to Virginia's Cavalier heritage. Henry Hartwell, who with James Blair and Edward Chilton published *The Present State of Virginia* in 1727, emphasized the wasteful and lazy farming methods of Virginians more strongly than their social origins; and Hugh Jones in his *Present State of Virginia*, printed in 1753, wrote only that the English Civil Wars had "enticed over several Cavalier families."[4]

Robert Beverley's *The History and Present State of Virginia*, published in 1705, is perhaps the most interesting as well as the most reliable of these early works. Like Hartwell, Blair, and Chilton, Beverley did not hesitate to criticize Virginians for what he considered their failings. He also refused to support the popular belief that the colony had been settled by large numbers of noble Cavalier families who had fled to Virginia after the defeat and execution of Charles I by Cromwell's Roundheads. Virginia, Beverley observed, had received alike very few

2. William Bullock, *Virginia Impartially Examined* (London, 1649), 14.

3. John Hammond, *Leah and Rachel; or, The Two Fruitful Sisters Virginia and Maryland: Their Present Condition, Impartially Stated and Related. Narratives of Early Maryland, 1633–1684*, ed. Clayton Colman Hall (1656; rpr. New York, 1910), 284.

4. Hugh Jones, *Present State of Virginia: From Whence Is Inferred a Short View of Maryland and North Carolina*, ed. Richard L. Morton (1753; rpr. Chapel Hill, 1956), 8–16.

criminals or Cavaliers. The great majority of settlers were of low or modest circumstances. "Nor was it hardly possible it should be otherwise," he realistically reflected, "for 'tis now unlikely that any Man of plentiful Estate, should voluntarily abandon a happy Certainty, to roam after imaginary Advantages, in a New World."[5]

Probably the most damning indictment of the aristocratic pretensions of Virginia's colonial gentry is contained in a manuscript by James Reid that remained unpublished until this century. Reid has been provisionally identified as an indentured servant of Scottish origin who in the 1760s lived on the Sweet Hall plantation of the Claiborne family in King William County, probably employed as a tutor. In his manuscript, entitled "The Religion of the Bible and the Religion of K[ing] W[illiam] County Compared," Reid observed bitterly that money, slaves, and land entitled even the dullest and crudest to call himself a gentleman. This so-called Virginia gentleman, he observed, inflated with self-esteem, "drinks, fights, bullies, curses, swears, whores, games, sings, whistles, dances, jumps, capers, runs, talks baudy, visits Gentlemen he never saw, has the rendez-vous with Ladies he never spoke to, writes Billets-dou to filles des joies whom he stiles women of Quality, eats voraciously, sleeps, snores, and takes snuff. This comprehends his whole life, and renders him a Polite Gentleman." Noting that a slave master "commonly impregnates his own wenches," Reid concluded that "an ignorant, vicious, rich Gentleman differs in nothing from his ignorant, vicious, poor Negro, but in the colour of his skin, and in his being the greater blacguard [*sic*] of the two."[6] Allowing these vituperative descriptions to be the product of a sour and perhaps unconsciously envious Calvinist mentality, it is probable nevertheless that Reid's manuscript tells us more about the manners and morals of the Old Dominion's colonial squirearchy than Caruthers' and Cooke's later embellished fictional portraits.

5. Robert Beverley, *The History and Present State of Virginia*, ed. Louis B. Wright (1705; rpr. Chapel Hill, 1947), 287–88.

6. James Reid, "The Religion of the Bible and the Religion of K[ing] W[illiam] County Compared," in Richard Beale Davis (ed.), *The Colonial Virginia Satirist: Mid-Eighteenth Century Commentaries on Politics, Religion, and Society* (Philadelphia, 1967), 48–49.

Though there were, as we have seen, a number of interesting and far from glossily heroic descriptions of Virginia's inhabitants in the seventeenth and eighteenth centuries, the version of Virginia's history that most Americans received during the nineteenth century was filtered through the pages of historical romances or from historical treatments that were nearly as subjective as the fictions.

John Esten Cooke, turning from novel writing, published a popular history of his state in 1883, entitled *Virginia: A History of the People*, which served to preserve romantic legend behind the shield of scholarship. Cooke accepted the theory that his native state had been settled by large numbers of King Charles's Cavaliers. He referred to the immigration as a "great tide of fugitive Cavalierdom" and added this final assessment: "Of the extent of the Cavalier immigration between 1650 and 1670 there can be no doubt whatever. It was so large and respectable in character that the Kings'-men speedily took the direction of social and political affairs. Few Commonwealthmen came to a country where the air was full of Church and King influences; and the Cavaliers were completely in the ascendency."[7]

A few native Virginians did raise voices of protest in the nineteenth century against this uncritical aggrandizement of their state's past. George W. Bagby, popular writer of local color sketches, wrote an essay for the Richmond *Whig* in 1859 entitled "The Unkind but Complete Destruction of John Esten Cooke" in which he good-naturedly attacked Cooke's presentation of colonial Virginia in *The Virginia Comedians*, a popular historical romance which had appeared in 1855. Cooke's eyes, Bagby sarcastically observed, were probably located in the rear of his head and were undoubtedly covered with rose-colored glasses. That "such a set of homely, selfish, money-loving cheats and rascals as we are should have descended from such remarkably fine parents" might be "good noveling," but it was just as plainly "wretched physiology."[8]

7. John Esten Cooke, *Virginia: A History of the People* (1883; rpr. Boston, 1894), 228.
8. Quoted in Jay Broadus Hubbell, *The South in American Literature, 1607–1900* (Durham, 1954), 516.

George Bagby's iconoclastic attitude toward his colonial ancestors was at least partly the result of eleven years of living outside Virginia in New Jersey, Pennsylvania, and Delaware, where he attended preparatory school, college, and medical school from the ages of ten to twenty-one. During this time he acquired, as he admitted in his Introduction to "The Old Virginia Gentleman," a keener sense of the defects of the Old Dominion. Bagby's keen satiric sense produced such early essays as "The Virginia Editor," a portrait of a "young, unmarried, intemperate, pugnacious, gambling gentleman" who ends his life with "half an ounce of lead . . . 'honorably and satisfactorily adjusted' in his heart or brain."[9] This essay, by the way, ironically resulted in a challenge from a properly offended Virginia editor and in a barely averted duel. Bagby's realistic impulse also resulted in the popular *Letters of Mozis Addums*, letters in dialect spelling written by a character who was modeled after the backwoodsmen and small farmers Bagby had known as a youth in Buckingham, Cumberland, and Prince Edward counties.

Yet, in spite of George Bagby's realistic proclivities, even he eventually succumbed to the siren call of Virginia's romantically colored past. His conversion from genial satirist to zealous defender of Virginia tradition was precipitated by the Civil War. Increasingly alienated by the antislavery fervor emanating from the North, he assumed editorship of the *Southern Literary Messenger* in Richmond in 1860 and used his position to denounce the perfidious Yankee and to urge secession. In January, 1861, he called for the fifteen stars of the South to be torn from the flag and arrayed in a Southern Cross. Under this holy and sublime banner the South would, in his words, "fight for our wives, our children, and our aged sires, whom the mercenary hordes of the North would fain deliver over to the sword of the invader and the pike of the negro insurrectionist."[10]

Bagby was never again able to completely recapture the good-humored detachment of many of his earlier essays. His later work re-

9. George William Bagby, Introduction to his *The Old Virginia Gentleman and Other Sketches*, ed. Thomas Nelson Page (New York, 1910), 66–67.
10. George William Bagby, "Editorial," *Southern Literary Messenger*, XXXII (January, 1861), 71.

veals a curious mixture of precisely observed realistic detail, suggestive of his earlier method, with a tone that frequently becomes emotionally and embarrassingly panegyric. "The Old Virginia Gentleman" illustrates as vividly as any of Bagby's later essays this paradoxical treatment. Written for the lecture circuit in 1877, this essay has served as the title for the three collections of his writings which have been published in this century.

The plantation described in "The Old Virginia Gentleman" is much like that of Bagby's earlier and more realistic description, "My Uncle Flatback's Plantation" (1863). In describing the drive that leads to the big house through miles of slash pine and scrub oak Bagby's meticulous narrative eye does not fail to note the numerous potholes "that make every vehicle, but chiefly the bug-back carriage, lurch and careen worse than a ship in a heavy sea." Threading through such realistic descriptions, however, is a strongly elegiac note for a vanished way of life. In the last analysis it is this mourning for a lost time—for "a beauty, a simplicity, a purity, an uprightness, a cordial and lavish hospitality, a warmth and grace which shine in the lens of memory"—that turns "The Old Virginia Gentleman" into an unabashed celebration of the perfection of antebellum Virginia.[11]

The men and women of Bagby's plantation become romantic stereotypes. The plantation matron is placed upon a pedestal as "mother, mistress, instructor, counsellor, benefactress, friend, angel of the sick room" (21). Her Virginia gentleman becomes a representative of a glorious race of men, of a "breed of human animals" as fine as any the world has ever seen, characterized by courage, pride, honesty, honor, and integrity of character. This gentleman becomes inextricably identified with a belated and defiant justification for the plantation system. "If slavery accompanied here, as in Greece, the development of a splendid breed of animals, say so; if it helped that development, say so fearlessly" (41). The destruction of the plantation system, in Bagby's view, has ended Virginia's golden age and rendered inexpedient the noble virtues which once characterized her ladies and gentlemen.

11. George William Bagby, "The Old Virginia Gentleman," in his *The Old Virginia Gentleman*, 4, 44, hereinafter cited in the text by page number only.

Looking over the whole of Bagby's output one is struck by a recurring tension in his essays between the impulse to see precisely and accurately and the impulse to sentimentalize and mythologize. This tension is revealed in the letters Bagby wrote to the Richmond *State* during the final years of his life. On one hand, he is capable of flying "into a violent passion about our Virginia laziness, our ignorance and indifference in regard to the arts or ornamentation." Yet Bagby also is convinced that plain industry and Yankee earnestness will not restore Virginia to its antebellum state of grace. "Were the Commonwealth one solid mass of factories from Alexandria to the Carolina line," he observes, "it would not requite the loss of men like Patrick Henry and John Randolph of Roanoke."[12] This tension between Bagby the realist and Bagby the romantic, between Bagby the astute critic of Virginia foibles and Bagby the celebrator of the Old Dominion's mythical past, is never resolved in his writing. Indeed, this is a tension which, as we shall see, characterizes all of Virginia's writers to a greater or lesser degree.

Considering the course of George Bagby's career, it is hardly surprising that few voices of literary or historical realism were raised in Virginia in the concluding decades of the nineteenth century. Thomas Nelson Page's inflated vision of Virginia's historical destiny, presented at the three hundredth anniversary of the founding of Jamestown, in 1907, reflected the conventional intellectual attitudes of this period in the Old Dominion. Page pronounced that God had "prepared Virginia to place the seal of His favor on, and the Virginia colonists and their successors as His instruments to accomplish His mighty work."[13]

Not until the beginning of the twentieth century was the intellectual climate favorable for the application of the new methodology of historical scholarship to the Old Dominion. Philip A. Bruce's *Social Life of Virginia in the Seventeenth Century*, published in 1907, and Thomas Jefferson Wertenbaker's *Patrician and Plebeian in Virginia*, published in 1910, were pioneering works which helped to dispel the romantic haze

12. Quoted in Joseph Leonard King, *Dr. George William Bagby: A Study of Virginia Literature, 1850–1880* (New York, 1927), 174, 175.
13. Thomas Nelson Page, *Address at the Three Hundredth Anniversary of the Settlement of Jamestown* (Richmond, 1919), 28.

surrounding Virginia's settlement and cleared the way for further research. Bruce exhaustively detailed the similarities between social life in England and Virginia in the early decades of the colony's existence, and Wertenbaker established, among other things, the fact that the Old Dominion's planter-aristocracy had been far outnumbered by yeomen farmers.

Slowly the aristocratic Cavalier was whittled down to what historians considered a more realistic size. Francis Pendleton Gaines declared that history's emphasis on the contribution of Virginia's first families in the Revolutionary War had necessarily neglected the great mass of small farmers from the state who had fought with equal heroism and sacrifice. The typical Virginian, he asserted, had little in common with Caruthers' gay bird of aristocratic plumage. Wilbur J. Cash, in his penetrating analysis of the southern mind, noted that even in its heyday Tidewater Virginia was a new society perched perilously close to the frontier. "Most of the Virginians who counted themselves gentlemen," he declared, "were still, in reality, hardly more than superior farmers."[14]

Cash's judgment perhaps reflects more the iconoclasm of a North Carolinian than a measured historical judgment. More recent historical analyses, however, have confirmed the relatively modest origins of Virginia's early settlers. Bernard Bailyn observes that the colony's dominant families can largely be traced to a third-generation wave of immigration that arrived from England between 1645 and 1675. Many of these men were "younger sons of substantial families well-connected in London business and government circles." Though not in the strictest historical sense Cavaliers, they were qualified to reproduce the governing patterns of the English gentry, and they quickly set about to do so. But this Virginia aristocracy was different in several important ways from its English model. Virginia planters were of necessity hardworking men involved with the task of developing a wilderness and blessed with little time for the leisurely pursuits of the English country squire. Rapid exhaustion of the soil combined with an enormous supply of new land to effectively eliminate the need for primogeniture and entail.

14. Gaines, *The Southern Plantation*, 187; Cash, *The Mind of the South*, 8.

Thus economic and political power was not concentrated, as it was in the mother country, in the stem family. The distribution of lands to all of a planter's children and intensive intermarriage between families produced a broad and diffuse leveling among Virginia's ruling gentry. Finally, the Virginia planter, unlike his English counterpart, was subject to an external political power in London that lay beyond his control; so that the highest political authority in the Old Dominion was not, as in England, synonymous with social class.[15]

In a more recent compilation of documentary evidence, Warren Billings confirms the idea that the bulk of Virginia's early immigrants "were rather ordinary, middling sorts of Englishmen." Those who became great planters were not markedly different in social origin from those who became small or middle planters. However, most of the men whose families came to dominate Virginia's social and political life had financial resources or connections at home or in the Old Dominion which "gave them a competitive edge over the others, and they used this advantage to push their way to the top. . . . Their claim to leadership did not have the sanction of ancient usage or custom: it was founded upon nothing else than their having outstripped their rivals."[16] Wesley Frank Craven provides the best thumbnail sketch of this first Cavalier aspirant:

> He was young but not a child; he may have come from any part of England but in most instances probably from the southeastern section of the kingdom. His religious convictions might speak for any of the divergences of opinion that beset the English church in that century but in the act of migrating he belonged to no organized religious movement. As for his political opinions, he may have supported the king, he may have backed parliament, even Cromwell, or he may simply have displayed the ambivalence of attitude which so many men through the course of his-

15. Bernard Bailyn, "Politics and Social Structure in Virginia," in James Morton Smith (ed.), *Seventeenth-Century America: Essays in Colonial History* (Chapel Hill, 1959), 98, 106–14.
16. Warren M. Billings (ed.), *The Old Dominion in the Seventeenth Century: A Documentary History of Virginia, 1606–1689* (Chapel Hill, 1975), 105, 109.

tory have shown when living in the midst of a revolution. Certainly, he was rarely a zealot. Primarily, he was an adventurer, and in the fullest sense of the word, a man seeking the main chance for himself in that part of the new world which at the moment seemed to offer for him the best chance.[17]

Historians have thus determined with increasing accuracy the social origins of the men who ultimately composed Virginia's ruling planter class. For the best overall description of the kind of society the sons, grandsons, and great-grandsons of these early immigrants developed in Tidewater Virginia in the eighteenth century, we can turn to Carl Bridenbaugh's *Myths and Realities*. Bridenbaugh concludes that colonial Virginia was overwhelmingly middle class in its social composition, not aristocratic. The "poor white" class of landless or nearly landless farmers—shiftless, swinish, but docile—was never large. At the opposite end of the spectrum, only about three hundred families in the entire Tidewater area possessed large plantations worked by numerous slaves and indentured servants. There was, however, a large middle class, holding small to medium estates of from two hundred to five hundred acres and owning few or no slaves.[18]

The large landowners, though few in number, nonetheless exerted a powerful influence on the economic, social, and cultural life of the colony. As we have seen, they sought to re-create in the Old Dominion the pattern of English rural life dominated by the ruling gentry and the code of the gentleman. But as Bernard Bailyn has also noted, there were important differences between Virginia and England. English estates were farmed by freemen, Virginia plantations by an unassimilated slave population which by 1775 constituted nearly half of the colony's population. The English gentry were by and large rooted to the land through generations of ownership. In contrast, Virginia at the peak of its opulence in 1750 could boast few "aristocratic" families who had been established in the colony for more than seventy-five years. Tide-

17. Wesley Frank Craven, *White, Red, and Black: The Seventeenth Century Virginian* (Charlottesville, 1971), 30.
18. Bridenbaugh, *Myths and Realities*, 8–10.

water society was thus much less rigid in its social structure than that of rural England. There was, observes Bridenbaugh, "a considerable amount of moving upward from servitude to the rank of lower planter, and rather more from lesser to greater planter occurred than might be expected."[19] Virginia society was stratified, as all societies are, but far from ossified.

An example of New World class mobility was William Carr of Prince William County. Inheriting 150 acres from his father, Carr steadily improved his social standing. He was addressed in correspondence as "gentleman" in 1762, "captain" in 1767, and "merchant" in 1773. When he died, he held an estate of nearly one thousand acres.[20] Edmund Pendleton's rise in Tidewater society was even more dramatic. From a propertyless apprentice to the clerk of the Hanover County Court, Pendleton rose by his own professional skill and personal merit to become a member of the House of Burgesses, a member of the Continental Congress, first speaker of the Virginia House of Delegates, and president of the Virginia Ratification Convention. "Thus," he observed with justifiable pride, "without any classical education—without patrimony—without what is called the influence of Family Connection, and without solicitation, I have attained the highest offices in any Country."[21]

The cultural achievement of the Cavalier is often assessed by the sprightly, graceful prose of William Byrd or by the light, pleasant verses of the *Virginia Gazette*. Yet Bridenbaugh observes that Byrd was not typical of the kind of gentleman Tidewater produced, and the verse and essays in the *Gazette* were lifted more often than not from the pages of the *London* and *Gentleman's* magazines. "Literary achievement," he reflects, "is not to be expected from an aristocracy whose members are concerned with politics and the extroverted life of a rural people."[22]

More recently Richard Beale Davis has challenged Bridenbaugh's

19. *Ibid.*, 18. See Bailyn, "Politics and Social Structure in Virginia," 106–14.

20. Robert E. Brown and B. Katherine Brown, *Virginia, 1705–1786: Democracy or Aristocracy* (East Lansing, 1964), 39.

21. David John Mays (ed.), *The Letters and Papers of Edmund Pendleton, 1734–1803* (Charlottesville, 1967), II, 606.

22. Bridenbaugh, *Myths and Realities*, 42.

assessment of Tidewater culture. Focusing on the planters' houses and gardens, on their love of music, their theaters, their sermons, their essays, diaries, and letters, Davis contends that "for the two generations preceding the Revolution and the decade thereafter, that is, from about 1720 to 1789, there was in actuality a strong expression of discriminating taste in the arts, as high a proportion of well-educated men as existed anywhere in the colonies."[23] To say that the variety of cultural expression in Tidewater Virginia was as high as or higher than in other colonies is not, however, to advance great claims for Virginia. The American colonies were a cultural backwater, and the paucity of genuine literary achievement in the Old Dominion lends support to Bridenbaugh's conclusion that Tidewater planters were not as a rule distinguished by their interest in belles lettres.

Although sons of the more substantial families received from private tutors the equivalent of a grammar school education, relatively few Virginians could afford to send their children to England to complete their studies. College records indicate only a handful of students at William and Mary attended that school for more than a year or two. Original wills and inventories show that the typical plantation library contained a limited number of books. The planter usually purchased works that would aid him in the running of his estate. Therefore, legal and medical titles were far more liberally represented on Virginians' bookshelves than were novels or collections of poetry.[24] It would appear that the average Virginia gentleman's knowledge was limited in its scope and distinctly practical in its application.

Although the economy of Tidewater Virginia flourished for one hundred years and produced a number of large planters, it was doomed by its enslavement to a one-crop tobacco economy. Planters were completely dependent on their English creditors for nearly all their manufactured goods and many of their foodstuffs. They could purchase the goods they needed only with tobacco—a product which brought grad-

23. Richard Beale Davis, "The Intellectual Golden Age in the Colonial Chesapeake Bay Country," in his *Literature and Society in Early Virginia, 1608–1840* (Baton Rouge, 1973), 151–52.
24. Bridenbaugh, *Myths and Realities*, 35–41.

ually diminishing prices on the London market and quickly exhausted the once-fertile land. The planters worked endless hours supervising their estates, trying to keep their huge farming operations financially afloat.[25] Yet by the end of the Revolutionary War—a war in which the Virginia planter had played such a distinguished role—many of the state's most prominent families faced bankruptcy.

Colonial Virginia was therefore neither so aristocratic nor so opulent as romance fiction has pictured it. Neither was the Cavalier the epitome of grace, refinement, and culture. The ruling class was not a class of vast wealth and unlimited leisure. Bridenbaugh summarizes the contribution of Tidewater society in this way: "The genius of this people lay in agriculture and politics; it displayed itself to the world as *noblesse oblige*, gracious hospitality, zest for living, effortless courtesy—all forms of action befitting their way of life. The Chesapeake Society produced a unique bourgeois aristocracy with more than its share of great and noble men; they were, however, men of intellect, not intellectuals."[26]

Recent scholarship has carried Bridenbaugh's conclusions even further. Robert and Katherine Brown question the actual existence of a ruling class of first families. Even more than Bridenbaugh, the Browns emphasize the middle-class nature of Virginia society and the limitless opportunity for prosperity and social advancement the colony afforded. They reject the idea that Virginia was controlled by an aristocracy of large merchant planters and underline what they consider the fluidity of class structure. Though there was an upper class, they conclude, it cannot legitimately be considered an aristocracy.[27]

In the most recent assessment of Virginia's legendary plantation aristocracy, Rhys Isaac argues that the Old Dominion's planters did strive, with initial success, to establish a hierarchical society along English lines in the colony. Yet Isaac also contends that this order was subject to disintegrating forces almost as soon as it had been established.

25. For a revealing look at the unremitting toil of both planter and slave, see Rhys Isaac's description of Landon Carter in *The Transformation of Virginia, 1740–1790* (Chapel Hill, 1982), 22–30.
26. Bridenbaugh, *Myths and Realities*, 53.
27. Brown and Brown, *Virginia, 1705–1786*, 307.

After 1740, he observes, the planter aristocracy, "only just settling into its newly built Classical mansions, courthouses, and churches of brick, began to undergo radical changes."[28] The loss of control of credit by the gentry over the smaller planters combined with the popular rejection of the established Anglican church and the patriot movement of the 1760s and 1770s to produce a postrevolutionary Virginia far more socially fractured than the colonial society of 1740.

In spite of the bourgeois origins of Virginia's Tidewater elite and in spite of the relatively brief time during which they exercised firm control over the colony's social structure, there can be no doubt that the Old Dominion produced a significant number of men who lived on vast estates in considerable style. Except on the rice and indigo plantations of coastal Carolina, this impressive accretion of land and wealth was unmatched in colonial America. Berkeley, Shirley, Westover, Carter's Grove—the stately mansions that still line the north bank of the James— bear witness that colonial Virginia was something more than merely a rural society composed of middle-class farmers. These surviving homes remain expressions of architectural and decorative taste and proportion. William Byrd II personally supervised the building of Westover, with its fine stone chimneys, its exquisite doorways, its carefully handcrafted gates and mantelpieces, its elegantly formal garden. He amassed one of the largest and most diverse collections of books in the New World, a collection large enough to require the services of a full-time librarian. Byrd's Westover remains a visual symbol of that perfect fusion of wealth and taste which few societies, least of all frontier societies, attain. Granted, Westover was not a typical estate; yet its presence cannot be dismissed as insignificant in assessing the quality of Tidewater civilization.

Perhaps, as historians suggest, the Virginian of fortune was not often a polished and cultured gentleman. It is clear, however, that he thought, or liked to believe, he was. This self-image is clearly displayed in the poems and essays which decorate the pages of the *Virginia Gazette*, published in Williamsburg from 1736 to 1778. One writer com-

28. Isaac, *The Transformation of Virginia*, 137.

plains of hearing "the Word *Honour* frequently profaned in the Mouths of the Vulgar and inferior sort of people." Another bemoans the degeneration of the Virginia gentleman. He attacks the excesses of gaming, cock-fighting, horse-racing, drinking, and blasphemy which currently are tolerated among the leading citizens and fears lest the term *gentleman* sink into absolute contempt. From the *Gazette* of April 4, 1751, comes the tragic story of a young Italian lady "of noble Extraction, but, it seems not of noble sentiments [who] forgot her Rank so far as to fall in Love with one of her Footmen."[29]

John C. Miller has demonstrated that aristocratic sentiments such as those expressed in the *Virginia Gazette* were not limited to the Old Dominion and the southern colonies. Puritans saw a hierarchical society as part of the divine plan, and northern merchant as well as southern planter sought to assert claims of birth and social class in an emerging frontier democracy. One might assume that a social code based on traditional European notions of fixed status and inequality would be doomed in a much less structured frontier society, and indeed the northern merchant never successfully imposed the notion of aristocracy of birth on his region. But the southern planter managed to claim a considerably larger measure of social prestige and political power, primarily because he championed the popular causes of his colonial constituency.[30]

Edmund Morgan sheds further light on the commonality of interests between large and small planters in Virginia. In an electorate dominated by small landowners, the planter aristocracy was notably successful in convincing the voters that it spoke for the interests of all. Large as well as small farmers opposed the attempts of London to regulate their land, and all planters shared a dependence on tobacco as a primary income producer. An even more significant factor, Morgan believes, is that by the eighteenth century the great planter was content to extract wealth from his slave labor, rather than from rents and taxes on small farmers. Ironically, then, slavery cemented the bonds among all

29. "Essay on Honor," *Virginia Gazette*, July 27–August 3, 1739, p. 1; "To the Printer," *ibid.*, July 11, 1751, p. 1; "London," *ibid.*, April 4, 1751, p. 2.

30. John C. Miller, *The First Frontier: Life in Colonial America* (New York, 1966), 108–11.

landowning Virginians and "became an essential, if unacknowledged, ingredient of the republican ideology that enabled Virginians to lead the nation."[31]

Although property qualifications were not restrictive in the colony and nearly all landowners could vote, the political power of the planter aristocracy was clearly displayed in the county courts, where appointed justices of the peace with lifetime tenure wielded wide executive, judicial, and legislative authority. These justices owned an average of nine hundred acres of land and twenty-five slaves, statistics which suggest that the typical county justice was drawn from the upper rather than the middle or lower planter class. Moreover, certain families tended to be represented again and again on the county courts. In the twenty years before the Revolution, 25 percent of Virginia's county justices came from fifty-five families, and 75 percent were chosen from fewer than four hundred families. "In most elections," Charles Sydnor points out, "all the candidates were members of the gentry. . . . In effect, the gentry provided the candidates and the freeholders made choice among them."[32]

The success of the planter aristocracy in capturing the allegiance of the yeoman and in thereby perpetuating their political ascendency probably explains the distinctively elitist ambiance which a French visitor, the Marquis de Chastellux, detected in Virginia at the time of the Revolution. There Chastellux observed a willingness of the masses, unlike those of other colonies, to be led by the few. He offers as illustration this statement of support made by Virginia citizens to Benjamin Harrison, Richard Henry Lee, and Thomas Jefferson before they left to attend the First Continental Congress in Philadelphia. "You assert that there is a fixed intention to invade our rights and privileges; we own that we do not see this clearly, but since you assure us that it is so, we believe it. We are about to take a very dangerous step, but we have confidence in you and will do anything you think proper." Such implicit

31. Edmund S. Morgan, *American Slavery, American Freedom: The Ordeal of Colonial Virginia* (New York, 1975), 386.

32. Charles S. Sydnor, *Gentlemen Freeholders: Political Practice in Washington's Virginia* (Chapel Hill, 1952), 10.

confidence in the colony's leaders led Chastellux to conclude that though "the government may become democratic, as it is at the present moment . . . the very spirit of the government, will always be aristocratic."[33]

It should be pointed out that Chastellux noted less pleasing aspects of Virginia life, which he also associated with the dominance of the planter aristocracy—vanity, sloth, slavery, and the poverty of many white people. Indeed, visitors to eighteenth-century Virginia frequently noted the pride and pretensions of the wealthy planters. An interesting critique of the pride and vanity of the Virginia gentry can be found in the pages of Philip Fithian's diary. Fithian, New Jersey born and Princeton educated, lived for about one year at Robert Carter's Nomini Hall as tutor of Carter's children. He came to know intimately and to admire the Carter family, one of Virginia's finest. Yet though he enjoyed his time in Virginia, Fithian preferred life in New Jersey, where he felt there was a comparatively level distribution of wealth and where thrift and industry purchased a man's ticket to social acceptance. In Virginia, he noted, "such amazing property . . . blows up the owners to an imagination, which is visible in all, but in various degrees according to their respective virtue, that they are exalted as much above other Men in worth and precedency, as blind stupid fortune has made a difference in their property."[34]

A scrutiny of the colonial period results in contrasting pictures of Tidewater civilization. On one hand Virginia seems to have been a rural society poised close to the wilderness and composed mainly of farmers of modest fortunes; yet Virginia was also a land of large estates owned by proud and powerful families—a land where the code of the gentleman and aristocratic notions exerted considerable influence on the conduct of its citizens. Although these pictures are different, neither is historically inaccurate. By 1750 the Old Dominion was paradoxically both a frontier land of opportunity and a land of established and inherited wealth and privilege.

33. Marquis de Chastellux, *Travels in North America in the Years 1780, 1781, and 1782*, trans. Howard C. Rice, Jr. (Chapel Hill, 1963), II, 429, 435.
34. Hunter Dickinson Farish (ed.), *Journal and Letters of Philip Vickers Fithian, 1773–1774: A Plantation Tutor of the Old Dominion* (Charlottesville, 1957), 161.

Nothing illustrates the peculiar mixed nature of Virginia's past more clearly than the backgrounds of the men who came to dominate her. Historians have shown that relatively few men of noble birth actually emigrated to the colony from England. On the other hand, the founders of Virginia's first families were not indentured servants or penniless soldiers of fortune. The most important requirement for success in Virginia was not noble birth, but capital. With a comparatively modest sum at one's disposal one could purchase indentured servants, buy a large tract of land, and set oneself up as a gentleman farmer. It is therefore not surprising that many younger sons of the English gentry, desirous of acquiring fortune and maintaining their social position, came to Virginia. The Lees and Randolphs were of such genteel origin. Nor is it surprising that merchants, tradesmen, and sea captains found it easier to rise to gentility in the new colony than in England. The Ludwells, Spencers, Steggs, Bollings, Bookers, Carys, Brents, Byrds, and Carters all were of such middle-class origins.[35] As Robert Beverley correctly noted, Virginia was not settled by noblemen, but neither was it settled by refugees from London's sewers.

Virginia's finest families were clearly of middle-class origin, and the aristocracy they established was, as Bridenbaugh terms it, a bourgeois aristocracy. The early planters were not ashamed of making profits or of engaging in commerce. Indeed, the terms *gentleman* and *merchant* were used synonymously in the colonial period. *Merchant* was not, as it was in later times, an odious appellation. The plantation owner's wharves, storage houses, and gristmills made him a factor and tradesman for the smaller surrounding farms, as well as a planter.[36]

Yet the larger planters, regardless of their bourgeois origins and bourgeois pursuits, quickly established themselves in positions of power and influence in the colony and only infrequently relinquished that power, passing it on to son and grandson. In the sense that this control tended to assume a hereditary prerogative, the leading families of Virginia did form a kind of aristocracy. By the end of the seventeenth cen-

35. Wright, *First Gentlemen of Virginia*, 44–47.
36. Richard Beale Davis (ed.), *William Fitzhugh and His Chesapeake World, 1676–1701: The Fitzhugh Letters and Other Documents* (Chapel Hill, 1963), 14.

tury, this aristocracy was firmly established. Its presence was most immediately visible in the families who were represented in the Governor's Council from generation to generation. As the price of tobacco dropped through the eighteenth century, those men who weathered the economic storm most successfully were those who owned the largest estates. Thus, declining economic prosperity tended to consolidate and even more firmly perpetuate the power of the wealthiest families.[37] The term *bourgeois aristocracy* is itself a paradox, but it probably best describes the ruling class in colonial Virginia.

The process by which the merchant planters of the Old Dominion established their wealth and social position can be demonstrated by examining a few of the men who built their family dynasties in this virgin land. The Fitzhugh fortunes were established in Virginia by William, the youngest son of a Bedford woolen draper, born in 1651. William obviously brought with him to the new world a respectable sum of money, for he purchased a rather large tract of land in Northern Neck Virginia around 1670. He had also received legal training in England that led him to a distinguished career before the bar in Virginia. Boasting an estate and legal expertise, Fitzhugh married the eleven-year-old daughter of the well-established Mrs. Rose Tucker Gerard in 1674, further consolidating his social position in the Northern Neck. In 1677, only about seven years after having arrived in Virginia, he was elevated to the House of Burgesses. By 1686 Fitzhugh possessed a working estate of one thousand acres farmed by twenty-nine slaves. He had erected a commodious house of thirteen well-furnished rooms, boasting brick chimneys and walls hung with tapestries. This estate was complemented by "four good Cellars, a Dairy, Dovecoat, Stable, Barn, Hen house, Kitchen and all other conveniencys."[38] Fitzhugh's wealth continued to increase dramatically during his lifetime. When he died in 1701, he owned, in addition to his house and plantation buildings, 54,000 acres of land, 51 slaves, 6 indentured servants, 122 pieces of silver plate, a large amount of household furniture, 2 coaches, and a study full of books.

37. Wright, *First Gentlemen of Virginia*, 52–57.
38. Davis (ed.), *William Fitzhugh and His Chesapeake World*, 175.

In only slightly more than thirty years Fitzhugh amassed a tremendous amount of private wealth. He also succeeded through his children's marriages in interweaving his fortunes with those of other established Virginia families, thereby ensuring the perpetuation of a dynasty that he had founded. His eldest son, also named William, followed him in the House of Burgesses and represented the Fitzhughs for the first time on the Governor's Council in Williamsburg. This son married Ann Lee, daughter of Colonel Richard Lee, scion of one of the Northern Neck's wealthiest families. His brothers, Thomas and George, married the daughters of another prominent Virginian, George Mason. Already by 1700 the Virginia aristocracy, founded on enormous holdings of land and slaves and sustained by the calculated unions of family blood and fortune, was assuming a recognizable shape.

Robert "King" Carter was representative of the second generation of bourgeois aristocrats who piled up fortunes that far surpassed even those of their immediate predecessors. Robert's father, the son of a London wine merchant of modest means, had settled in the Northern Neck around 1640. At his death, he bequeathed to his son more than five thousand acres of land and more than one hundred slaves. On this auspicious foundation Robert continually built and enlarged, increasing his wealth through hard work and shrewd business acumen. By his death in 1732 Robert, now known as "King," owned more than 1,000 slaves and more than 300,000 acres of land.

Robert Carter's letters reveal the complex attitudes that characterized Virginia's newly emergent bourgeois aristocracy. A shrewd businessman, ever alert to the price for his tobacco on various English markets, Carter discusses with his agents the most prudent investment of his profits, warning them against sinking too much of his money in the South Sea Company. He demands full accounts of his son John's expenses in England, continually chiding him for his spendthrift ways. Whether writing about the price of land, the rate of return on an annuity, or the means employed to collect debts, Carter's letters are those of a businessman, with a businessman's concern for profit and loss. Nothing expresses Carter's shopkeeper mentality more clearly or humorously than the following passage written to his agent, William

Dawkins, concerning his son's behavior in England: "You please me very well in the commendable character you give me of my son. 'Tis no small satisfaction to me to have a pennyworth for my penny. To have spent so much money upon a dunce or a blockhead had been most intolerable."[39]

Yet if his correspondence reveals Carter the shopkeeper, it also reveals Carter the Virginia aristocrat, the man who became known as "King." His capacity for gentlemanly hauteur is vividly conveyed in a letter of reproof to Dawkins. Apparently Carter believed Dawkins had become too presumptuous and expected too much gratitude for managing his sons' affairs in England. With reference to a prior letter that Dawkins had written, Carter directs his rage and disdain toward his agent: "Now pray, upon the whole, where was your prudence, or rather manners, to use me with the language that was hardly fit for your footman, if you keep one? You might remember I was your master's equal and all along have lived in as good rank and fashion as he did, even when you were something like Grave's cabin boy."[40] Interestingly, in this passage Carter does not claim to be a nobleman, but he leaves no doubt that he considers himself a gentleman, due all the status and esteem of his counterpart in England.

Carter blood probably flows in the veins of more Virginia aristocrats than that of any other family. King Carter's sons founded Sabine Hall and Berkeley; his grandsons built equally magnificent dwellings at Shirley, Nomini Hall, and Carter's Grove. This venerable patriarch claimed many illustrious descendants. Two of his grandsons, Carter Braxton and Benjamin Harrison I, signed the Declaration of Independence. Harrison later became Virginia's first governor. Great-grandson William Henry Harrison was president of the United States. But Carter's most famous descendant was a great-grandson who led the armies of the Confederacy—Robert E. Lee.[41] In the marital alliances of suc-

39. Louis B. Wright (ed.), *Letters of Robert Carter, 1720–1727: The Commercial Interests of a Virginia Gentleman* (San Marino, Calif., 1940), 3–4.

40. *Ibid.*, 81–82.

41. For a concise sketch of Carter's descendants, see Clifford Dowdey, *The Virginia Dynasties: The Emergence of "King" Carter and the Golden Age* (Boston, 1969), 362–

cessive generations of Carters, one sees most clearly how the best Virginia bloods were blended to form a self-perpetuating aristocracy.

Of all the stars in colonial Virginia's cultural constellation, perhaps none shone more brightly than William Byrd II. Byrd was the most famous of Virginia's early planter aristocrats. In his successful blending of sound business sense and organizational skill with political, scientific, and cultural distinction, Byrd perhaps most closely approximated the Cavalier ideal.[42] Indeed, one might consider him the representative figure of the Virginia Cavalier in history.

Byrd's father, William Byrd I, was the son of a London goldsmith. From an uncle he inherited land and a trading post at the falls of the James, where Richmond now stands. The elder Byrd made his fortune by trading rum and guns for furs with the Indians and slaves for tobacco with surrounding planters. He left over 25,000 acres of land to his son in 1704. Young William was carefully prepared by his father for a future role as a leader in the Virginia colony. He was sent to England as a child and attended the well-known Felsted School in Essex. At sixteen, he traveled to Holland to study business and trade. In 1692 he returned to England and entered Middle Temple. He was admitted to the bar in 1695. Thus when Byrd returned to Virginia in 1696 at the age of twenty-two he had been properly groomed for a seat in the House of Burgesses, to which he was promptly elected. He followed his father to the Governor's Council in 1708.

Byrd's business and legal training was complemented by literary and cultural triumphs in London. His protector in England during these years was the distinguished diplomat, Sir Robert Southwell. Young Byrd was well acquainted with Wycherley, Congreve, and other literary lions. After his return to America, he corresponded extensively with such famous figures as Charles Boyle, earl of Orrery; Lord Oxford; Robert Walpole; and Hans Sloane, later president of the Royal Society.

---

69. Nathaniel Burt's *First Families: The Makings of an American Aristocracy* (Boston, 1970), 23–26, contains a brief but engaging description of Virginia's river mansions and the complex family ties among their builders.

42. The best brief description of Byrd's life can be found in Wright, *First Gentlemen of Virginia*, 312–47.

Byrd's supreme intellectual triumph was his induction at the age of twenty-two into the Royal Society.

When he returned to Virginia, however, Byrd did not content himself with luxuriating in the triumphs of his youth. Throughout his life he worked hard in the service of his colony. In 1697, after less than a year's stay in Virginia, he returned to London, acting as agent for the colony until 1705. From 1715 to 1720 he was again in England to represent the planters before the Board of Trade. He returned to Virginia in 1720, but in the same year he reluctantly agreed to represent the colony again in London as colonial agent, a post which he held until 1726. In 1728 he served on the Virginia Boundary Commission, personally supervising the arduous surveying of the boundary between Virginia and North Carolina. In 1736, at the age of sixty-two, he was again called to serve on the commission that surveyed the Northern Neck. During his last years Byrd was senior member of the legislative council and presided in that capacity over the General Court of Virginia. In addition to these time-consuming public duties, Byrd also supervised and maintained his own vast estates.

To the end of his life, Byrd remained a man of indefatigable energy who conscientiously maintained his cultural contacts in spite of his distance from London and the pressing weight of plantation business and governmental duties. For over thirty years he corresponded with Hans Sloane, physician and botanist, supplying him with animal, vegetable, and mineral specimens from the new world. His own private diaries reveal the systematic and rigorous study habits, the early morning hours given to readings in Hebrew, Greek, Latin, and Italian. His huge personal library testifies to the extent of his literary interests, and his unpublished manuscripts, including the "Dividing Line Histories," demonstrate a sprightly and sure command of English prose. Though situated perilously near the savage wilderness thousands of miles from the mother country, Byrd successfully maintained his stance of the cultured and refined gentleman of the world. His was an assertion of civilization that demanded the full expenditure of his own remarkable energies.

Such were the Virginia aristocrats; such were the men who shaped, molded, and eventually came to represent for their nineteenth-century descendants the Virginia Cavalier. They were assuredly not Cavaliers in the literal sense of the term. They were by and large men of distinctly bourgeois origin, and they established their dynasties in Virginia through a remarkable combination of skill, will, and stamina. In spite of their relatively undistinguished origins, however, they considered themselves gentlemen, creators of a new dispensation in Virginia. The social ideals and the code of conduct which shaped their lives came from England, and they sought to affirm in the New World the rightness of the patterns which they had inherited from the Old. Because of the difficulty of maintaining the old pattern on the edge of the wilderness, they were highly conscious of what was civilized and proper. Thus William Fitzhugh, in spite of his extensive wealth and comfortable situation, bemoaned the lack of good society and the scarcity of good books and adequate schools. Commenting apprehensively on the education of his children, he wrote, "Better be never born than ill bred."[43]

If most wealthy Virginians were not in fact of aristocratic origin, nearly all of them acted as if they were. William Byrd was the son of an immigrant trader and grandson of a goldsmith. But from his position of wealth, privilege, and eminence in the colony, he was able to forget his own modest origins and make this harsh judgment of a young lady's elopement with a plantation overseer without the least sense of incongruity or irony: "Had she run away with a gentleman or a pretty Fellow, there might have been some excuse for her, tho' he were of inferior Fortune; but to stoop to a dirty plebeian, without any kind of merit, is the lowest Prostitution."[44]

In a sense Byrd was entitled to his judgment because he consciously adhered to the code by which he judged others. It would be false to claim that Virginia developed in the seventeenth and eighteenth centuries a highly aristocratic and cultured society. Yet, as Louis Wright says, there was a germ of truth in the legendary picture of life in the Old

43. Davis (ed.), *William Fitzhugh and His Chesapeake World*, 203.
44. Quoted in Marshall Fishwick, *Virginia: A New Look at the Old Dominion* (New York, 1959), 197.

Dominion. "Virginia did develop an aristocracy of wealthy planters who, in time, came to live in considerable splendor, who established a pattern of life modeled after the English gentry, who ruled the destinies of the colony as by inherited right."[45] The original Virginia planters were only men, but they were men of stature and vitality who were easily transformed into legends by their descendants.

Virginia's aristocracy as it existed in history was far removed from the aristocracy that flourished on the pages of nineteenth-century romantic novels. The Old Dominion was not Arcadia, and her merchant-planters were not silken-coated grandees who whiled away their time with various civilized amusements. Neither were they directly descended from English lords. Yet the Cavalier myth, as we have seen, still stubbornly clings in the popular imagination. By the same myth-making process these noble Cavaliers have spread from Tidewater Virginia all over the South. Historical studies continue to pile up, and still the myth retains much of its vigor and its appeal. Perhaps it is true, as Francis Butler Simkins contends, that historians "forget that what is often important to Southerners is not what actually happened but what is believed to have happened."[46]

Southerners would seem always to have had an impatience with the limitations of reality, for by the beginning of the nineteenth century, the earliest period to which most historians trace the rise of southern regional consciousness, her writers were at work creating a magnificent planter aristocracy. In no state was this process more productive than in Virginia, the home of the original plantation idea. Here, a precipitous decline in the state's economic fortunes and a loss of cultural vitality coincided with the appearance of several writers who created the earliest plantation fiction and the first of the South's fictional Cavaliers. The Old Dominion's economic eclipse almost certainly influenced the tone of these early novels, for in them the Cavalier is viewed as a romantic figure doomed by the progressive forces of history.

45. Wright, *The First Gentlemen of Virginia*, 38–39.
46. Francis Butler Simkins, "Tolerating the South's Past," in Gerster and Cords (eds.), *Myth and Southern History*, 317.

THREE

The Cavalier's Developing Image

TUCKER AND KENNEDY

THE romantic embellishment of the Cavalier figure in early nineteenth-century Virginia fiction is paradoxically linked with the very unromantic economic and cultural decline of Tidewater rural society during the same period. This decline had set in by the end of the Revolutionary War. Its most debilitating effects were extensively noted and bemoaned during the first quarter of the nineteenth century by both natives and visitors. But the economic and social catastrophe this depression brought to rural Virginia was in part irremediable. Large landowners in the Old Dominion never made a complete financial recovery and never reattained the opulence and power they had enjoyed during the first three-quarters of the eighteenth century.

59

Rural Virginia's decline was the joint product of a wearing out of the once-fertile land, brought about by the unceasing planting and replanting of tobacco, and of the unreliability of the foreign export market, on which Virginia's one-crop economy was absolutely and helplessly dependent. The economic and agricultural sins committed by the commonwealth's fathers during the eighteenth century were visited on her sons in the nineteenth. The once-flourishing Tidewater ports of Alexandria, Tappahannock, Yorktown, and Norfolk declined in population and prosperity. By 1800, for example, Yorktown retained only one-third of its 1770 population. Norfolk, the largest town in the state, had only four hundred residences. Even Williamsburg, the once-thriving and active center of government, was spotted with deserted or ruined houses. Its church, Bruton Parish, stood neglected and sadly out of repair.[1] Twenty years later population statistics and economic indices continued to tell all too clearly Virginia's sad story. From 1819 to 1833 the price of tobacco remained prevailingly low. As a result exports from the state were worth no more at the end of this period than they had been in the beginning. Between 1820 and 1830 Virginia's rate of population growth, even including the still-developing transmountain region, was less than half the national average of 33 percent. During the next decade growth was even lower, creeping at the rate of approximately 2 percent.[2]

Visitors from Europe noted definite signs of economic depression in Virginia as early as the 1780s. Jacques Brissot de Warville's *New Travels in the United States of America* contrasted the fertile farms of the Middle Atlantic states with the dilapidated condition of Virginia's agricultural economy. Instead of well-tilled acres, he found "a starved soil, bad cultivation, houses falling to ruin, cattle small and few, and black walking skeletons; in a word, you feel real misery, and apparent luxury, insulting each other." Isaac Weld, an English traveler who visited the Old Dominion in the mid-1790s, noted very few tracts of well-cultivated land. These occasional fertile acres, he observed, were "so intermixed

1. Eaton, *The Growth of Southern Civilization*, 5.
2. Charles S. Sydnor, *The Development of Southern Sectionalism, 1819–1848* (Baton Rouge, 1948), 250–51.

with extensive tracts of waste land, worn out by the culture of tobacco, and which are almost destitute of verdure, that on the whole the country has the appearance of barrenness."[3]

Europeans who traveled to the Old Dominion in the opening decades of the nineteenth century found economic conditions as bad as or worse than those of the postrevolutionary period. Englishman Edward Abdy quoted in his diary an article in the *American Quarterly Review* of 1832 which revealed that Virginia's total yearly agricultural production was less valuable than the yearly exports of the 1740s and 1750s, when the state had contained only a sixth of its present population. These figures tallied with Abdy's own personal notations of the state's stagnating agricultural economy. Other English travelers made similar observations. Adam Hodgson, for example, reported that numbers of planters were abandoning the cultivation of tobacco in desperation.[4]

Visitors from the northern states were no less quick than their European counterparts to note signs of economic and social decline. Arthur Singleton described the "loose, uncompacted, unappropriated appearance" of Virginia's plantation homes and villages. "The ancient Episcopal churches," he wrote, "which were once so predominant, are mostly in a state of dilapidation. The rank weeds rustle around the doors; the fox looks out at their windows." James Kirke Paulding was a more sympathetic observer of Virginia life than Singleton. He was drawn to the carefully measured pace of living and the ease, grace, and good manners with which Virginians invested their social relations. Yet even he could not avoid the brutal reality that the plantation system, which had nourished this way of living, was collapsing. A few of the old plantations had managed to survive, he observed, "but many of the houses are shut; others have passed into the hands of the industrious, or the speculating, whose modes of thinking, feeling, and acting are totally different. . . . Nothing now remains, but the traditionary details of

3. Jacques Pierre Brissot de Warville, *New Travels in the United States of America, Performed in 1788* (London, 1792), 288; Isaac Weld, *Travels Through the States of North America and the Provinces of Upper and Lower Canada* (1799; rpr. New York, 1970), 151.

4. Jane Louise Mesick, *The English Traveler in America, 1785–1835* (New York, 1922), 138, 157.

some aged matron, who lives only in the recollections of the past, of ancient modes, and ancient hospitality."[5]

Virginians themselves were not unaware of the grave economic conditions which were being described by visitors. John Randolph of Roanoke, in a letter to Josiah Quincy, gave this mordant view of his native state: "The old mansions, where they have been spared by fire . . . are fast falling to decay; the families, with few exceptions, dispersed from St. Mary's to St. Louis; such as remain here sink into obscurity. They whose fathers rode in coaches and drank the choicest wines now ride on saddlebags, and drink grog, when they can get it. What enterprise or capital there was in the country retired westward." Even those who stayed behind and strove manfully to restore their lands through innovative farming techniques, such as John Taylor of Caroline, were forced to confront, as Taylor did in the introduction to his *Arator* essay, "the terrible facts, that the strongest chord which vibrates on the heart of man, cannot tie our people to the natal spot, that they view it with horror, and flee from it to new climes with joy, determine our agricultural progress, to be a progress of emigration, and not of improvement."[6]

Virginia's deteriorating economic fabric had its inevitable effect on the cultural tone of the upper class of planter-aristocrats—those Virginians who had led the colony with such skill before the Revolution, contributed so worthily to national independence, and asserted themselves with such distinction in directing the nation's destiny after the Revolution. As Clement Eaton has pointed out, the serious decline in the commonwealth's tobacco trade contributed to a growing isolation not only from her northern neighbors but also from England and the Continent. This isolation, with its mental concomitant, provincialism, embedded itself so deeply in the texture of Virginia's culture that not even the introduction later in the century of the steamboat and the railroad suc-

5. Arthur Singleton, *Letters from the South and West* (Boston, 1824), 61; James Kirke Paulding, *Letters from the South, Written During an Excursion in the Summer of 1816* (New York, 1817), 42.

6. Randolph and Taylor quoted in Russell Kirk, *John Randolph of Roanoke: A Study in American Politics* (Indianapolis, 1978), 197, 14–15.

ceeded in significantly reducing it. Virginians were in fact becoming increasingly less cosmopolitan in outlook.[7] By 1820, notes Vernon Parrington, intellectual brilliance and the catholicity of taste which had marked Jefferson's generation were fading, replaced by increasing isolation and sectionalism.[8]

Virginia's provincialism, her tendency to retreat into an attitude of complacency, was reflected in the anemic condition of education in the state. In 1824, for example, William and Mary College had only eleven students enrolled. At the same time it was estimated that nearly a third of the Commonwealth's adult white population was illiterate.[9] In an effort to improve educational opportunities, Thomas Jefferson waged a long and eventually successful fight to establish the University of Virginia. But in waging his battles, Jefferson was forced to combat the ingrained indifference of the legislature. In 1820 the venerable politician expressed his disgust over the state's unwillingness to provide funds for the establishment of the university. He noted that Kentucky, a state settled long after Virginia, already had a flourishing university with over two hundred students, and concluded pessimistically: "All the States but our own are sensible that knowledge is power, and we are sinking into the barbarism of our Indian aborigines, and expect, like them, to oppose by ignorance the overwhelming mass of light and science by which we shall be surrounded. It is a comfort that I shall not live to see it."[10]

Travelers' diaries suggest that intellectual sophistication and openness to new ideas, which had been characteristic of a significant number of the planter-aristocrats of the eighteenth century, were less evident in the nineteenth. Arthur Singleton complained that at fish fries the men talked only of slaves, crops, and shooting matches. He concluded that as

7. Eaton, *The Growth of Southern Civilization*, 4.

8. Vernon L. Parrington, *The Romantic Revolution in America, 1800–1860* (New York, 1927), 30, Vol. II of Parrington, *The Main Currents of American Thought: An Interpretation of American Literature from the Beginnings to 1920*.

9. Sydnor, *The Development of Southern Sectionalism*, 59–64.

10. Philip Alexander Bruce, *History of the University of Virginia, 1819–1919: The Lengthened Shadow of One Man* (New York, 1920–22), I, 292.

a group the Virginians were intellectually undistinguished: "Their gymnastic education insures all to be bold riders, and brave fighters; but leaves a more than moiety suprisingly wanting in literature. Latin is not uncommon, but rare is any Greek. At William and Mary College, where the course is but *three*, instead of *four* years as with us, there is now no funded professorship of languages. They boast of their Virginia Presidents, but by whom were they educated? They care but little for belles-lettres." Of course Singleton was a New Englander, and residents of this region tended to echo Ralph Waldo Emerson's judgment that southerners were uncivilized "bladders of conceit."[11] Yet even allowing for exaggeration on the part of an unsympathetic outside observer, one may reasonably assume that Singleton's criticisms were not altogether unfounded and that Virginia culture had in fact suffered from economic depression and the corresponding weakening of the state's commercial links with the outside world.

The decline in the intellectual tone of Virginia society can be most conveniently illustrated by comparing the Constitutional Ratification Convention of 1788 with the State Constitutional Convention of 1829 – 1830. The 1788 convention was attended by James Madison, James Monroe, Edmund Pendleton, John Marshall, Edmund Randolph, George Wythe, Patrick Henry, and George Mason. These names, which read like an honor roll of revolutionary heroes, did not include the Old Dominion's most illustrious sons, for neither George Washington, in Mount Vernon, nor Thomas Jefferson, in Paris, was present at the convention, though their spiritual presence was real. By 1829, however, Washington and Jefferson were dead. Only Madison, Monroe, and Marshall were present at the 1829 convention, elderly survivors from Virginia's impressive group of revolutionary leaders. During the intervening forty years, Virginia had produced only two men of significant political stature—Abel P. Upshur, who contended that Virginia's Declaration of Rights was a collection of metaphysical subleties, and John Randolph, who declared at the convention that "if there be any

11. Singleton, *Letters from the South and West*, 67; Merton M. Sealts, Jr. (ed.), *The Journals and Miscellaneous Notebooks of Ralph Waldo Emerson* (Cambridge, Mass., 1965), V, 388–89.

point in which the authority of Mr. Jefferson might be considered as valid, it is in the mechanism of a plough." [12] These were the men whose spirits moved the convention of 1829–1830. Needless to say, they were men who, unlike their predecessors, left no profound or lasting imprint on our nation's political heritage.

Virginia was clearly undergoing a transformation during this period. Economic stagnation and decreasing wealth were pushing her away from the intellectual liberalism and from the cosmopolitan and confident spirit which had characterized many members of her upper class during and immediately after the Revolutionary War. Liberalism was frequently being replaced by virulent conservatism; confidence, by reaction and bitterness. The changing intellectual climate produced men like John Randolph, a gifted—perhaps brilliant—statesman who renounced the Jeffersonian political philosophy of his youth, blamed the collapse of Virginia's plantation economy on the abolition of primogeniture, and pronounced as his "great cardinal principle" this precept: "Never without the strongest necessity to disturb that which is at rest." It was no accident that by 1820 voting restrictions were more prohibitive in Virginia than in any other southern state, so that, as Jefferson sorrowfully admitted, the majority of free white males were excluded from the polls. [13]

But though Virginia had declined both economically and culturally since the Revolution, her native sons seemed no less devoted to her in the nineteenth century. As Joseph Glover Baldwin wittily observed, "patriotism with a Virginian is a noun personal." Hard times and limited opportunities might drive him from his beloved homeland, but wherever he went, the Virginian carried his spiritual allegiance to the Old Dominion with him. To paraphrase Baldwin, he might breathe in Alabama, but he lived in Virginia. The Virginian, therefore, whether a resident of Tidewater or of the southwest wilderness, retained a fierce loyalty to his native state, a loyalty that easily translated itself into a reverent worship of her glorious past. This past was but a few decades re-

---

12. Quoted in Kirk, *John Randolph of Roanoke*, 540.
13. *Ibid.*, 217–18; Sydnor, *The Development of Southern Sectionalism*, 47.

moved from the present; yet its close proximity did not deter the Virginian from seeing his homeland through a soft and blurring gauze of romance. He might leave behind the decaying village of Williamsburg, but as Baldwin discerned, he carried an altogether different image of that village with him to the frontier: "A hallowed charm seems to rest upon the venerable city, clothing its very dilapidation in a drapery of romance and of serene and classic interest: as if all the sweet and softened splendor which invests the 'Midsummer Night's Dream' were poured in a flood of mellow and poetic radiance over the now quiet and half 'deserted village.'"[14]

Thus, even as early as 1800 the Virginian had developed a unique way of viewing his history. The economic collapse which followed the brilliance of the revolutionary period had a direct impact on the way he interpreted his past. As Jay Hubbell has observed, the Virginian from this point in his history became a deteriorationist. He tended then and has tended through succeeding generations to view the past as inherently superior to and more interesting than the present.[15] The economic recession of the opening decades of the nineteenth century confirmed him in a view of history that was ideally suited to historical romance. For inevitably it was Virginia's completed destiny, not her present or future destiny, that appealed to her writers as the subject matter most worthy of fictional treatment.

Virginia was the first of the original states to experience serious and culturally destabilizing economic decline. The Old Dominion thus produced the first Americans to view history as a process of deterioration. By 1800 Virginians had begun to think about the relationship of past and present in a significantly different way from that of most other Americans. The Virginian's highly nostalgic and strongly melancholy sense of the past is perfectly illustrated by a story Jacob Harvey told about his traveling companion, John Randolph. At the time of Randolph's visit to England he was widely known to be a Jeffersonian Democrat. Yet at a dinner party Randolph, according to Harvey, ex-

14. Joseph Glover Baldwin, *The Flush Times of Alabama and Mississippi: A Series of Sketches* (Americus, Ga., 1853), 73, 74.
15. Hubbell, *Virginia Life in Fiction*, 12.

posed his English listeners to "what he termed the sad degeneracy of Old Virginia, and became quite pathetic, in mourning over the abolition of the laws of primogeniture. Some of the company thought this a strange complaint from a republican; and, before we separated, they really had nearly mistaken Randolph for an aristocrat!"[16] Well might the English have been confused. What they did not realize was that circumstances had combined to produce a Virginia gentry as conservative, as traditionalistic, and as nostalgic for the past as the most Tory of English squires.

William Wirt's *The Letters of a British Spy* (1803) is one of the earliest works to exhibit the Old Dominion's nostalgic attitude toward her past. This collection of essays uses the narrative frame device of having a British visitor comment on Virginia in letters ostensibly written to his friends in England. Eighteenth-century writers such as Montesquieu, D'Argens, and Goldsmith had successfully used this technique as an ingenious means of satirizing contemporary society. Continuing in this tradition, Wirt employs the formula at scattered points in his essays to level mild criticisms at Virginia. Letter I, for example, contains an indictment of the unequal distribution of property in the state. Yet as a whole the *Letters* make remarkably little use of the satiric resources inherent in the narrative point of view. For in several of his letters Wirt seems more concerned with analyzing the significance of Virginia's glorious past than with criticizing her present social structure.

The relationship of past to present is vividly set forth in Letter VI. Here the writer wanders among the ruins of Jamestown, whose church steeple is the only architectural survivor of a once-bustling village. In tones explicitly evocative of Lawrence Sterne, Wirt reflects upon the great nation that has sprung from such a "feeble, sickly germ." He realizes that Virginia has good reason to be proud of her past, a past which has been so intimately entwined with the nation's destiny. Yet today, he admits, Virginia is lacking in the bravery, enterprise, and public spirit of her forefathers. "There seems to me to be but one object throughout the state," he concludes, "*to grow rich*." As a result, Virginia lacks the

16. Kirk, *John Randolph of Roanoke*, 88.

public improvements, the roads and canals, which she needs to keep abreast of other developing states. And her educational institutions, such as William and Mary, have fallen into sad decay. In *The Letters of a British Spy*, Wirt's view of Virginia's present is negative. Significantly, he does not look with hope to the future; rather he dwells lovingly on the Old Dominion's illustrious past. As Richard Beale Davis has pointed out, Wirt's backward-glancing essays give an early indication of the direction in which Virginia fiction would develop.[17]

If *The Letters of a British Spy* offers an interesting preview of what was to be the dominant tone of Virginia fiction, *First Settlers of Virginia* (1806) claims our interest as the first narrative to suggest the important role the Cavalier figure would play in Virginia's historical romances. An expanded version of a novelette entitled *Captain Smith and Princess Pocahontas* (1805), *First Settlers of Virginia* was written by John Davis, an English-born writer and teacher who spent most of his American years (1798–1817) living in the Old Dominion. In Davis' novel John Smith amply fills the role of dashing Cavalier gentleman-explorer and is described in highly idealistic and romantic terms: "The person of Smith was tall, graceful and manly. His visage was striking. He had an eye to command, to threaten, or soothe. His aspect bespoke a man ready to face his man, yet capable of moderation; a character comprehending both firmness and refinement; blending taste with energy, and while ready to hit, yet able to forbear."[18]

Playing opposite Smith is Pocahontas, who has been called the earliest fictional embodiment of the Virginia belle.[19] "If not so beautiful as Venus," Davis describes her, "she was more simple than her doves, and her voice was not less sweet than a seraph" (39). Though bred of a savage race, Pocahontas is presented as a genteel lady of the wild. She is sensitive and refined in her passion for Smith, a passion she demonstrates

17. William Wirt, *The Letters of a British Spy* (1803; rpr. Chapel Hill, 1970), 191–92; Richard Beale Davis, "Literary Tastes in Virginia Before Poe," *William and Mary Quarterly*, n.s. XIX (1939), 58.

18. John Davis, *The First Settlers of Virginia: An Historical Novel* (New York, 1806), 37, hereinafter cited in the text by page number only.

19. Richard Beale Davis, *Intellectual Life in Jefferson's Virginia, 1790–1830* (Chapel Hill, 1964), 300–302.

by saving his head from being dashed open and by alluring him with a "thousand wild charms." Smith, in turn, pays her the respect appropriate for a gentleman to give a lady. But though Pocahontas is entirely worthy of the worship of her Cavalier, the only real object of Smith's heart is "the colony he has founded." And so the Indian maid ultimately gives her love to another gentleman, John Rolfe, in a refined courtship that includes the penning of love sonnets and the meeting of passionate yet pure lovers amidst Virginia's virgin forests. In this version of the founding of Jamestown, Rolfe fills the role of the Cavalier lover of noble sentiments, while Smith serves a more soldierly function; he is an absolute leader totally responsible for the colony's survival.

By 1805, then, essays and narratives featuring Virginia's colorful past were being written by men who, if not natives of the Old Dominion, had spent a significant portion of their lives there. The economic decline which beset Virginia after 1780 clearly fostered a nostalgic and wistful backward glancing toward the Old Dominion's past, toward the material luxury, the social sophistication, and the political triumphs of the colonial and revolutionary eras. Paradoxically Virginia's economic and cultural regression resulted in a minor but nonetheless historically significant effusion of writing which included the South's first plantation novels and the first fictional depictions of the Cavalier, a figure who would soon come to represent, not only Virginians, but all southerners.

George Tucker and John Pendleton Kennedy are the most significant of these early portrayers of the fictional Cavalier, of interest to literary historians because of their relatively complex and partially realistic treatment of their subject. There are two primary reasons for these elements of objectivity in their fiction. The opening decades of the nineteenth century were the last years that the state's writers were free to create fiction without tieing that fiction at least implicitly to the larger social and political concerns of the South. Virginia writers would become passionately involved both before and after the Civil War with defending their native state and the South from northern attacks and with justifying their way of life, even after its destruction. In contrast, the writers of the early nineteenth century wrote in an atmosphere relatively free of sectional animosity. Though they shared with later generations a proclivity for romantically rendering the Old Dominion's past, they were also more inclined to view the economic dislocations of the present with candor. No matter how sympathetically they identified with Virginia, they recognized that the plantation system and the type of gentleman that system had produced were in deep trouble. Already they understood that a way of life was rising in the North founded on the commercial-industrial order which seemed destined to destroy the paternalistic agrarian society of the southern plantation system, and they conveyed this understanding in their fiction.

The ability of Tucker and Kennedy to achieve a measure of distance from their subject can also be explained by the fact that neither writer was a native of the state, though Tucker spent most of his life in the commonwealth and Kennedy was tied to Virginia by strong family ties. The importance of this fact can scarcely be overstated. Both Tucker and Kennedy loved Virginia, but they did not have all of their emotional and intellectual stock invested in her. The circumstances of their lives made it possible for them to achieve a degree of objectivity. They were both inside and outside their subject and were therefore blessed with a quality of authorial double vision which, although not highly refined, nonetheless gave their works an element of irony and elevated them above the level of simple panegyric.

A striking quality of both Tucker's *Valley of Shenandoah* and Kennedy's *Swallow Barn* is the element of frankness which exists amid the romance and nostalgia. Less encumbered with the obligation to defend and glorify the Old Dominion, these writers are freer to investigate the somber social implications of their narratives. One of the most interesting features of these novels, as William R. Taylor observes, "is not their advocacy of the Southern position on such sectional issues as slavery and secession, but rather their introspection." This introspection, in turn, results in especially interesting projections of the Cavalier figure. Both Tucker and Kennedy approach their Cavalier characters with decided ambivalence. Though they admire and identify with their planter-aristocrats and even romantically inflate their characters, they also seem to understand that these men are fated to be destroyed by the progressive movement of history. They ultimately see the Cavalier as "doomed aristocrat."[20] These counter tendencies toward romantic inflation and realistic introspection are never successfully resolved in the fiction of either Tucker or Kennedy. But it is the palpable strain, the scarcely concealed tension between realism and romance in these novels, which makes them fascinating social and historical documents.

GEORGE TUCKER

In 1824, eighteen years after the publication of *First Settlers of Virginia*, two new novels with Virginia settings appeared. One of these novels, entitled *Tales of an American Landlord*, was anonymously written. At the time of its publication, some American readers considered it a serious rival to the works of Walter Scott.[21] Today one can easily see why *Tales of an American Landlord* has been almost totally forgotten. Set in country inns and plantations of Northern Neck Virginia, the novel is outrageously pompous in style and cluttered with extraneous characters, overcomplicated action, and romantic plot clichés. In addition, its author seems not to have been able to decide whether he wanted to write a plantation romance or a religious tract. As a result *Tales* incongruously combines an elaborately wrought picture of Virginia plantation life with a heavy overlay of evangelical Christian sermonizing. It certainly marks the first and last time in Virginia fiction that a Cavalier hero is transformed into a pious convert to Methodism.

Of much greater interest to contemporary scholars is the second Virginia novel published in 1824, George Tucker's *The Valley of Shenandoah*. The creator of this novel was not a Virginian by birth. George Tucker immigrated to the Old Dominion from Bermuda in 1795 when he was twenty. He immediately entered William and Mary College and graduated two years later in 1797. Tucker's close relationship with his wealthy and influential relative, St. George Tucker, undoubtedly explained his choice of law for a career and his subsequent marriages to two young ladies with impeccable social credentials, Mary Byrd Farley

20. Taylor, *Cavalier and Yankee*, 151, 52.
21. Richard Beale Davis, *Intellectual Life in Jefferson's Virginia*, 302–305.

and Mary Ball Carter. After leaving Williamsburg, Tucker became an integral part of the Richmond social scene, but extravagance and financial reverses forced him to quit the capital for rural southside Virginia, near present-day Danville. Here he practiced law, managed his farms, and represented his district in Congress. During this period he also completed his first novel. The public indifference which greeted *Shenandoah* was undoubtedly a factor in Tucker's acceptance of an appointment as professor of moral philosophy at the University of Virginia. During his years there he wrote books in the fields of economics, history, and biography on which his limited reputation is chiefly founded today. He retired from teaching in 1845 and spent most of his last sixteen years living in Philadelphia.[22]

The Valley of Shenandoah contains two plots of nearly equal importance that interact contrapuntally. One tells the sad story of the financial collapse of the venerable and aristocratic Grayson family. This collapse is precipitated by the mismanagement and reckless generosity of Colonel Grayson, a character who is dead before the action begins in the early nineteenth century but whose unfortunate excesses haunt his unhappy heirs and remorselessly motivate the tragic plot. A second and parallel plot follows the progress of two love affairs. The participants of one are Edward Grayson, a young heir of the plummeting family fortunes, and Matilda Fawkner, daughter of the Grayson's less socially distinguished but more financially stable neighbors. The second affair develops between Edward's college friend, James Gildon, a smooth-talking but insidious Yankee roué from New York, and Louisa Grayson, Edward's sweet, innocent, and initially chaste sister. The unhappy conclusion of this second affair brings personal disaster to all the major characters which parallels the economic disaster that has already struck the Grayson family.

Tucker's novel is thus a strange mixture of social history and sentimental melodrama. Judged by the tastes of modern readers, it is, alas, an unsuccessful mixture. For although the author's presentation of the

22. The best brief biographical sketch of George Tucker is Donald Noble's Introduction to George Tucker, *The Valley of Shenandoah; or, The Memoirs of the Graysons* (1824; rpr. Chapel Hill, 1970), hereinafter cited in the text by volume and page number.

financial ruin of an aristocratic Virginia family is still interesting, the tortuous working out of Tucker's romance is definitely not. Had Tucker concentrated on developing the decline of the Graysons, his novel might be more widely appreciated today.

Taken in the context of its age, *The Valley of Shenandoah* is surprisingly factual in the presentation of certain narrative details connected with the economic decline of the Graysons. This aristocratic family has been forced to abandon its expensive mansion on the James River and now inhabits a "modest mansion of rough blue limestone" in the Shenandoah Valley. The house is pleasant, but not palatial. The mistress of the house, Mrs. Grayson, is presented more as a domestic household manager than as an aristocratic lady of refinement and unlimited leisure. She can, if called upon, adequately discourse on Mrs. Radcliffe's *The Mysteries of Udolpho*, but she is much more at home in the kitchen. As Tucker writes, "In the mysteries of the dairy, the kitchen, in all its branches of roast, boiled, and stewed; of potting, pickling, and preserving; of making bread, beer, soap, candles, and curing bacon . . . Mrs. Grayson was a perfect adept" (I, 14). Mrs. Grayson presides unostentatiously over the bountiful and hospitable table of a genteel Virginia rural family.

Tucker juxtaposes the well-born Graysons with the less-distinguished but solidly middle-class Fawkner family and gives this family an important role in the novel. Here again the novelist violates a central precept of Virginia fiction writers, for not even in Kennedy's reputedly realistic *Swallow Barn* are middle-class characters allowed such a significant role. Of course, Tucker never lets his reader forget that the Fawkners are slightly beneath the Graysons in social status. Fawkner is a major, Grayson a colonel. During the Revolution, Fawkner had served in the southern campaigns; Grayson had fought in the North, serving personally under General Washington. Grayson's home occupies a hilltop; Fawkner's slightly smaller home rests on bottomland. Fawkner's middle-class heritage is further emphasized by his union with a lady of German origin. Mrs. Fawkner exhibits all the unrefined qualities which Tucker attributed to the Germans who settled in the valley. She is totally materialistic, "narrow-minded and ambitious, priding herself on her own wealth, and graduating her respect to others by theirs" (I, 20). When she learns of the Grayson's financial difficulties, she demands that her daughter cease to encourage the affections of the unhappy Edward.

Yet in spite of his unflattering portrait of Mrs. Fawkner, Tucker did not consciously intend to satirize the Fawkner family or to damn them for their middle-class origins. It is true that they are devoid of noblesse oblige, that they are more calculating and less generous with their money. Yet these very qualities enable them to survive and to avoid the disaster that strikes the Graysons. They do not represent the finest traditions of the Tidewater culture, but they are not therefore an unacceptable lot. To the contrary, Tucker approves their frugality and leaves no doubt that Matilda Fawkner is completely worthy of Edward Grayson. In his willingness to include middle-class characters as a significant element in his novel, Tucker stands virtually alone among Virginia's nineteenth-century fiction writers.

Although Tucker exercises an uncharacteristic degree of objectivity in his presentation of the Grayson and Fawkner families, it is his relatively complex and fresh approach to the problem of slavery in the novel which has attracted most modern critical comment. The enlightened attitude toward slavery that Tucker shared with Jefferson and other Virginians is clearly present in his description of Edward Grayson's semiannual visit to his family's Tidewater estate. This estate is managed by a grasping, dishonest, and opportunistic overseer named Cutchins, who is far less generous to and more demanding of the slaves than was the deceased Colonel Grayson. Cutchins is cheating his employer and profiting from the sweat of the Grayson slaves. Edward is partially aware that conditions on the estate are not what they should be. "He found them," Tucker writes, "more uncomfortable in clothing, and in their little dwellings, than he had ever before seen them. Several were sick with agues; these were badly nursed, and ill supplied with medicines, and their little articles of diet, which are of still more importance in slight diseases. Throughout the whole body of them, an air of sadness, and sometimes of sullen discontent, manifested itself in their behavior towards him" (II, 44–45). Yet though Edward is aware of a certain hostility, he cannot fully understand or appreciate the plight of his slaves because he visits his estate only a few days each year. In implying the evils of absentee ownership and the hostility of the slave toward the master that such a practice induces, Tucker shows a far more critically searching attitude than John Pendleton Kennedy would later display in *Swallow Barn*.

Tucker not only honestly depicts many of the inhumane aspects of slavery, but he also infuses the question with a quality of irony that is not present in other Virginia novels of the period. His most powerful irony is reserved for the aristocratic Graysons. These high-born, high-minded Virginians are both sympathetic and sensitive to the plight of their slaves; yet they are forced by economic conditions and by their own weakness and mismanagement to submit them to the ultimate horror of being sold. Edward and his mother seek to make the conditions of the sale as humane as possible. Most of the Negroes are sold in a group to a planter from Georgia who has a good reputation for his kindly treatment of slaves. Those who do not want to go to Georgia are allowed to be sold in Virginia, and Mrs. Grayson's executor, Mr. Truehart, with the aid of kindly neighbors, sees to it that husband is not separated from wife. Yet all the good intentions of the white man cannot prevent the dissolution of friendships and of family ties, and the terrible uncertainty of being sold "down South" into an unknown land.

The elements of realism and objectivity in Tucker's novel have led Jay B. Hubbell to conclude that there is no attempt in *The Valley of Shenandoah* to exaggerate the realities of plantation life or to gloss over unpleasant details. "Tucker," he concludes, "had no part in the building up of the romantic plantation tradition."[23] Despite Hubbell's judgment, however, there is much in the novel that is obviously and grossly overromanticized. This tension between objectivity and subjective romanticism is indeed the most striking characteristic of the book. Tucker, for example, is capable of a fairly rigorous examination of the evils of slavery; on the other hand, he insists at key points in the novel on subscribing to the notion that the slave loves his master and is absolutely

23. Hubbell, *The South in American Literature*, 252.

dependent on him. Mrs. Grayson, who must leave her estate, offers to allow her house servant, Granny Moll, to remain in her old cottage on the plantation. But the old lady rejects the proposal. She loves her home, but she must live and die by her old master's child. "What should I do for my coffee?" she weeps. "And who is to nurse the old woman when she's sick?" (II, 199). Devotion of slave to master was undoubtedly an element of the plantation system in the South, but the modern reader must object to the cloying sentimentality of the scene and to the insidious manner in which Tucker seems to be romantically coloring a relationship which, elsewhere in the novel, he strong-mindedly calls into question. Such sentimental scenes seem to indicate that Tucker was not always clear about what his attitude should be toward slavery.

It is, however, in his romantic depiction of the Virginia gentleman that Tucker seems to work most at cross-purposes with his objective presentation of Virginia society. Whatever Tucker's thoughts about slavery and about the economic collapse of the Tidewater culture may have been, he was an unqualified admirer of the end product of that culture: the planter-aristocrat, or Virginia Cavalier. He describes the gentlemen who inhabited the Old Dominion around the turn of the nineteenth century as men "remarkable for their urbanity, frankness, and ease" (II, 105). They possessed, in Tucker's eyes, "a nice sense of honour; a hatred of all that was little or mean," and they were "great epicures at table; great lovers of Madeira wine, of horses and dogs; free at a jest, particularly after dinner; with a goodly store of family pride, and a moderate portion of learning . . . kind and indulgent, rather than faithful husbands" (II, 105).

Unlike the later fictional portraits of William Alexander Caruthers and John Esten Cooke, Tucker's description does not create a paragon of moral perfection. There are cracks in the Cavalier's armor. But the description is nevertheless warm and sentimental in tone, and the author admits no serious or critical flaws. Tucker's gentlemen, in short, possess those "luxurious and social habits" which give them "all that polished and easy grace, which is possessed by the highest classes in Europe," without the numbing formality and restraint of the European (II, 106).

Tucker's hero, Edward Grayson, is the most complete embodiment of the Cavalier figure in *The Valley of Shenandoah*. To show Edward to best advantage the novelist makes a deliberate and sustained comparison with the low-minded Yankee villain of the novel, James Gildon. The contrast is made explicit from the opening pages of the book. Edward is described as a tall, thin, blond, and handsome young man who reflects in his deportment and bearing a character guided by a "refined and high-minded standard of right." He is the perfect Cavalier, "reserved, somewhat haughty in his manners to those who were not acknowledged inferiors (to whom he was all mildness and condescension), and possessed of the most scrupulous and fastidious honour" (I, 3). James Gildon is shorter and stouter than Edward, with a florid complexion, black hair, and black eyes. He is witty, lively, and cheerful, with "genteel and insinuating manners" (I, 3). From the beginning of Tucker's novel there is a suggestion, through physical description, that the Yankee visitor is a glib and possibly treacherous character, with not a fraction of Edward's strength and nobility. Gildon's baseness is eventually confirmed when he ruins and betrays Edward's sweet, pure, and equally fair sister, Louisa.

As in the other novels of the Virginia tradition which were to follow, the Cavalier best expresses his superior qualities in pure and worshipful wooing of the only object worthy of his interest—the equally refined, pure, and exquisite Virginia belle. In this novel the belle is a member of an unpretentious, middle-class farming family, but this inconsistency does not seem to bother Tucker. Matilda acts as though she comes from the most lordly plantation mansion. In one excessively dramatic scene she gives her lover a locket containing a curl of her hair as a token of her affection. Edward forthwith experiences, in Tucker's words, "that delight which can be known only to those whose feelings have been refined and sublimated by sentimental love." He ecstatically kisses "the little present again and again, with the most rapturous joy." (I, 307). This strange and, to modern taste, amusing response was evidently an appropriate way for a Cavalier to express his love for his lady.

To assert, as Jay Hubbell does, that Tucker contributed nothing to the plantation tradition is to ignore the hero of the novel. For Edward

Grayson is as much a part of the Cavalier literary tradition as John Esten Cooke's Champ Effingham. He does not have the vibrant, swashbuckling energy of Champ, but in his feelings and actions he exists on an exalted level, as removed from reality as Cooke's hero. Tucker could probably never have imagined that the least interesting and most preposterous portions of his book to today's reader would be those which concern the scheming lust of Gildon or the noble passion of Edward. Here the reader is depressingly aware that he is dealing with character types, not human beings. Edward Grayson is clearly a romantic and exaggerated beau ideal, and Gildon, his cardboard foil. It is hard to believe that a writer who was capable of a penetrating analysis of social decay and slavery could be equally capable of creating such a stiff and lifeless character. Yet Tucker seems to have been as fictionally committed to his Cavalier ideal as he was to an objective analysis of the society which produced that ideal. In the long run these commitments were flatly contradictory, and this contradiction explains in part why, with all its admirable attempt at social critique, the novel failed its ultimate test—to engage and maintain the interest of the reader.

Critics of nineteenth-century American literature are fond of contemplating what might have been, particularly in analyzing the careers of promising minor American writers. So too with Tucker, a critic is likely to feel that this writer possessed a potential that unfortunately was not realized. This potential took the form of a view of the progression of history which, if adequately translated into literature, could have made Tucker an important historical novelist.

As an economist Tucker knew that history told the story of the rise and fall of successive civilizations. In his essay "On the Future Destiny of the United States" he predicted that the eventual rise of industrialism in America would decrease its dependence on Europe for manufactured goods and would inevitably bring the decline of the European superpowers. "Perhaps," he concluded, "it is unalterably decreed that communities, like individuals, should have not only their periods of infancy and manhood, but also of old age and dissolution." Tucker had in fact arrived at the same theory of history that Walter Scott used effectively in his series of Scottish historical novels. Georg Lukács has brilliantly defined the historical novel that Scott created as a work that develops out of the clash of cultures, bringing the destruction of the antiquated by the more progressive civilization.[24] Tucker brought a significant measure of this view of history into his *Valley of Shenandoah*. Robert McLean has correctly noted that the novel's study of Virginia society at the turn of the century "rests upon the assumption that the laws which control the progress of a society are unalterable and impersonal."[25] The Graysons are in many respects the most admirable characters in the book, but insofar as they are representatives of a class and a way of life, there is a kind of historical necessity in their decline.

Certainly Tucker possessed a view of history that could have made him an important chronicler of the decline of Tidewater civilization before the onrush of a more commercial, progressive, competitive national spirit. But *The Valley of Shenandoah* failed to successfully incorporate this view into fiction. Part of Tucker's problem undoubtedly lay in his inexperience as a novelist and in his lack of creative genius. But the factor which probably most weakened Tucker as a writer was his emotional commitment to the myth of the Old Dominion, which manifested itself in wooden, idealistic characterization and which undermined the effectiveness of the writer's admirable attempt at social analysis. The unsuccessful portrayal of the Cavalier-hero, Edward Grayson, represents a clear example of this failure.

George Tucker died two days before the bombardment of Fort Sumter. He never lived to see the fissure of the Union that commanded his solid allegiance. Perhaps it is not too bizarre to see in Tucker's writing a reflection of the tensions and unresolved conflicts which eventually split the nation—tensions between the commitment to status quo and the commitment to progress, between slavery and abolition, between a past- or future-oriented time perspective. Tucker never resolved these tensions in *The Valley of Shenandoah*.

24. George Tucker, "On the Future Destiny of the United States," in his *Essays on Various Subjects of Taste, Morals, and National Policy, by a Citizen of Virginia* (Georgetown, D.C., 1822), 23; Georg Lukács, *The Historical Novel*, trans. Hannah and Stanley Mitchell (Boston, 1962), 32–33.

25. Robert Colin McLean, *George Tucker: Moral Philosopher and Man of Letters* (Chapel Hill, 1961), 85.

JOHN PENDLETON KENNEDY

In 1832, eight years after the publication of *The Valley of Shenandoah*, a new work of fiction dealing with Virginia rural life, entitled *Swallow Barn*, was published. Its author, John Pendleton Kennedy, like the author of *The Valley of Shenandoah*, was not a Virginian. He was a native of Baltimore, and his father was a merchant who had immigrated to America from Northern Ireland after the Revolution. Yet his links with the Old Dominion were strong. His mother, Nancy Pendleton, came from the distinguished Virginia family that had produced Nathaniel and Edmund Pendleton. His maternal uncles were landed gentry of the Shenandoah Valley, and here John spent a portion of each of his boyhood summers. His parents eventually retired to this region, and his brothers became permanent residents of Virginia. Kennedy's upbringing thus involved the interplay of conflicting influences. Through his mother's family he was exposed to the southern plantation culture. But his life in Baltimore immersed him in a rich, bustling, cosmopolitan, and commercially oriented city which was fast sloughing off the traces of its southern heritage.

Ultimately Kennedy became the only member of his immediate family to throw in his professional lot with this raw and still-developing society. He became a lawyer in Baltimore, eventually serving in the Maryland legislature and in Congress as a Whig. His political fortunes peaked in 1852 with his appointment to President Fillmore's cabinet as secretary of the navy. After leaving that office in 1853 he retired from politics, but he continued to play a leading role in the commercial and cultural life of his native Baltimore. At the outbreak of the Civil War he unhesitatingly supported the Union side. During these later years he was accorded the respect due to a major American writer. He received the LL.D. degree from Harvard in 1863, and in the same year was entertained by Boston's prestigious Saturday Club. He died in 1870, one of Maryland's most respected citizens.

Kennedy's close identity with the urban life of Baltimore did not erase his affection for and emotional attachment to the civilization below the Potomac. As Charles Bohner has observed in his biography of

Kennedy, he continued all his life to be drawn to the grace of Virginia's culture, "its devotion to the good life, its delight in humor founded on the premise that in society one should make oneself agreeable." [26] These social qualities appealed to Kennedy, as they appeal to Mark Littleton, the narrator of *Swallow Barn*.

Swallow Barn is essentially a collection of essays held together tenuously by two thin plot strands. Written from the viewpoint of a northern relative, Mark Littleton, it describes Virginia rural life in the early nineteenth century at Swallow Barn, the James River estate of the Hazard family now transferred by marriage to the ownership of Frank Meriwether. In the course of his narrative Littleton gives a detailed view of the economy, customs, and manners of his Virginia cousins. Chapters directly descriptive of local life are interspersed with those that develop two separate plots: the boundary dispute between Frank Meriwether and Isaac Tracy, owner of the neighboring plantation, The Brakes; and the uncertain development of a love affair between Ned Hazard, Frank's brother-in-law, and the sprightly but hard-to-please Bel Tracy.

Structurally the book suffers from Kennedy's inability to decide whether he is writing a novel or a collection of descriptive essays. The epistolary technique which allows Mark Singleton to write informative letters to a northern friend is abandoned after the first chapter, and the Ned Hazard–Bel Tracy romance is abruptly stopped short at the end of the novel, a brief "Postscript" serving to hastily tie together the loose ends. Yet *Swallow Barn* is, for the most part, charmingly written. It contains an entertaining number of humorously developed incidents. And most of all, it provides an informal and fairly intimate view of plantation life in the Old Dominion that assured it an immediate appeal for northern readers. Thus Kennedy's work rewarded him with a solid literary reputation that matched the professional success he had already attained in Baltimore in 1832.

In their examination of *Swallow Barn*, modern critics have tended to concentrate on the question of the book's fidelity to antebellum rural Virginia. Alexander Cowie believes that *Swallow Barn* is basically true

26. Charles H. Bohner, *John Pendleton Kennedy, Gentleman from Baltimore* (Baltimore, 1961), 8.

to the realities of that culture. "Kennedy," he concludes, "was the first to reveal Virginians in their homes much as they really were." Charles Bohner agrees with Cowie's interpretation, citing the pervasive presence of a genial Addisonian satire as proof of the novel's essential accuracy of portrayal. William S. Osborne makes an interesting comparison between Kennedy's book and Washington Irving's *Bracebridge Hall*. Osborne contends that *Swallow Barn* is a deliberate burlesque of Irving, providing a realistic counter commentary to that author's romantic inflation of the English squirearchy. Kennedy's picture, he argues, is more valuable because it reflects "accurately the times in which it was written," while *Bracebridge Hall* does not. Yet at least one important critic, Francis P. Gaines, has rejected the view that Kennedy's work is realistic. Gaines contends that, although there are frequent touches of irony and laughter in *Swallow Barn*, the novel is far from accurate in its portrayal of Virginia manners and customs, and it contains no deep or telling criticism of Tidewater society. Kennedy's purpose, he feels, is not so much to realistically depict Virginia society as "to idealize with his own culture and art an example of plantation life at its best."[27]

Much of *Swallow Barn* is realistic and objective in tone, however. The opening description of the plantation house, for example, encourages the reader to admire its stateliness without turning the dwelling into a faultlessly beautiful palace. The house is "an aristocratical old edifice" which sits "like a brooding hen" overlooking the James. The association of *aristocratical* with the homely term *brooding hen* does not undercut the dignity of the mansion; it merely renders the description of the house believable, allowing it to be appreciated as both beautiful and real. This conscious attempt to define a scene more sharply and realistically continues in the sentences which immediately follow. The main door is a gigantic and "ancient piece of walnut" which, in spite of its impressiveness, has loosened from its hinges and furrowed the hall floor. The pillars which support the small porch are "massive columns

27. Alexander Cowie, *The Rise of the American Novel* (New York, 1948), 262; Bohner, *John Pendleton Kennedy*, 88; William S. Osborne, Introduction to John Pendleton Kennedy, *Swallow Barn; or, A Sojourn in the Old Dominion* (1832; rpr. New York, 1962), xxxi; Gaines, *The Southern Plantation*, 23.

of wood" which are crowned by a classically carved pediment. Yet Kennedy takes care to note that these columns are "somewhat split by the sun," once again skillfully removing the scene from the realm of the ideal and intimating that Swallow Barn is a real plantation inhabited by real human beings.[28]

Kennedy eschews idealization in his character sketches as well as in his descriptive scenes. Louisa Meriwether, for example, is presented in an unassuming manner that reminds one of Tucker's portrait of Mrs. Grayson. Louisa is the industrious, early-rising director of the plantation's domestic enterprises. From supervising the waxing of floors and the grinding of coffee to administering her own home remedies, she is the epitome of competence. She is not the immaculately coiffured mistress of the tea table. Her figure is thin and her face marred "from the paths worn across it, in the frequent travel of a low-country ague" (38–39). In short, Kennedy portrays in his character the hard work and physical sacrifices that contribute to the making of a competent plantation lady.

Kennedy is at his best, however, in his sketch of the character of the plantation master, Frank Meriwether. Here the successful combination of light satire with genial humor most impressively demonstrates the author's command of Addisonian wit. Frank is a good-looking Virginia squire of magisterial presence who stands at the meridian of his age. His two most obvious characteristics are the bountiful hospitality he extends to both friend and stranger and the kind and considerate manner with which he rules both his family and his slaves. From the beginning the reader is thus disposed to like Meriwether, and this disposition enables him to laugh at Frank's faults, rather than to become upset by them or overly critical of them.

In numerous respects Frank's character is far from ideal. His education as a lawyer, Kennedy tells us, consisted primarily of smoking "segars in a lawyer's office in Richmond; and eating oysters once a week in a cellar" with fellow members of a law debating society (33). He has

28. John Pendleton Kennedy, *Swallow Barn: A Sojourn in the Old Dominion* (Rev. ed.; Philadelphia, 1861), 27, 28, hereinafter cited in the text by page number only. All references are to this edition unless otherwise noted.

seldom removed himself beyond the borders of Virginia and has never traveled to New England. Like a true provincial, he considers Richmond "the centre of civilization," and like a true planter-aristocrat, he "thinks lightly of the mercantile interest, and, in fact, undervalues the manners of the large cities generally" (34–35). He is totally devoted to the genius of Virginia and totally dogmatic in his opinions on all important subjects. As Kennedy ironically observes, "For unextinguishable pertinacity in argument, and utter impregnability of belief, there is no disputant like your country-gentleman who reads the newspapers" (35–36). The heat of his political opinions, in fact, is only matched by the distinct coolness of his religious affections.

In his descriptive essay on Frank Meriwether, Kennedy displays an amiable and gentle satiric touch which stands in the best tradition of the *Spectator* essays. The reader likes Meriwether but, at the same time, is laughingly made to see his inadequacies. The technique, in other words, cuts two ways simultaneously. Kennedy uses this approach not only to poke light fun at his character but, beyond this immediate target, to level light satiric thrusts at the entire Virginia way of life. For Frank Meriwether is both an individual and a representative spokesman for a whole class of planter-aristocrats. Meriwether, for example, distrusts the newly invented steamboat. "I don't deny that the steamboat is destined to produce valuable results," he opines, "but after all, I must question . . . if we are not better without it. I declare, I think it strikes deeper at the supremacy of the States than most persons are willing to allow. This annihilation of space, sir, is not to be desired" (72). This quixotic attitude, which is at the same time humorous and rather pathetic, tells the reader much about the conservative, inbred nature of the culture represented by Swallow Barn and its inhabitants.

In the story of Bel Tracy's hawk, Kennedy most skillfully and effectively satirizes the sentimentalized, lotus-land mentality of Virginia's inhabitants. Like many of her fellow Virginians, Bel has fallen under the baleful influence of Walter Scott and is addicted to romantic dreaming. Thus she fancifully transforms her pet marsh hawk into a medieval hunting falcon and decorates the unlikely bird with leather jesses and a silver ring on which is inscribed the name of the hawk, Fairbourne, and

84

a properly chivalric slogan, "I live in my lady's grace." Kennedy skillfully extracts the maximum comic effect out of this ridiculous situation.
For example, when Bel casts her gallant bird to the air, he ignobly flops
to the earth a few paces away. One day, however, Fairbourne breaks his
string in a rare burst of flight and escapes into the woods. This unfortunate incident opens the stage for Bel's would-be lover, Ned Hazard.
Ned, like a true Cavalier, offers to recapture the bird and promptly sets
forth on his chivalric quest, scouring the neighboring farms for the de-
linquent hawk. In a chapter ironically titled "Knight Errantry" the
brave knight finds his prize in an appropriately unheroic spot—perched
in an apple tree above a mockingbird's cage in the backyard of a Negro
shanty.

Of course, Kennedy's message through these episodes is clear: Virginia is not Camelot. And yet many of her citizens in *Swallow Barn* act
as though they were living in another time and age and adopt standards
of conduct which are both ridiculous and hopelessly inappropriate for
the occasion. At one point in the novel Ned beats up an insolent wastrel
for insulting Bel's father. But later he tosses in an agony of apprehen-
sion, fearing that Bel will blame him for using his brute fists and for
fighting publicly in front of a country store. "Now if I had encountered
an unknown ruffian in the woods," he muses, "with sword and lance, on
horseback, and had had my weapon shivered in my hand, and then
been trussed upon a pole ten feet long,—Gad, I believe she would be
thrown into transports!—that would be romance for her" (370). In ir-
reverently laughing at Virginia's obsession with chivalric honor and romance, Kennedy uncovered a subject which Mark Twain would later
develop with greater force and blacker humor in *The Adventures of
Huckleberry Finn*.

One could hardly deny, therefore, that *Swallow Barn* contains a
good amount of light but telling satire aimed at its Virginia subjects.
On the other hand, it is hard not to notice a countercurrent of undiluted
admiration for the Virginia way of life. Joseph V. Ridgely has dis-
cerningly observed that the characteristic of Tidewater society which
Kennedy most effectively criticizes—its provincial and indwelling self-
sufficiency—is the same characteristic which makes possible the lei-

sureliness and the sense of social stability the author most strongly admires.[29] The admiration for the tasteful beauty that such a poised culture can produce is evident in Kennedy's description of the interior of the neighboring plantation house, The Brakes. On these pages the author describes in loving detail the elaborately hand-chiseled pediments, cornices, window-frames, and mantels and the hand-carved furniture, black with age, yet still affording "glimpses of the lacker and varnish that gave effulgence to Virginia's days of glory" (219).

It is in the chapter entitled "The Dinner Table," however, that Kennedy describes most lyrically and admiringly the hospitality and good manners that are the essence of the Swallow Barn tradition. Frank Meriwether holds a dinner for all the people of quality in the county. Dinner, Virginia style, begins before noon with the arrival of the numerous guests. After ample time has elapsed for the convivialities of social intercourse, a midafternoon meal is served on a huge banquet table stored "rather with a reference to its own dimensions than to the number or wants of those who were collected around it" (326). The guests are regaled with ham, mutton, fried chicken, oysters, crabs, innumerable vegetables from the garden, and a profusion of pickles and relishes. They are attended by a "bevy of domestics" and entertained by the merriment and wit of Virginia temperaments that command a sure instinct for pleasing. After dessert and iced wine the gentlemen retire to the oak-paneled study to savor whiskey punch, cigars, and good fellowship among men who respect each other and enjoy each other's company to the fullest. "Such," concludes Kennedy, "are the images that gladden the old-fashioned wassail of Virginia" (345).

The Addisonian quality of Kennedy's satire so evident in such portions of the book as the description of Frank Meriwether and the capture of Fairbourne vanishes in chapters like "The Dinner Table." Kennedy's persona, Mark Littleton, is not able to maintain his satiric mask because he lacks the emotional distancing from his subject that Addison was capable of maintaining with his famous creation, Sir Roger de Coverley. As C. S. Lewis has observed, Addison, as a member of the

29. Joseph V. Ridgely, *John Pendleton Kennedy* (New York, 1966), 60.

ascendant commercial Whig establishment, was able to consistently view the Tory Sir Roger "as an archaism, a lovely absurdity."[30] But Kennedy, speaking through Mark Littleton, was not able to attain this consistency of satiric point of view because he emotionally identified with some of the most basic characteristics of the culture he was examining.

Throughout *Swallow Barn* Kennedy adheres to his general thesis that Virginia society is permeated and dominated by aristocracy. "Her population consists," he tells his reader, "of landholders, of many descents, unmixed with foreign alloy." In such a society the forms of government may be democratic, but "in temper and opinion, in the usages of life, and in the qualities of her moral nature, she is aristocratic" (71). From his personal visits to the Shenandoah homesteads of the Pendletons, Kennedy would have observed that the majority of Virginia's landholders were small farmers who more than likely owned no slaves. He would have been equally aware that the earlier English composition of the valley, and indeed of all parts of Virginia, had been significantly diluted by Scotch-Irish and German immigration. His demographic survey is thus patently oversimplified and weighted to produce the picture of a land dominated by large landowners of long, aristocratic English ancestry.

Here and there in his sketches Kennedy leaves the world of the plantation long enough to give the reader glimpses of the white masses. But these glimpses are so few and the people are described so hazily that they all seem to coalesce into a single vague outline, a poor-white stereotype. Referring to them as "rustics," Kennedy describes them at a Fourth of July celebration "laughing boisterously, drinking, and making ribald jokes" and dressed in garish, cheap finery (160). There seems to be a vast gulf between these rustics and the plantation folk. For example, in their political arguments they defer with near reverence to the opinions of Ned Hazard, whom they are always careful to address formally as "Mr. Ned Hazard." One feels that there must exist in Swallow Barn country a class of farmers without either the wealth and aristocratic airs of the large plantation owners or the ignorance, obsequi-

---

30. C. S. Lewis, "Addison," in James L. Clifford (ed.), *Eighteenth-Century English Literature: Modern Essays in Criticism* (New York, 1959), 146.

ousness, and imputed shiftlessness of the rustics. But they are nowhere to be seen.

Kennedy obviously prefers to spice his narrative, not with drab middle-class characters, but with colorful manifestations of the Virginia gentleman. Rather than create one character to embody all the characteristics of this type, the author skillfully presents a series of diverse figures. Frank Meriwether represents the typical middle-aged Virginia squire, a man of good looks, good disposition, good manners, and adequate learning—a man who easily fills his authoritative positions as estate manager and as arbiter of local public opinion. In Frank's neighbor, Isaac Tracy, Kennedy sketches his version of the old Virginia gentleman, a crusty royalist who stands like a rock in the stream of time, spurning changing modes, and adhering to his traditional dress and his scrupulous manners. Mr. Tracy's lawyer, Singleton Oglethorp Swansdown, is a slightly effeminate and decidedly foppish character who, with all his polished manners and his casual references to poets and philosophers, is obviously a brainless, though harmless, fool. Perhaps the most appealing of these characters, however, is Meriwether's brother-in-law, Ned Hazard, an amiable young man of dark laughing eyes and a lover of dogs, horses, and hunting. It is Ned who roughly woos and eventually wins the sprightly Bel Tracy.

To Kennedy's credit, he allows none of his characters to act in a preposterously romantic fashion. Unlike Tucker, Kennedy does not create moral paragons or beau ideals, and unlike John Esten Cooke, he does not set up his characters with ruffles, plumes, powdered wigs, and polished swords. Ned Hazard, the closest approximation to these two characters, is, after all, only a Princeton dropout. He rescues marsh hawks, not damsels; and he defends his lady's honor, not in a duel, but in a fistfight at a country crossroads. Yet beneath the blemishes, foibles, and humorous eccentricities of these characters, the broad outlines of the Cavalier figure can be perceived. Kennedy's gentleman is neither flawless nor heroic in dimension. On the other hand, none of his flaws seriously impairs his basically admirable character. He is incapable of being heartless, cruel, or villainous. We smile at him, but essentially we admire him because we know that he is an aristocrat, or as close to an aristocrat as our country can produce. Ned goes in knightly quest of a marsh hawk, and Kennedy expects us to laugh at the irony. But he does not expect our laughter to extend to the sincere feeling that motivates that quest.

Kennedy's depiction of the boundary dispute between Swallow Barn and The Brakes shows more clearly how the writer mixes humor and gentle reproof with a deeper vein of idealization in presenting his aristocratic characters. Isaac Tracy has for decades been pressing a suit which disputes ownership of a few worthless acres of swamp land. On one level we are expected to interpret this dispute as another example of the Virginian's distorted sense of values. But on another level Kennedy invites us to examine Tracy's pertinacity and dedication to principle and Frank Meriwether's grace, good manners, kindliness, and tact. Thus, in spite of the absurdity of the dispute, Kennedy would have us admire certain abstract and noble qualities in his characters. "Never," says the narrator, "were there, in ancient days of bull-headed chivalry, when contentious monk, bishop, or knight appealed to fiery ordeal, cursed morsel, or wager of battle, two antagonists better fitted for contest than the worthies of my present story" (149). Tongue in cheek? Most certainly. Ironic? No doubt. But there coexists with this tone a feeling of admiration and respect for Kennedy's latter-day adversaries that make his evocation of chivalry and nobility much more than the simple play of satiric irony. Tracy and Meriwether carry their code of conduct, like the tattered flag of a dying way of life, into battle over a piece of swamp land. They are antique Cavaliers who have somehow stumbled into the nineteenth century, hopelessly unequipped to deal with a modern world that demands progressive vision and flexible personal standards. Yet Kennedy is by no means certain that the values they represent are necessarily inferior to the values which are replacing them. Thus, though his characters become objects of gentle satire, their underlying nobility is untarnished. In them we find distinct traces of Caruthers' and Cooke's idealized Cavalier figures.

Joseph Ridgely, noting his tendency both to satirize and to celebrate Virginia life, attributes Kennedy's "double focus" to an inability to decide which view was valid. *Swallow Barn*, Ridgely concludes, "is a valid reflection of the divided mind of John Pendleton Kennedy, a man who looked forward but understood the pragmatic value of legend— one who, like many of his countrymen, yearned for roots in the past and for the America that was to be, and was not at all sure how the two could be reconciled."[31]

Kennedy's earlier drafts of *Swallow Barn* give concrete evidence of this internal tension. An extant first writing of the opening chapter clearly indicates that the author originally planned a much harsher satire of Virginia society. This fragment introduces the reader to the bigoted master of Hoppergallop House, Frank Oldstock. Throughout this version there is a sustained ironic contrast between Oldstock's pomposity and the abject poverty of his plantation, described as a decaying mansion surrounded by "fields producing a sickly crop of diminutive corn or some scragged rows of tobacco."[32] Yet at the conclusion of his finished draft Kennedy had immeasurably softened his satire, a softening objectively represented by the transformation of the observing narrator from an outside traveler to a visiting relative. Mark Littleton is far enough removed from his kin to laugh in a lightly irreverent manner at their faults, but his blood ties enable him to appreciate their virtues more thoroughly. Indeed, in the course of his visit Mark comes to realize that life in the Old Dominion "has a winning quality that already begins to exercise its influence upon his habits" (311). There are times, in fact, when the narrator is convinced that he could want nothing more than "a thousand acres of good land, an old manor house, on a pleasant site, a hundred Negroes, a large library, [and] a host of friends" (311). Kennedy was capable of writing a much more vigorous satire, and certainly a part of his nature prompted him to do this. But in the end his admiration for Virginia overcame his critical doubts.

The tension within Kennedy's personality between romanticism and pragmatism—a tension suggested by the double focus of *Swallow Barn*—is given even more intriguing expression in *Horse-Shoe Robin-*

31. Ridgely, *John Pendleton Kennedy*, 64.

32. John Pendleton Kennedy, "Hoppergallop House," in his *Swallow Barn* (1962), liv.

son, a Revolutionary War novel that Kennedy published three years after *Swallow Barn*, in 1835. Although set primarily in South Carolina, the novel's hero, Arthur Butler, is cut from essentially the same cloth as the Virginia aristocrats of *Swallow Barn*. However, it is the juxtaposition of, and the consequent character contrast between, Cavalier Arthur Butler and frontier yeoman Galbraith "Horse-Shoe" Robinson that gives the novel its chief interest today.

The main plot line of *Horse-Shoe Robinson* concerns the misadventures of Arthur Butler, a Revolutionary War officer from the low country of South Carolina. During most of the novel Butler is a captive of the British and their American Tory allies. Not until the climactic Battle of King's Mountain is he freed; whereupon he is reunited with Mildred Lindsay, a Virginia belle who hails from Dove Cote Plantation. Mildred is the daughter of a Tory gentleman, whose convenient death at King's Mountain allows Butler to reveal that they have been secretly married for a year. One may well wonder why, in a novel that focuses on the fate of Arthur Butler, Kennedy titled his narrative *Horse-Shoe Robinson*. The answer is that Robinson, who is Butler's military guide and companion, is responsible for efforts to free the officer and dominates the action while Butler languishes as a prisoner during the major portion of the novel. The title represents Kennedy's own understanding that the yeoman frontiersman, and not the aristocratic young officer, is the de facto protagonist of his narrative.

Horse-Shoe, William R. Taylor observes,

is the Southern Yeoman become Chevalier Bayard; he is the wild Scot become gentleman warrior. Horse-Shoe Robinson is to the South what Harvey Birch of James Fenimore Cooper's *The Spy* was to the North: a defensive fiction. Harvey was a triumph over predatory greed. Horse-Shoe was a triumph over back-country brutality. Each in his own way held the American wildness at bay. Horse-Shoe's superiority to Butler lay in the fact that he belonged to the American present and future, while Butler took his gentlemanly social values from the European chivalric past.

Horse-Shoe was a Scotch-Irishman's symbol of hope; Arthur Butler was a part Englishman's idea of a conventional gentleman. Horse-Shoe accommodated to the American present those qualities which Kennedy admired in his Pendleton ancestors; he promised to carry these qualities into the future. He was a mounted knight with his feet on native ground, a Cavalier who could shoe, as well as ride, a horse.[33]

There is ample evidence in Kennedy's novel to support Taylor's view of Horse-Shoe Robinson as representative of a kind of compromise between the extremes of aristocratic chivalry, on one hand, and uncivilized frontier brutality, on the other. Representing the chivalric attitude, of course, is Arthur Butler. Although Butler is not subjected to the kind of gentle satire which Kennedy directs toward his aristocrats in *Swallow Barn*, it is not difficult to identify the quixotic aspects of his character that make him—conventional hero though he may be—a less effective soldier than Robinson. Butler is brave and honorable. As he warns his Tory captors, "If aught be said against me that shall be intended to attaint my honor as a gentleman, I will, in the same presence and before God, throw the lie in the teeth of my accuser."[34] Butler's chivalric bravado, however, cannot deliver him from the British. In fact it is the timely intercession of Horse-Shoe Robinson, who is one of the leaders of a raid on the Tory camp, that saves Butler moments before he is to be executed as a traitor.

Butler's sense of honor and of noblesse oblige, though perhaps worthy of a certain admiration, can also be judged as ill adapted to the kind of irregular guerrilla warfare that rages across the interior of South Carolina. For example, Butler is rescued at one point in the novel by John Ramsay, a yeoman farmer who sacrifices his life in the rescue attempt. Unfortunately, Butler is almost immediately recaptured because he insists on remaining in hostile territory to give John a proper mili-

33. Taylor, *Cavalier and Yankee*, 197.
34. John Pendleton Kennedy, *Horse-Shoe Robinson: A Tale of the Tory Ascendency in South Carolina, in 1780* (1838; rpr. New York, 1928), 218, hereinafter cited in the text by page number only.

tary burial. This is a ritual that includes the firing of muskets over John's grave, firing that immediately brings British troops to the scene. One cannot help but feel that Butler's behavior is more stupid than noble and that his chivalric attitude in this instance is simply self-destructive.

If Butler represents the chivalric extreme, Wat Adair embodies the savagery of the uncivilized frontiersman. He is a man who sells his loyalties to the highest bidder and whose only concern is for himself. He represents a kind of lower-class brutality, the reverse or the shadow of Thomas Jefferson's noble yeoman figure. Cooper had recognized this darker element of American democracy and had given it fictional substance, most notably in the characterization of Ishmael Bush in *The Prairie*. Later Mark Twain brought the type violently to life in *Huckleberry Finn*. In the twentieth century William Faulkner would describe the same viciously solipsistic character in the Deep South and give him a name and a label—Snopes.

Wat Adair's identification with the Snopesian characters who have both preceeded and come after him in American fiction is dramatized in a scene of shocking savagery, one of only a few scenes in an otherwise pedestrian and formulaic romance that conveys the power of truly felt experience. Just before Adair betrays Butler and Horse-Shoe to the Tories, we see him reveling over the capture of a she-wolf who has long eluded his traps. Ignoring Horse-Shoe's admonition to kill the animal quickly, Adair proceeds slowly and methodically to skin the miserable creature alive. Kennedy describes the process with clinical precision:

> Adair proceeded with his operation with an alacrity that showed the innate cruelty of his temper. He made a cross incision through the skin, from the point of one shoulder to the other, the devoted subject of his torture remaining, all the time, motionless and silent. . . . He applied the point of his knife to separating the hide from the flesh on either side of the spine, and then, in his eagerness to accomplish this object, he placed his knife between his teeth and began to tug at the skin with his hands, accompanying

the effort with muttered expressions of delight at the involuntary and but ill-suppressed agonies of the brute. (131)

In the face of such a disgusting and perverse scene, Butler can only "withdraw himself from a sight so revolting to his feelings" (131).

Kennedy seems to understand that in a head-to-head confrontation between Cavalier and Snopes, the ferocity of the savage frontiersman would be more than a match for the chivalry of the gentleman warrior. Only a man like Horse-Shoe Robinson, who combines earthy strength and pragmatism with moral principle, can contend with the likes of Wat Adair. Horse-Shoe displays on occasion a hard resolve that borders on cruelty. He warns a British officer whom he has captured that if a hair of Arthur Butler's head is hurt, "I myself will drive a bullet through from one of your ears to the other" (210). Later in a raid on British forces, he urges his men to cut the enemy down without mercy. Kennedy tells us that "he accompanied his exhortation with the most vehement and decisive action, striking down, with a huge sabre, all who opposed his way" (260).

In spite of a bloodthirsty quality that attaches to his yeoman hero in certain scenes, Kennedy would have his reader understand that there is a clear distinction between Horse-Shoe's ferocity and that of Wat Adair. Horse-Shoe's methods are dictated by the particularly savage nature of the conflict between Patriot and Tory in frontier South Carolina. He understands that the "game of war is a stiff game" and that he must play the game according to the rules currently in force. He does not simply kill for the joy of killing, and he does not derive unhealthy pleasure in inflicting pain. His severity of character is modified by a humane concern for others. In contrast to Arthur Butler's unbending principle, Robinson displays flexibility and pragmatic shrewdness at every turn. When the British officer who is his prisoner pledges upon his honor that he will make no attempt to escape, Horse-Shoe sensibly replies: "I can take no pledge in the dark; daylight mought make a difference. If we should happen to fall in with any of your gangs I'm thinking a pledge wouldn't come to much more than a cobweb when I ax you to gallop out of the way of your own people. Flesh is weak when the arm is strong or the foot swift. . . . No, no, Mr. Ensign, you may get away, if you can; we'll take care of you whilst we're able—that's a simple understanding" (241). Arthur Butler, like a true gentleman, would have accepted the British officer's pledge without question. Yet we must feel that Horse-Shoe's response is an eminently practical and reasonable one and that a certain kind of honor must attach to a character who thinks with such clarity, honesty, and wisdom.

There are indications in the novel that Kennedy sought to enlarge his yeoman figure as Cooper had ennobled the character of Leatherstocking. Like Leatherstocking, Horse-Shoe expresses his wisdom in long rambling discourses delivered in homely dialect. His entrance into the novel—silhouetted against a door, a venerable hero of a revolution fought forty years before—recalls Cooper's initial description of Leatherstocking in *The Prairie*, silhouetted and enlarged against a setting sun. "What a man I saw!" exclaims the narrator of Kennedy's novel. "With near seventy years upon his poll, time seemed to have broken its bellows over his front only as the ocean breaks over a rock. There he stood—tall, broad, brawny, and erect" (8).

Unlike Cooper's Leatherstocking, however, Kennedy also seems interested in grafting specifically chivalric qualities onto his frontier hero. At one point as Robinson sets out on an adventure he is described as riding forth "with as stout a heart as ever went with knight of chivalry to the field of romantic renown" (288). Passages such as this one remind the reader that Horse-Shoe is not a simple reproduction of Leatherstocking. He is not merely a frontier hero. He is a southern frontier hero, and as such, he carries with him at least a faint aura of the Cavalier figure. This suggestion of knightly grandeur, however, does not significantly qualify our understanding of his character as a fundamentally pragmatic one. Thus one may question the accuracy of William R. Taylor's description of Robinson as a "mounted knight." But it would be hard to disagree that he is a warrior with "his feet on native ground."

Horse-Shoe Robinson provides an interesting contrast with *Swallow Barn*. Together the two novels might be said to externalize the conflict within Kennedy between romantic and pragmatic attitudes. *Swallow Barn* is completely dominated by the Cavalier stereotype. The yeoman figure is at best shadowy and unsubstantiated in this narrative. Three years later, however, Kennedy would write a novel in which the Cavalier type is pushed into the background and in which the plot is dominated by a yeoman hero.

Yet this dichotomy is not so clearly pronounced as it may at first seem. One must remember that even in a novel in which Kennedy celebrates the virtues of the yeoman he feels it necessary to pay proper reverence to the aristocratic ideal. Horse-Shoe dominates the action, but the novel remains essentially the story of aristocratic lovers tragically separated and then, at long last, joyfully reunited. The slighting of Horse-Shoe's character within the scheme of a typically romantic plot is nowhere more evident than at the conclusion. Here Horse-Shoe's story is simply dropped. Instead, the reader is given a description of the death of Mildred Lindsay's father. He also learns that Arthur Butler becomes a colonel and later serves in Virginia. Of course, if anyone is made a colonel it should be Robinson. But Kennedy cannot make Horse-Shoe a colonel because he is not, like Butler, a gentleman. Robinson is fit to fight bravely and to save Butler's life; he is fit to demonstrate resolve, wisdom, and humanity under the most trying of circumstances. But he is categorically denied the option of leading men, for only true gentlemen can lead men. In spite of Kennedy's honest attempt to create a yeoman hero, he cannot ultimately avoid casting his protagonist in an inferior role. For elevating Horse-Shoe above Butler would require either the repudiation or the radical redefinition of the Cavalier ideal, and Kennedy is not willing to tackle either of these tasks. Arthur Butler is not as effective a character as Horse-Shoe. Kennedy must have realized this. Yet Arthur, not Horse-Shoe, must be made colonel, if only because "his sufferings in the cause certainly deserved such a reward" (483). It is a lame excuse for a promotion but one that Kennedy and his readers no doubt preferred to a more candid explanation.

In the final analysis Horse-Shoe Robinson is not exactly the "Southern Yeoman become Chevalier Bayard" that Willliam R. Taylor describes. Those chivalric aspects of his character which are stressed seem to bear only a superficial relation to his strongest qualities, which are those of the yeoman class from which he comes. Though the yeoman ideal is given much more exposure in *Horse-Shoe Robinson* than in *Swallow Barn*, there remain tensions between Kennedy's admiration for the yeoman character type and his emotional commitment to the Cavalier figure that resonate with the conflicting tones of irony and romantic idealization that one encounters in *Swallow Barn*. Kennedy's problem in *Horse-Shoe Robinson* is that he must pretend that the two mythical types he dramatizes in his narrative are not in fundamental opposition to each other. He seems to perfectly illustrate the southern paradox that Richard Gray describes in *The Literature of Memory*. Fearing the expanding industrial power of the North, the South embraces the agrarian ideal and the concept of the noble yeoman; yet at the same time it refuses to turn its back on the aristocratic plantation ideal. It insists on embracing both the yeoman and the Cavalier ideals.[35] So too does Kennedy insist on identifying with both character types in *Horse-Shoe Robinson*, ignoring as best he can the deep gulf between Arthur Butler's perspective and Horseshoe Robinson's. Kennedy could have bridged this gulf only by molding Robinson into a genuine Cavalier-Yeoman. To effect this transformation he would have had to make Horse-Shoe's character, rude though it is, worthy of a lady's love. He would have had to elevate his yeoman to a position of command over others, even over those more conventionally defined as gentlemen. But Kennedy was too committed to the standard definition of southern Cavalier to attempt to synthesize the best qualities of that type with the best qualities of the yeoman type.

John Pendleton Kennedy did not successfully forge a Yeoman-Cavalier, but he did make an earnest attempt to celebrate the virtues of both types. As the South moved toward the Civil War her writers became less inclined to feature the yeoman ideal and more inclined to apotheosize the Cavalier, though, as we shall see, William Alexander

35. Gray, *The Literature of Memory*, 13–15.

Caruthers would struggle even less successfully than Kennedy with the same Yeoman-Cavalier problem in *The Knights of the Golden Horseshoe*. Not until the beginning of the twentieth century was a successful amalgam of Cavalier with common man achieved. Ironically, the achievement would be a northern writer's, Owen Wister's, and the novel would be a western, *The Virginian*.

The uneasy coexistence of critical objectivity with romantic idealization is, as we have seen, a characteristic of both Kennedy's and Tucker's fiction. Indeed, there are a number of similarities between these two writers. Both men, though not native sons of the Old Dominion, were closely linked to Virginia. Tucker spent most of his life in the state, and Kennedy was tied by the strong links of blood and heritage. Both men used Virginia as a setting for their fiction. *The Valley of Shenandoah* was fundamentally a historical novel, while *Swallow Barn* basically consisted of a group of descriptive essays; yet both writers attempted through these differing forms to present what they thought was an objective and accurate picture of Virginia society. In both books, however, there was an unresolved tension between the desire to criticize Virginia objectively and the desire to idealize and sentimentalize her. Both writers clearly ascribed idealized characteristics to their Cavalier characters, and ultimately identified themselves with the Cavalier's aristocratic ethos.

Compared to the later creations of William Alexander Caruthers and John Esten Cooke, however, Kennedy's and even Tucker's portraits strike the modern reader as much less inflated character types. Edward Grayson, it is true, is an idealized representative of a venerable Tidewater culture. The men of Swallow Barn and The Brakes have no serious character defects; they sympathetically evoke the best of what Kennedy felt was the Virginia aristocratic tradition. Yet both Tucker and Kennedy pull back from presenting their characters in the full blaze of romantic glory. Edward Grayson, though his actions are always above reproach, ironically seems to be weakened by his virtues. His social and moral code does not adapt him for the modern competitive world in which one must cagily fight Yankees like James Gildon to survive. There is an aura of defeat and doom about Edward that under-cuts him and denies him the quality of romantic grandeur. Kennedy's characters share this aura. The writer of *Swallow Barn* would have us appreciate his characters' virtues and their noble, aristocratic senti-ments. At the same time he understands that they are cultural anoma-lies, fated in the long run to extinction. In *Horse-Shoe Robinson* the Cavalier serves a secondary role to the yeoman protagonist through most of the novel. As in *The Valley of Shenandoah*, the idealized portrait of the southern gentleman is denied the complementary qualities of strength, dramatic presence, and grandeur.

In their aristocratic heroes Tucker and Kennedy first delineated some of the fundamental characteristics of the Cavalier figure—cour-age, generosity, hospitality, high moral standards, impeccable manners, and an instinctive capacity for charming and pleasing others. Caruthers and Cooke subsequently took these characteristics and created fully de-veloped, swashbuckling Cavalier heroes. Tucker and Kennedy were in-capable of such creations because they were objective enough about their subject to perceive the economic and social decay which restricted the dimensions of their characters. Their objectivity was not compre-hensive or sustained; yet its limited presence in their novels was never-theless remarkable. For by 1832 there were precious few minds capable of being objective about Virginia, and in the following three decades objectivity in Virginia fiction vanished altogether.

Indeed, the publication in 1828 of James Ewell Heath's *Edge-Hill; or, The Family of the Fitzroyals* provided an excellent indication of things to come in antebellum Virginia fiction. Avoiding Virginia's present or near past *Edge-Hill* moves back in time to the exciting conclusion of the Revolutionary War. The title is taken from the name of the James River plantation of Launcelot Fitzroyal. Launcelot is an "opulent" royalist and a descendant of the original founder, Sir Rupert Fitzroyal, "a loyal Cavalier and gentleman of wealth and family" who named his planta-tion for the battle in which he almost died fighting for King Charles. Much more explicitly than either Tucker or Kennedy, Heath empha-sizes the aristocratic backgrounds from which his Virginians are descended, and Launcelot expresses precisely this aristocratic point of view: "I venerate those worthies of the olden time . . . those true Cavaliers, who were firm supporters of Church and State against the levelling assaults of roundheads and puritans."[36]

Naturally, Launcelot Fitzroyal supports the Crown in its attempts to exterminate the American rebellion, and he warmly greets the officers of Cornwallis' army when they arrive at his estate. However, Charles Fitzroyal, Launcelot's only son, entertains very different political principles, having gained, presumably from his late mother, a downrightness and a love of liberty which place him at bitter odds with his father. The events of the highly melodramatic plot detail Charles's brave exploits in the service of Lafayette and explain how he eventually becomes reconciled with his father. By the end of the novel the Revolutionary War has been concluded and Charles has settled happily on the Fitzroyal estate with his bride, a young woman of noble character but obscure parentage whom Launcelot had originally forbidden Charles to marry.

What interests a reader today about *Edge-Hill* is not its highly mannered dialogue or the complicated workings of its plot but the remarkable way James Ewell Heath establishes and then completely turns away from a potentially important social conflict in his narrative. The opposition of a rigidly Tory father with his liberty-loving son would seem to provide an ideal context for analyzing the conflict between past and present in Virginia and for suggesting the inevitable movement of history toward liberal political principles. This is the sort of analysis which characterizes *The Valley of Shenandoah* and *Swallow Barn* to some degree. Yet by the end of *Edge-Hill* all problems have been neatly solved by the deathbed reconciliation of father and son. Set against the panorama of events leading to Yorktown, Heath's story completely ignores the ultimate effect of these events on the characters. It does not investigate the ironic relationship between the aristocratic life of Edge-

36. James Ewell Heath, *Edge-Hill; or, The Family of the Fitzroyals* (Richmond, 1828), 48.

Hill, which it lavishly describes, and the triumph of the ideals of liberty and equality, which attends victory in the War of Independence. Neither does it analyze the conflict between Charles Fitzroyal's libertarianism and the role of planter-aristocrat which he seems willingly to assume at the novel's conclusion.

Edge-Hill shares much more with the novels of Caruthers and Cooke than with *The Valley of Shenandoah* or *Swallow Barn*. A significant indicator of the movement of Virginia's writers toward simple romance and uncomplicated glorifications of their state's past, it reflects the increasing difficulty Virginia's novelists would have dealing with the decline of the Old Dominion. *Edge-Hill*, like the novels of Caruthers and Cooke which followed, was a work more harmoniously in keeping with Virginia's increasingly reactionary social and intellectual climate than those of Tucker and Kennedy.

The Virginia State Constitutional Convention of 1829–1830 marked the political consolidation of these conservative attitudes in the state. Two events quickly followed which mirrored the rising tensions between black and white, northerner and southerner, and which helped crystalize Virginia's conservatism into self-defensive reactionism. On January 1, 1831, the first issue of William Lloyd Garrison's *Liberator* appeared. This event was scarcely noted at first in the South, but it was emblematic of the gradually growing opposition in the North to slavery. Shortly after the *Liberator* was published, in August of 1831, the myth of the happy, placid Negro slave was rudely shattered by Nat Turner's bloody rebellion.[37] Turner's insurrection resulted in what historians have called the last lengthy and free discussion of slavery in the South. The debate took place in the Virginia legislature in January, 1832, and resulted in the defeat of the antislavery forces. For all practical purposes the slave question was closed in Virginia.[38] With the continued profitability of slave sales to the Deep South and with the increased attacks on slavery from the North, the Old Dominion eventually turned her back

37. Rollin G. Osterweis, *Romanticism and Nationalism in the Old South* (New Haven, 1949), 54–55.
38. Sydnor, *The Development of Southern Sectionalism*, 226–29.

upon the Union, adopted the bitterly belligerent attitude of her southern sister states, and expressed herself politically through a philosophy which ignored the realities of nineteenth-century American society.

But Virginia's economic and political situation was even more desperate than that of other southern states. Watching the steady loss of their population to the expanding territories, forced by economic distress to sell their slaves to the Deep South, increasingly attacked by northern abolitionists—it is not surprising that Virginians turned in their fiction toward an ideal vision of social stability and order. To create this vision, Virginia novelists William Alexander Caruthers and John Esten Cooke delved deeper into Virginia's colonial past. And to give it more potent expression they drew the Cavalier in his most highly romanticized form. Tucker and Kennedy, because of their capacity for partial objectivity, created characters who merely suggested or broadly hinted at their aristocratic heritage without directly representing that heritage in its most exalted form. Caruthers and Cooke, freed from any superficial obligation to objectivity, moved beyond these characters and developed full-blooded, one-hundred-percent Cavaliers, undiminished by economic failure or social obsolescence.

FOUR

The Apotheosis of the Cavalier

CARUTHERS AND COOKE

ANTEBELLUM FICTION AND THE WALTER SCOTT SYNDROME

IN THE summer of 1845 Fauquier White Sulphur Springs, a popular Virginia spa, hosted a "Tournament of Knights." The object of competing cavaliers was to spear from the back of a galloping horse a small ring which dangled from a cord eight feet above the ground. The knight who successfully speared the ring presented it to his lady and crowned her "The Queen of Love and Beauty." Competitors included gentlemen with the assumed names of Brian de Bois-Guilbert, Wilfred of Ivanhoe, and the Knight of La Mancha. They were urged on by a crowd of genteel spectators, who shouted: "Love of ladies—glory to the brave!"[1]

The tournament at Fauquier White Sulphur Springs was typical of a host of such equestrian competitions which were being held through-

1. Osterweis, *Romanticism and Nationalism in the Old South*, 4.

out the South at that time, merely one symptom in antebellum Dixie of what might best be described as the Walter Scott cultural syndrome. Goaded by attacks from the North, accused of maintaining an inhuman and immoral social institution, southerners turned in their literature to Scott's romantic rendering, in ballad and novel, of medieval Scottish and English society. In these colorful period pieces the South found not only an escape from increasingly bitter sectional tensions but also a justification of its way of life. For in southern eyes Scott's courageous and honorable feudal lords and Scottish chiefs had been reborn in the nineteenth century in the person of the southern planter. The planter's slaves, like the feudal lord's medieval serfs, reasoned southerners, were necessary to nurture the flowering of the South's aristocratic society.

Mark Twain, in his *Life on the Mississippi*, has probably given the most entertaining, if not the most accurate, estimate of Scott's profound influence on the southerner's self-image. "It was Sir Walter Scott," he wrote, "that made every gentleman in the South a major or a colonel, or a general or a judge, before the war; and it was he, also, that made these gentlemen value these bogus decorations. For it was he that created rank and caste, and pride and pleasure in them. Enough is laid on slavery, without fathering upon it these creations and contributions of Sir Walter." Of course, Scott's enormous popularity in the South was as much a manifestation as a cause of Dixie's newly discovered reverence for the aristocratic ideal. But there can be no doubt that his novels and poems gave impetus to the creation of a southern myth expressive of cultural ideals which were radically opposed to corresponding democratic ideals in the North and West. So pervasive was Sir Walter's influence on the southern mind that many of the region's writers sought determinedly, if unsuccessfully, to incorporate his word coinages into their vocabulary. Thus in many formal essays "The Chivalry" came to stand for the southern planter, and northerners became barbarous "Saxons" and "Goths."[2]

This surge of interest in things medieval in the southern states paralleled a strong medieval revival in England. As Mark Girouard has

2. Samuel L. Clemens, *Life on the Mississippi* (New York, 1927), 376; Osterweis, *Romanticism and Nationalism in the Old South*, 46–48.

noted, the cult of antique chivalry among the nineteenth-century English aristocracy was used as a kind of talisman to ward off the unpleasant realities of rapid industrialization, democratic political reform, and the threat of extinction which these social changes posed for the old order.[3] In a similar manner, medievalism served a talismanic purpose in antebellum southern society. It offered to southerners a kind of psychological compensation for the steady erosion of their region's economic and political power in the Union, and it was an integral part of their justification of a social system that was being attacked in the North as outmoded and barbarous.

Failing to develop an industrial base comparable to that which was being established in the North, the South began to perceive itself as part of a nation increasingly dominated by northern interests. The cultural and political isolation of the southern states was exacerbated by the eventual merging of midwestern with northern economic interests, a union ordained by such technological triumphs as the completion of the Erie Canal, tieing the Great Lakes region with New York, and by the subsequent forging of numerous east-west rail links between the Midwest and the Northeast. As Charles Sydnor notes, the South had begun to view itself as both a distinct and a beleaguered region by the 1830s. "Perhaps the chief product of the troublesome early 1830's," Sydnor writes, "was the strong charge of emotion added to matters that had hitherto been on the level of thought and calculation. In the previous decade, something of a Southern platform on national issues had evolved. Clashes over that platform convinced many Southerners that their interests were seldom respected by the rest of the nation and that the fabric of their way of life was being destroyed. A feeling of oppression, of defeat, and even of desperation was engendered."[4]

The medieval revival which swept the South from the 1830s to the coming of the Civil War must be understood, not as an expression of cultural stability and harmony, but rather as a fabrication by a culture which felt its very foundations being undermined. After 1830 north-

3. Mark Girouard, *The Return to Camelot: Chivalry and the English Gentleman* (New Haven, 1981).
4. Sydnor, *The Development of Southern Sectionalism*, 220.

erners found themselves more and more inclined to agree with a writer in *Harper's Weekly* that southern civilization was like a mermaid—"lovely and languid above, but ending in bestial deformity."[5] In response to this progressively more malignant judgment, southerners retreated further into their medieval fantasy land of gallant knights and winsome ladies. One result, as Henry Nash Smith has observed, was that the South eventually became "actively hostile to the yeoman ideal which had been developed as a rationale of agricultural settlement in the Mississippi Valley."[6] Against the concept of the yeoman, which continued to be embraced by the midwestern states, southerners from Baltimore to Little Rock defiantly held up the idealized Cavalier figure. After 1830 the Cavalier, rather than the yeoman, became a central element in the South's justification of its way of life.

The siege mentality which was beginning to grip the South was given early literary expression in 1836 by a Virginian, Nathaniel Beverley Tucker, with the publication of *The Partisan Leader*. He was the son of William and Mary law professor St. George Tucker, kinsman of George Tucker, and half brother of John Randolph, whom he reverenced and whose strict-constructionist, states' rights doctrines he adopted. A resident of Missouri for sixteen of his middle years, he vigorously opposed the Missouri Compromise and remained convinced after its implementation that secession would eventually be the South's only recourse. Tucker—whom Vernon Parrington has described as "so completely and exclusively Virginian as to deserve the epithet 'Virginianissimus'"[7]—thus became the South's first radical spokesman for secession, and he used *The Partisan Leader* as a fictional forum for his extreme sentiments.

The Partisan Leader is set in the near future in 1849. After twelve years of Jackson–Van Buren political hegemony during which Van Buren has acquired the power of a de facto monarch, the states of the mid and lower South have broken from the Union, formed a Confederacy, and quickly concluded a favorable commercial treaty with Great Brit-

5. Quoted in Williams, "Romance and Realism in Southern Politics," 115.
6. Smith, "The South and the Myth of the Garden," 122.
7. Parrington, *The Romantic Revolution in America*, 35.

ain. Virginia remains undecided, her leaders intimidated by the stationing of large numbers of federal troops in the state. Against this background Virginian Douglas Trevor, a federal officer, renounces his allegiance to the Union and eventually leads his partisan guerrilla bands into battle against the occupying army.

Today *The Partisan Leader* is less interesting as fiction than as a statement of certain economic and political precepts that would gain more and more credence in the South as the region moved toward secession. Beverley Tucker believed, for example, that Virginia and the other states of the South would always remain agricultural societies. "Apart from the influence of artificial causes," he wrote, "it is not certain that any labor can be judiciously taken from the soil to be applied to any other object whatever." Given its inherently agricultural nature, Tucker believed, Dixie was being systematically impoverished to provide cheap raw materials for the developing industrial centers of the North. After independence, Tucker opined, the historical commercial interchange between Britain and the southern states should have been restored. However, to satisfy agricultural interests in Britain and manufacturing interests in America, artificially high import duties had been imposed in both countries which had placed a double burden upon the South, forcing it to accept low prices for its agricultural products and to pay high prices for the manufactured goods it purchased. After secession, Tucker prophesied, this historical interchange would be restored; Britain "would be the work-house, and here would be the granary of the world."[8]

Many southerners would have entertained reservations about an economic exchange that would, in effect, relegate the South to the role of an underdeveloped colonial economy. This was the kind of lopsided economic theory, however, best suited to defend the region's patriarchal plantation system. Indeed, in *The Partisan Leader* Tucker found it convenient to ignore many realities that were uncongenial to his vision of the plantation South. He ignored the considerable commercial and industrial activity in his own native state, and he refused to believe that

8. Nathaniel Beverley Tucker, *The Partisan Leader: A Tale of the Future* (1836; rpr. Chapel Hill, 1971) 242, 247, hereinafter cited in the text by page number only.

the planters' slaves could be anything other than happy with their lot in life. Four years after Nat Turner's bloody insurrection, Tucker's novel presents its readers with faithful and contented slaves who, in one instance, are given weapons to defend a plantation from an incursion by Yankee troops and who actually succeed in capturing the entire body without firing a shot. In *The Partisan Leader* the South is a bucolic Eden in which slaves "are one integral part of the great black family, which, in all its branches, is united by similar ligaments to the great white family" (204).

Despite its almost complete deficiency of characterization, Tucker's novel makes it abundantly clear that the foundation of the plantation system is the noble and chivalric personal qualities of the South's aristocracy. In contrast to Martin Van Buren, whose genteel exterior masks a rapacious and totally unprincipled character, we are presented with a number of fine southern gentlemen, chief among them Douglas Trevor. Trevor's chivalric nature is epitomized by the incident which eventually causes his dismissal from the Union army. When an unmannered unionist insults a southern lady by damning her secessionist father to her face, Trevor threatens the man—who is, naturally, a coward—with a duel and forces him to apologize to the lady. She is properly impressed by "the delicacy which, at once, veiled and adorned his chivalrous character" (89). This same delicacy compels Trevor to resign from the army to avoid giving the lady's name at a formal inquiry into the incident. Trevor's northern superiors—Martin Van Buren among them—cannot understand his refusal to testify because, not being gentlemen, they cannot appreciate the dishonor which would justly accrue to a man who stooped to "the public use of a lady's name." Expelled from the Union army, Trevor heads South to align himself with true gentlemen who are sensitive to the intricacies of the chivalric code.

Beverley Tucker's Douglas Trevor earns the distinction of being the first fictional Virginia Cavalier to go to war against the gothic hordes of the North. He would not, of course, be the last. Beneath the surface of its polemic, *The Partisan Leader* clearly indicates the manner in which the chivalric ideal was being used as early as the 1830s to justify the southern plantation system. Of course, in 1836 few Virginians or southerners favored the expedient Tucker proposed in his novel—secession. Twenty-five years later, however, most of them did.

The South's chivalric fantasies were therefore played out against the background of increasingly ominous sectional tensions. In order to entertain their readers and at the same time to defend their region, southern writers fashioned an aristocratic South steeped in the traditions of chivalry. Of all southern states, however, no state was more fitted by history and tradition to furnish the background for these fictional visions of Cavalier splendor than Virginia. The crumbling mansions which still dotted Tidewater river shores gave mute but effective testimony that the region had enjoyed a past grander and more glorious than the prosaic and trouble-beset present. Under such circumstances it is not surprising that Virginians tended to magnify the accomplishments of eighteenth-century Tidewater society, turning the inhabitants of that period into epitomes of noble excellence on the model of Scott's fictional heroes.

As they had done earlier in the century, Virginians found a sentimentally elegiac tone best suited for reflections on their past. "How many spacious structures are seen there," mused Landon Carter, "hastening to decay, which were once the seats of grandeur and a magnificent hospitality! The barons of old were scarcely more despotic over their immediate demesnes, than were the proprietors of these noble mansions, with their long train of servants and dependents; their dicta were almost paramount to law throughout their extensive and princely possessions."[9]

A comparison of Carter's observations with those made by William Wirt nearly thirty years before reveals an interesting contrast. Wirt and Carter both emphasize Virginia's past grandeur, but Carter, unlike Wirt, describes Virginia's past in terms much more evocative of medieval feudalism. "Noble," "princely," "barons," "despotic," "dependents," "demesnes"—Carter's vocabulary seems explicitly designed to link

9. [St. Leger Landon Carter?], "Interesting Ruins on the Rappahannock," *Southern Literary Messenger*, I (August, 1834), 9–10.

eighteenth-century Virginia society with Europe of the Middle Ages. Of course, in spite of slavery and the dominance of the plantation system, historians would agree that Virginia's social organization was far from feudal in its character. Yet by the 1830s Virginians increasingly tended to interpret their society as an island of medieval order in a chaotic sea of classless modernism.

Virginia fiction of the antebellum period between 1830 and 1860 thoroughly reflected the South's obsession with Scott's medieval romances. As Jay B. Hubbell has observed, Virginia writers could easily translate Scott's character types to the Virginia scene, for rough equivalents of medieval classes might be drawn with felicity from the Old Dominion's colonial social structure. Thus in the novels of Virginia writers, "the aristocratic planter replaces the English baron and the Scottish laird; the indentured servant and the Negro slave take the place of the vassal and the serf; and the Indian and the mountaineer sometimes assume the role of the outlaw of the Scottish Highlands."[10]

Under the influence of Walter Scott and the medieval revival, Virginia's antebellum writers, like those from other sections of the South, added two significant appendages to the eighteenth-century concept of the gentleman. These additions were already present in George Tucker's *Valley of Shenandoah* and in John Pendleton Kennedy's *Swallow Barn*, but they were much more colorfully developed in the generation of plantation novels which followed Tucker and Kennedy. The first of these appendages was the code duello. Although the seventeenth and eighteenth centuries had frowned on dueling as a rather barbarous medieval practice, the nineteenth century found it an indispensable instrument for the maintenance of a gentleman's personal honor. During the period from 1830 to 1860, a dramatic confrontation on the oakshadowed dueling ground became a part of the conventional background of the Virginia plantation novel. The Old Dominion's novelists utterly ignored in their fiction the disturbing implications of the revival of this supposedly aristocratic custom in their state. They turned a

10. Hubbell, *Virginia Life in Fiction*, 8.

blind eye to the coercive societal spirit, the summary justice, and the primitive notion of honor which the duel emblemized.[11]

The second appendage was the Cavalier's reverential love for a chaste and refined plantation lady. William R. Taylor has perceptively noted that in "having the Cavalier kneel down before the altar of femininity and familial benevolence" writers were able to associate their aristocratic characters with the qualities of "moral consciousness, sentimentality, introspection and benevolence" without robbing them of their manly powers.[12] Indeed, this combination of martial vigor and chivalric love had been a central characteristic of the earliest medieval romances. Beverley Tucker's *The Partisan Leader* demonstrates, however, that the pedestal upon which the worshipful Cavalier placed his lady had the effect of rigidly restricting her role.

Tucker believed that not only "the public use of a lady's name" but any kind of activity which drew a woman away from home and hearth was incompatible with the idea of the lady. As he pungently observed in his novel: "A woman exposed to notoriety, learns to bear and then to love it. When she gets to that, she should go North; write books; patronize abolition societies; or keep a boarding school. She is no longer fit to be the wife of a Virginia gentleman" (123). Whatever the attitudes of women may have been toward their role in plantation society, antebellum fiction in Virginia and in the South uniformly interpreted them as idealized symbols of social virtue and racial purity.[13] As Tucker describes them, they were women who "continued to walk in the steps of their chaste mothers . . . safe in that high sense of honor which protects at once from pollution and suspicion" (130). The southern lady represented a natural line beyond which the promiscuity of the lower orders—Tucker termed it "the gangrene of the social body"—could never pass.

11. For a perceptive and stimulating analysis of the darker side of the concept of southern honor, see Bertram Wyatt-Brown, *Southern Honor: Ethics and Behavior in the Old South* (New York, 1982).

12. Taylor, *Cavalier and Yankee*, 147–48.

13. Anne Firor Scott's *The Southern Lady: From Pedestal to Politics, 1830–1930*

Southern writers of the antebellum period thus set about purveying their idealized character types—the chivalric Cavalier aristocrat and the refined and exquisitely pure plantation belle. Of a number of novelists of this period, however, Virginians William Alexander Caruthers and John Esten Cooke most successfully conveyed the atmospheric romance of Walter Scott's novels to the southern scene. Caruthers' Nathaniel Bacon and Cooke's Champ Effingham thus became American equivalents of Wilfred of Ivanhoe and Quentin Durward. Writing under the influence of the master of historical romance, these Virginia writers apotheosized the Cavalier into a figure of unblemished nobility, providing at the same time a literary apologia for Virginia and the South.

WILLIAM ALEXANDER CARUTHERS

Curtis Carroll Davis noted the pervasiveness of the Cavalier figure in mid-twentieth-century Virginia. A young man of Richmond, for example, might smoke Cavalier cigarettes, skate at the Cavalier Arena, and have his pants cleaned at the Cavalier Cleaners and Dryers. Pursuing a weekend of fun, he might board the Cavalier railroad express and speed to Norfolk, thence to the Cavalier Hotel in Virginia Beach for several days of swimming and sun. The prevalence of the Cavalier motif in modern Virginia, concludes Davis, "if it can be ascribed to the work of any one man, is to be ascribed to that of William Alexander Caruthers."[14] Those acquainted with Virginia literature must take exception to the preeminence Davis ascribes to Caruthers in the molding of the Cavalier. Yet there is no doubt that Caruthers was one of the most important contributors in the literary development of this mythical figure. His second and most successful book, *The Cavaliers of Virginia*, was the first Virginia novel to portray the Virginia gentleman, magnified to

---

(Chicago, 1970) shows that the attitudes of southern women towards their prescribed roles were complicated and diverse.

14. Curtis Carroll Davis, *Chronicler of the Cavaliers: A Life of the Virginia Novelist Dr. William A. Caruthers* (Richmond, 1953), 130.

heroic proportions by historical distance. Caruthers was truly, as Davis has called him, the first "Chronicler of the Cavaliers."

It is interesting to note that the novelist was not a member of one of the Old Dominion's first families. His ancestors were of Scottish descent and came to the Shenandoah Valley of Virginia, as many of their fellow Scotsmen did, via Pennsylvania before the Revolutionary War. His father was, if not an aristocrat, a respected and financially secure merchant and farmer. William, as befitted a member of the middle class, attended Washington College (now Washington and Lee University) in his native Lexington and then went on to the Pennsylvania Medical College in Philadelphia.

Soon after becoming a physician, Caruthers married Louisa Gibson, a wealthy heiress from Sea Islands, Georgia. Louisa's money undoubtedly accounted for the Caruthers' extravagant standard of living in Lexington. But their financial profligacy seems to have driven Caruthers in 1829, at the age of twenty-seven, to New York in order to rebuild his depleted family fortunes. In 1835 Dr. Caruthers returned briefly to Lexington, and in 1837 he moved with his family to Savannah. All of these moves seem connected with the writer's difficulty in supporting his family. Caruthers died in Georgia of tuberculosis in 1846 at the age of forty-four. He left behind three novels which he had managed to complete during his years as practicing physician.

As Jay Hubbell has noted, Caruthers was in many ways strangely equipped for his role as chronicler of the Cavaliers. He was Presbyterian, not Episcopalian. He was a supporter of the commercially oriented Whig party, not an agrarian Democrat. Like many residents of western Virginia, he had no love for slavery and admitted the abuses of the system. Perhaps most significantly, he was an optimistic nationalist. He did not parochially brood over Virginia's decline; rather he championed the manifest destiny of the new republic.[15]

Caruthers' nationalistic, forward-looking vision is most clearly evident in his first novel, *A Kentuckian in New-York; or, The Adventures of*

---

15. Hubbell, *The South in American Literature*, 497.

Three Southerns, published in 1834. In this epistolary novel Caruthers sends two South Carolinians and a Kentucky backwoodsman north to New York and a Virginian south to South Carolina. Through their letters the novelist conveys the conciliatory message that sectional misunderstandings would be greatly diminished if northerner could view southerner and southerner could view northerner at first hand. In the letters of the Virginian, slavery is attacked as an institution which discourages the growth of a vigorous middle class. The South Carolinians, in turn, find that northern society possesses many admirable qualities which southerners would do well to emulate. As Vernon Parrington has discerned, Caruthers' theme of national unity finds artistic expression in the character of the Kentuckian. This product of the American frontier becomes a humorous, yet vigorous and sympathetic spokesman for the republic's unified and manifest destiny.[16]

A few months after *The Kentuckian in New-York* was published, Caruthers' second and most popular novel, *The Cavaliers of Virginia*, appeared. In tone and subject matter this novel is surprisingly and fundamentally different from Caruthers' first book. In *The Cavaliers* the novelist returns to Virginia's early history, 1676, the year of Nathanial Bacon's famous uprising against colonial governor William Berkeley. The novel is composed of three plot segments. The first presents the conflict between the Cavalier supporters of King Charles and the Roundhead insurgents. The second plot segment, which occupies the concluding two-thirds of the book, develops the tension between Nathaniel Bacon and Governor Berkeley over the suppression of hostile Indian tribes, which finally results in Bacon's expulsion of the governor from Jamestown and the burning of the city. A third plot line, which threads in and out of the first and second plots, revolves around the identity of Nathaniel Bacon and the complicated development of his love affair with Virginia Fairfax, daughter of Bacon's foster father, the aristocratic Gideon Fairfax. Uniting all these plots is the mysterious recluse of Jamestown, who turns out to be Edward Whalley, one of the infamous Puritan regicides. Whalley is a portentous and imposing fig-

16. Parrington, *The Romantic Revolution in America*, 41–45.

ure who seems to have been chastened and ennobled by past tragedy. He enters the narrative at crucial moments, turning the tide of battle, first against the Roundhead insurgents and later against the forces of Governor Berkeley, which seek to destroy Bacon.

As Curtis Carroll Davis has impressively and exhaustively demonstrated, Caruthers, in the exuberance of his romantic treatment, paid scant attention to historical details of Bacon's Rebellion. History tells us that the bloody conflict at Jamestown between Cavalier and Roundhead which the novelist colorfully describes never, in fact, transpired. In like manner, Caruthers grossly exaggerates the extent and severity of Bacon's battles with the Indians and with Governor Berkeley's troops. The real Bacon was not a romantic, dashing young bachelor of unknown parentage, but a well-established and ambitious gentleman of good family connections who was married at the time of his famous insurrection.[17] It is clear that Caruthers claimed a romancer's prerogative to alter facts to suit the exigencies of plot interest.

In setting, subject matter, and plot *The Cavaliers of Virginia* is far removed from *The Kentuckian in New-York*. Caruthers has abandoned the analysis of contemporary manners and social problems in favor of a historical romance with a sensational, colorful, and complicated plot. Yet at least one of Caruthers' themes, the theme of national unity and manifest destiny, recurs in his second novel. Caruthers' hero, Nathaniel Bacon, becomes an early leader of this momentous sweep westward when, in defiance of Governor Berkeley's wishes, he leads an army of Virginians against the massed Indian nations and drives them forever from the fertile lands along the Tidewater rivers. As Caruthers interprets it, Bacon's war with the Indians is the first in a long series of actions that will result in the inexorable movement of the white man across the vast North American continent.

Of course, this movement does not occur without tragic side effects, for it precipitates the destruction of the Indian aboriginal culture which had existed in America thousands of years before the coming of the white man. To make this sense of cultural disintegration more poignant

17. Davis, *Chronicler of the Cavaliers*, 147–62.

and more concrete Caruthers introduces the Indian squaw, Wyanokee, into his narrative. Wyanokee is a female Uncas; she is the last member of the ruling family of the Chickahominy tribe. Years spent among the whites at Jamestown have introduced her to the advantages of European culture. Yet when Bacon—whom she secretly loves—destroys the Indian confederation, Wyanokee realizes with bitterness that in the white man's world there is no room for the Indian. Torn pitifully between two worlds, she leaves Bacon and follows the retreating remnants of her people.

Bacon is Wyanokee's friend; he fully understands the incompatibility at the root of the clash between red and white races. Yet he is also aware of the historical necessity which impels and sanctions what to Wyanokee's limited viewpoint must seem unjustified aggression. The multitudes of Europe cry for new land and new opportunity; America offers both. "God's political Economy" is the justification that Bacon offers to the Indian maiden for the destruction of her people. He uses the same concept when he defends his attack on the Indians before the Governor's Council. Here again Bacon is conscious of his role as initiator of a vast and profound historical movement. "Future emigration," he prophesies, "must advance westward in a semicircular wave."[18] Caruthers clearly interprets Bacon's Rebellion as the first ripple in that wave, and Bacon himself becomes in the writer's imagination the nation's first spokesman of manifest destiny.

Bacon's championing of the nation's westward expansion in the novel has led Curtis Carroll Davis to conclude that *The Cavaliers of Virginia* is "Caruthers' most vivid and thorough-going interpretation of the American democratic ideal."[19] Davis believes that Caruthers develops this democratic theme through the presentation of three conflicts: the initial struggle between Cavalier and Roundhead (usurping tyrannous minorities); the major conflict between white man and Indian (America's enemies from without); and the final contest between the

18. William Alexander Caruthers, *The Cavaliers of Virginia; or, The Recluse of Jamestown: An Historical Romance of the Old Dominion* (1834; rpr. Ridgewood, N.J., 1968), II, 179, hereinafter cited in the text by volume and page number.

19. Davis, *Chronicler of the Cavaliers*, 140–41.

followers of Bacon and the forces of Governor Berkeley (the privileged elite).

Francis Pendleton Gaines, in contrast, finds little support for the idea that the novel is a paean to democracy. Gaines feels that Caruthers has glorified the inhabitants of early Virginia and emphasized a richness of culture in the developing colony which historians today know to be false. Far from supporting the democratic ideal, he believes that Caruthers' novel first and foremost projects the myth of Virginia's aristocratic settlement.[20]

In a more recent interpretation of *The Cavaliers of Virginia*, William R. Taylor has charted a critical course which steers between the extremes of Davis and Gaines. Taylor believes that there existed in Caruthers' mind two types of men on which he based the characters in his book. The first was the Cavalier figure, graced with aristocratic lineage and blessed by qualities of nobility, courtesy, and noblesse oblige but damned by an impractical nature and financial ineptitude to oblivion in the modern world. The second type of man was the Scotch-Irish settler of Puritan religious convictions, stalwart and hardworking, fanatical and intense, but capable of functioning effectively in a modern, competitive world. Neither figure, Taylor believes, was Caruthers' sole model; in *The Cavaliers of Virginia* he "sought to combine in his heroes the best qualities of both."[21]

Although Taylor's schema is oversimplified, it does at least partially explain the conflict that Caruthers has established. William Berkeley might be considered the prominent representative of the unadulterated Cavalier tradition in the novel. High-minded, aristocratic, opinionated, stubborn, short-sighted—he embodies both the virtues and the flaws of the aristocratic temperament. At the opposite end of the spectrum stands the mysterious recluse, a man whose past is vaguely but surely linked to the fallen Puritan Commonwealth and who seems to reflect single-minded Puritan conviction in his very strength and presence. In the middle of these contrasting elements stands the young hero of the

---

20. Gaines, *The Southern Plantation*, 23–24.
21. Taylor, *Cavalier and Yankee*, 208.

novel, Nathaniel Bacon. Bacon's unknown parentage makes it impossible to attribute to him a sure aristocratic ancestry. On the other hand, he is shunned by the party of Puritan zealots. He is, in Taylor's opinion, half Cavalier, half Roundhead.[22]

Bacon's unknown origins place him in a delicate position, for he must compete for the affections of the lovely Virginia Fairfax against Frank Beverley, an aristocratic snob, Governor Berkeley's nephew and protégé. Nature, Frank sneers, has "stamped Bacon for a Roundhead and a Crop-ear at his birth. Have you not observed how obstinately his curling locks are matted to his head?" (I, 107). Of course Miss Fairfax herself naturally prefers the noble and high-minded Bacon to the dandified and arrogant Beverley. But the opposition of the governor threatens the happiness of Caruthers' hero and heroine. After Gideon Fairfax's death, Berkeley warns Mrs. Fairfax, "Should you attempt to form an alliance with an individual who would disgrace my family . . . I will . . . with mine own hands tear him from the very foot of the altar" (I, 205).

Bacon therefore elicits sympathy as a social outcast. He stands in opposition to the haughty aristocracy represented by Frank Beverley and Governor Berkeley. It is therefore fitting that he should defy the governor on an issue connected to the very survival of the colony. Bloody Indian raids have penetrated to the very walls of Jamestown; yet the governor refuses to send an expedition to quell the depredations. Bacon is consequently appointed by popular voice as leader of a citizen's army. In his address to his supporters he complains of Berkeley's high-handed methods in ruling the colony and decries the unjust taxation and the abrogation of the citizens' right to vote. "There was a time," he thunders, "when both Cavalier and Yeoman dared to be free" (II, 58). Bacon subsequently leads an expedition against the Indians possessing interesting democratic political overtones.

Yet even though Bacon is alienated from the more arrogant of the Virginia aristocrats, he is far from being a political revolutionary or a fiery leader of the lower classes. He has been raised in the aristocratic

22. *Ibid.*, 211–15.

Fairfax household, and he shares the basic social code of his environment. As Caruthers portrays him, he has no political ambition and no desire to profoundly redistribute the political balance of power. It is Governor Berkeley's blind stubbornness and his refusal to defend the colony against Indian attacks that leads to the formation of Bacon's army, not the governor's political philosophy. In fact, Caruthers is careful to point out that most aristocratic Cavaliers fear Berkeley's peremptoriness as much as the lower classes do. Bacon's army includes ordinary citizens, but the posts of leadership are held by Cavaliers with the venerable names of Dudley and Harrison. The citizens' army is thus made up, in Caruthers' words, "of hardy planters and more chivalrous Cavaliers," while Berkeley's forces are composed primarily of mercenaries.

Caruthers does not reveal the origin of Bacon's birth until the end of his novel. But whether he be a natural or a blooded aristocrat, Bacon is clearly a hero shaped in the Cavalier mold. His aristocratic instincts are most apparent in his wooing of the fair belle, Virginia Fairfax. In this courtship Bacon assumes the role of reverent and humble acolyte to his divinely pure mistress, a role that nineteenth-century Virginians unanimously assumed was the proper fictional relationship between gentleman and gentlewoman. In an oration tailor-made to suit the more sentimental and mawkish tastes of readers, Bacon surrenders his affections to Virginia. "Mould them as you will," he exclaims, "reject me if you must, they are still yours. I swear never to profane the shrine of this first and only love by offering them upon any other" (I, 164).

Like all spirited Cavaliers, Bacon subscribes to the code of the duel. At one point in the novel, Virginia, fearing that Bacon and Beverley will settle their rivalry over her at swordpoint, promises to marry Nathaniel on condition that he never engage in a duel. Bacon, responding as any true aristocrat would, is horrified by her condition. "You cannot, you will not, require me to promise this," he cries. "One evidence I must and will give to the calumniator Beverley, that I come of no churl's blood" (I, 169). On the crucial point of honor Bacon thus proves himself as punctilious as the most pedigreed of gentlemen.

William R. Taylor's Cavalier-Roundhead thesis does not sufficiently explain the complexities of Caruthers' main character. There can be no doubt that Caruthers placed his hero into an ambiguous and ambivalent situation by design. It is also true that Bacon is an aristocratic figure who at the same time calls for a government more responsive to the needs of Virginia's citizenry than Berkeley's shortsighted autocracy. Yet to interpret him as a precisely defined amalgam of two distinct and differing cultures one must be able to distinguish definite elements in Bacon's character that are attributable to a "democratic" or "Puritan" tradition. One must also be able to recognize the recluse as a clear symbol of that Roundhead tradition of which Bacon supposedly partakes.

There is little, however, in the recluse's character to distinguish him clearly as a symbol of either Puritanism or democracy. True, Whalley's exile is tied to his dark past role in the execution of Charles, and at the end of the novel Caruthers does imply that he removes himself to New England, an environment presumably more congenial to his temperament. Yet his most striking characteristics seem more strongly colored by the romantic Promethean impulse than by Puritan asceticism. He is first described living deep within a cave in a vast chamber littered with weapons of war and scholarly volumes that indicate a vast and penetrating intellect. Caruthers does not fail to indicate that the recluse is descended from a noble family. The reader realizes that he suffers a terrible stain, a sin that has branded him, like Cain, a wanderer and an outcast. This terrible deed is, of course, regicide. But it is clear that the recluse fully repents and recognizes the horror of his deed.

In his portentous strength and awe-inspiring manner, in the mysterious gothic trappings which envelop him, the recluse seems much more obviously a Byronic superman than a spokesman for any tradition, Puritan or Cavalier. Interestingly enough, the most obviously Puritan character types—men with the names of Berkinhead, Goodenough, and Proudfit—are mercilessly satirized by Caruthers as bigots and fanatics. And it is the recluse himself who personally destroys their threats to the public order.

If it is difficult to interpret Whalley as a representative of the Roundhead tradition, it is even more difficult to view Bacon as an amalgam of two opposing traditions. Except for a single speech in which he complains of Berkeley's autocratic rule, Caruthers gives the reader no hint that his hero is anything other than a Cavalier, in word, thought, sentiment, and action. Caruthers might have chosen to emphasize the dual nature of Bacon's role by making him a common-born man who has been raised in an aristocratic environment. It is significant, however, that Bacon is at last revealed as the son of a gentleman. This gentleman, it is true, is a supporter of Cromwell, but he is nonetheless a man of reputable social standing and solid financial means. Nathaniel Bacon, far from being basely born, is a gentleman, entitled to all the rights of the Cavaliers around him. Thus the tension which centers around Bacon and tends to make him a man-in-the-middle hero vanishes and becomes superfluous with the revelation of his birth. Looking back at the novel, it is hard to imagine Bacon as anything other than a Cavalier. If there are Roundhead elements in his character, they are few and hard to detect.

It is probable that Caruthers intended what Taylor believes he accomplished in *The Cavaliers of Virginia*—to fuse Cavalier and Puritan traditions in the figure of the hero, Nathaniel Bacon, and to make Bacon a symbol of manifest destiny and national unity. It is also probable that he drew either a conscious or an unconscious association between the Roundhead tradition and personal qualities of strength and pragmatic decisiveness, qualities which a proud and headstrong Cavalier lacked. If this thesis is correct, it would indicate that Caruthers was moving toward an examination of the conflict between a practical and essentially middle-class ethic, represented by Whalley and Bacon, and an impractical and ineffectual aristocratic code, represented by Governor Berkeley and his followers. Caruthers' fellow Virginian, George Tucker, had explored a similar contrast ten years before in *The Valley of Shenandoah* through the Fawkner and Grayson families, and John Pendleton Kennedy had juxtaposed Cavalier and Yeoman in *Horse-Shoe Robinson*. *The Cavaliers of Virginia*, however, failed to materialize the conflict between Roundhead and Cavalier because Caruthers developed too few traits in either the recluse or Bacon that could be positively labeled as Roundhead in quality. In the course of writing his narrative he simply became too enamored of the Cavalier ideal to give the opposing Puritan tradition adequate attention.

The further one proceeds into the novel the clearer it becomes that Caruthers has abandoned what was probably his original intention in order to celebrate just one of the two figures he had originally posited— the Cavalier. The novelist frequently betrays his bias toward and his interest in his aristocratic characters in scenes such as the duel between hero Bacon and villain Beverley. Acting on his promise to Virginia, Bacon merely defends himself, refusing to take the initiative. But Beverley taunts him with the epithet of bastard, and the enraged Bacon quickly skewers his opponent. The gravely wounded Beverley then makes a speech which is totally out of character. "Bacon," he gasps, "forgive me; I wronged you both first and last. I see it now when it is too late, but it is never too late to ask forgiveness for an injury" (I, 188). This statement is rendered even more incongruous by the subsequent acts of villainy which Beverley perpetrates. The explanation for this inconsistency of sentiment is that Caruthers is describing, not how the character Beverley speaks, but how an ideal Cavalier wounded in a duel should speak. For Beverley, even though proud and cruel, is a Cavalier. At crucial points where the code of the Cavalier is exemplified, he must act, not as one might expect him to act, but as one might expect a gentleman to act. Caruthers, in short, never takes unfair advantage of prostrate gentlemen, even if they are villains.

Taken in its entirety *The Cavaliers of Virginia* provides ample support for Francis Pendleton Gaines's contention that the novel is first and foremost a celebration of the Old Dominion's rich aristocratic past—a past which we know today to be largely mythical. The little settlement of Jamestown, for example, is described as a "city" of "very imposing and romantic appearance." Caruthers' general and romanticized portrait bears no resemblance to the village which archaeologists and historians have recently restored. The society which inhabits Jamestown is depicted as divided simply into two classes, aristocrats and nonaristocrats. On the anniversary of the Restoration, Caruthers describes the daytime festivities of the plebeians. The night, however, is reserved for the aristocracy, who "roll along the streets in their carriages" toward the governor's ball.

Caruthers not only gave colorful and dramatic literary expression to the myth of Virginia's aristocratic settlement, but he also assured both northern and southern readers that the aristocracy still prevailed in Virginia. For, as he was careful to point out, the "generous, foxhunting, wine-drinking, duelling and reckless race of men" who had founded the Old Dominion still gave a distinct cast to contemporary Virginia society (I, 4). Nathaniel Bacon might be dead, but he had founded, in Caruthers' opinion, a race of men which continued to powerfully influence "the destinies of the Ancient Dominion from that day to the present" (I, 23). In *The Cavaliers of Virginia* Caruthers celebrated much more than manifest destiny and national unity. More profoundly he celebrated the birth and triumph of the Cavalier ideal as a part of Virginia's mythical past.

Caruthers' last novel, *The Knights of the Golden Horse-shoe*, was probably begun before the novelist left New York City in 1835. By 1838 he had settled in Savannah and had finished his book, but the financial panic which erupted in that year undoubtedly persuaded *Harper's* not to publish it. In 1841, however, it appeared serially in a small literary quarterly, the Savannah *Magnolia*, as "The Knights of the Golden Horse-shoe"; and in 1845 Charles Yancey, a printer from Wetumpka, Alabama, persuaded Caruthers to let him publish the book on his press. Unfortunately, Yancey lacked facilities for distributing the novel. It received only a few scattered reviews and was soon forgotten.

The book's fate was undeserved, for critics are in general agreement that *The Knights of the Golden Horse-shoe* represents Caruthers' best fictional effort. It develops two fairly self-contained plots. One, which takes up the first half of the novel, concerns the identity of the mysterious Henry Hall, a tutor to Governor Spotswood's son who has recently arrived from Scotland. After much confusion Henry reveals himself as Frank Lee, an aristocratic Virginian of noble character who, after traveling to Edinburgh to study at the university there, had unfortunately become involved in a plot to restore the Pretender. The death of Queen Anne produces a general pardon which enables Lee to reveal his true identity. The second and more interesting portion of the novel describes Governor Spotswood's bold expedition to the height of the Blue Ridge. This expedition drives the Indians westward and opens vast new territories for British colonization. Having disposed of the complicated and excessively melodramatic question of Frank Lee's identity, Caruthers re-creates the stirring events of Spotswood's tramontane expedition with a zest and vigor that reveal his writing talent at its best.

William R. Taylor has observed that in *The Knights of the Golden Horse-shoe* the Cavalier figure almost completely dominates. He attributes Caruthers' concentration on the Cavalier to his personal reaction to his own financial difficulties and to his sense of professional failure. In other words, Taylor feels that Caruthers used the Cavalier ideal as a means of escaping from the unpleasant day-to-day realities of his own life.[23] This theory is interesting and provocative, but it would probably be equally valid to look upon *The Knights of the Golden Horse-shoe* as a development and intensification of the bias and propensity toward the Cavalier which had already been apparent in *The Cavaliers of Virginia*.

The Knights of the Golden Horse-shoe employs many of the same themes and plot complications as *The Cavaliers of Virginia*. Frank Lee, for example, is cast into a socially ambiguous position that closely resembles the predicament of Nathaniel Bacon. Like Bacon, his origins are a mystery through much of the novel, and thus his social pedigree is questionable. But Lee, like Bacon, carries himself with the deportment and grandeur that mark him unmistakably as an aristocrat. "Our new tutor," remarks young Kate Spotswood, "has quite as aristocratic an air as any person at the table, and more of the camp grace about him than even Papa himself."[24] Caruthers, like many another romancer of his time, obviously believed that it was impossible to disguise an inherently aristocratic nature.

Ironically, Frank's bitterest enemy is his own younger brother, the

23. *Ibid.*, 217.

24. William Alexander Caruthers, *The Knights of the Golden Horse-shoe: A Tradition-ary Tale of the Cocked Hat Gentry in the Old Dominion* (1845; rpr. Chapel Hill, 1970), 40, hereinafter cited in the text by page number only.

proud and selfish Harry Lee. Because Frank's appearance has matured during his years in Scotland, Harry does not recognize the tutor as his brother. Instead he bitterly resents the growing friendship between this newcomer and the lovely Ellen Evylin and tries to sabotage the friendship by calling the tutor's obscure social origins into question. The conflict between Frank and Harry Lee is resolved dramatically at a meeting called to select young men for the governor's mountain expedition. Harry, with a few other snobbish supporters, forces through a resolution "that none but those of gentle blood should be admitted into this exclusive association" (162).

Here again, as in *The Cavaliers of Virginia*, Caruthers has dramatically developed a situation that might have conveyed an effective statement on the damaging consequences of haughty, aristocratic pride. And indeed, Harry Lee is frustrated in his selfish designs. However, it is not Frank Lee's personal merit, but the startling self-revelation that he is in fact as blooded and fine an aristocratic Cavalier as any in the assembly, which vindicates him before his peers, just as Nathaniel Bacon is vindicated in *The Cavaliers*. The resolution of the conflict suggests nothing about aristocratic pretensions except that good and well-mannered Cavaliers inevitably win out over bad and snobbish Cavaliers. And, as in Caruthers' previous novel, the Cavalier villain does not receive the just deserts usually accorded to such characters. Harry Lee simply fades into the woodwork and is heard from no more. One must assume that, although Caruthers was capable of making some of his Cavaliers villains, he was not capable of passing judgment on them.

Caruthers' felicitous resolution of the conflict between the Lee brothers reminds one of the superficial manner in which James Ewell Heath concludes *Edge-Hill*. Like Heath, Caruthers provides a solution to his protagonist's problem which has the effect of turning his narrative away from the examination of a serious social conflict. Indeed, this blunting or shunting aside of social problems that have become implicit in a narrative is one of the most notable characteristics of Virginia fiction after Tucker and Kennedy. After 1830 Virginia's writers seem less and less inclined to acknowledge social tensions in their idealized projections of the Old Dominion's past.

After Frank Lee's identity has been established, Caruthers moves on to the more exciting subject of Governor Spotswood's expedition to the Blue Ridge. Spotswood becomes Caruthers' spokesman for manifest destiny, just as Nathaniel Bacon had been in *The Cavaliers of Virginia*. The governor firmly believes that, if the British colonies are to avoid being hemmed in from the west by the French, Virginians must press an exploratory party to the Appalachian peaks and lay claim to the vast, unknown tramontane region. Although the more conservative planters scoff at his plan, Spotswood tenaciously fights for appropriations from the Burgesses. "Just as sure as the sun shines to-morrow," he declares, "I will lead an expedition over yonder blue mountains, and I will triumph over the French—the Indians, and the Devil, if he chooses to join forces with them" (28–29). The governor's unwilting determination finally wins him the support he needs from the government as well as the backing of most of the colony's young Cavaliers.

Caruthers attaches profound significance to this expedition, considering it another symbolic step forward in the conquering of a continent. Indeed, he favorably compares Spotswood's achievement with the accomplishments of other American explorers such as Daniel Boone. For this march, observes expansionist-minded Caruthers, was but the beginning of a grand procession that, renewed generation after generation, "would transcend the Rio del Norte, and which in half that time may traverse the utmost boundaries of Mexico" (161).

The Knights of the Golden Horse-shoe obviously intends to introduce a new figure into the pantheon of folk heroes, Alexander Spotswood. It is also obvious that Caruthers intends for Spotswood's character to dominate the portion of the narrative dealing with the tramontane expedition. Yet few who read the book can fail to note that as the expedition progresses Spotswood must share the limelight more and more with a humble, unostentatious, and quite ungentlemanly fellow named Red Jarvis. Jarvis seems to be Caruthers' answer to Natty Bumppo and Horse-Shoe Robinson. Simple, homespun, sententious, humorous, crafty in the ways of the wood—he contrasts vividly with the dandified Cavalier crusaders. In the course of the expedition Spotswood becomes more and more dependent on his guide's advice in the maintenance and provisioning of the army. Indeed, at a crucial point Jarvis literally saves Spotswood's undertaking. Used to the light, sandy Tidewater soil, the army's unshod horses are lamed by sharp, cutting mountain stones. Spotswood bitterly contemplates turning back, but the resourceful Jarvis solves the seemingly unsolvable problem by stripping metal from the supply wagon wheels, molding it into horseshoes, and teaching the noble Cavaliers how to shoe their mounts. In a scene heavy with irony Jarvis stands as supervisor while Frank Lee and Governor Spotswood kneel before their horses.

Like Natty, Jarvis is a creature of the wilderness who mourns the destructive forces of civilization. "There's scarce an elk or a buffalo to be found now this side of the hills," he muses, "and he's a gwine to drive them all clean over the ridge" (185). Yet like Cooper's Leatherstocking, Jarvis is the instrument, the pathfinder, the cutting edge of civilization's advance. Without his knowledge Spotswood's expedition would not have been successfully completed. Jarvis also suggests the leveling influence of the frontier, the democratizing influence of a land where a man can be judged only by his skills and human resources. At the beginning of the expedition the scout rightly predicts that aristocratic trappings will mean little in the wilderness. "You'll see who's the best man among us," he says, "when we get among the mountains, and when neither money nor larnin' can do much for a man" (185–86).

Of course, there are obvious differences between Caruthers' Jarvis and Cooper's Leatherstocking. Jarvis does not have the nobility and stature that Cooper was able to impart to his hero over a five-novel cycle. Yet for all his ignorance and limitations, Jarvis stands as the most appealing and interesting character in the book. Nathanial Bacon, Frank Lee, and Alexander Spotswood are three different characters, but essentially they think, feel, and act in distressingly similar and predictable ways. They do not come to life as human beings. They are cardboard characters cut from the pattern of aristocratic gentleman. One feels that one has met them a hundred times before in a hundred mediocre melodramas and romances. Of course, Jarvis himself is not a completely unique characterization, but he does contain a creative spark that the other characters in the novel lack. He is Caruthers' most successful creation, just as Horse-Shoe Robinson was Kennedy's most fully realized character.

Because he likes Jarvis, the reader is apt to be jolted by the character assessment that Frank Lee makes at the end of the expedition. Frank has been closely associated with Jarvis during this perilous journey. The hunter has personally initiated Lee into the mysteries of the forest and the art of surviving in the wilderness. Yet after the army returns to civilization Frank retains essentially the same condescending attitude toward Jarvis he had displayed at the beginning of the expedition. "I have learned to feel something like an attachment for the scout," he concludes. "The native soil is a good one, and with judicious attention and skilful guidance, he might be made a useful man in his sphere" (240). Frank speaks of Jarvis as if he were a strange sort of semihuman, to be appreciated at arm's length, to be valued with circumspection. Yet one must assume that the writer stands behind Lee's judgment. For Frank is a hero and a gentleman, and Caruthers' fictional world is structured around the values Lee and men like him represent.

Caruthers' novel ends on a grand scale with Spotswood's investiture of his Cavalier warriors as "Knights of the Horse-shoe." Lee, Page, Randolph, Byrd, Carter, Wythe, Washington, Pendleton, Beverley, Bland, Fitzhugh, Dandridge, Ludwell—each flower of Virginia Cavalierdom receives a golden horseshoe inlaid with precious stones. Spotswood challenges the young men to carry their tokens to King George and to tell him of the new empire they have added to his dominion. "He will recognize you," the governor proclaims, "as a part of the chivalry of the empire—of that glorious band of knights and gentlemen who surround his throne like a bulwark" (245).

Amidst all this pomp and splendor, it is ironic but not surprising that the man most responsible for the success of the undertaking, Red Jarvis, is absent. At this point in the novel Caruthers has no more use for his frontier scout. The Cavaliers take the stage in the final act; all along they have been the destined heroes of the novelist's parable of our nation's destiny. For it is not the rude frontiersman, but the polished Virginia aristocrat who most splendidly fulfills his role as leader of the westward continental expansion. The final chapters of *The Knights of the Golden Horse-shoe* serve to remind the reader, in case he has forgotten, that the laurels rest with Governor Spotswood and his Cavalier followers. It is Spotswood that Caruthers celebrates, with his uniformed bodyguard, his powdered footmen, his baronial hall hung with staghorns and war trophies. These are the scenes on which, in the end, Caruthers invites us to rest our eyes.

William Alexander Caruthers was a nationalist, but he could never be considered a champion of American democracy. The task he set for himself in fiction was a difficult one. He sought to create a counter myth to match the appeal of the myth of the American common man bravely encountering and subduing an uncivilized continent. He accepted the vision of America's manifest destiny, but in his version of our national crusade he substituted as leader and hero the aristocratic Virginia Cavalier for the democratic man of the people. Nathaniel Bacon, Frank Lee, and Alexander Spotswood were his answer to Davy Crockett and Daniel Boone. Caruthers' vision of America's growth was not convincing for the simple reason that aristocratic mythical figures could not be substituted as leaders of a historical movement profoundly democratic in its implications. In a national mythology Spotswood could never be as convincing a figure as Boone. Though he probably did not recognize it, Caruthers stumbled over this very problem in his appealing characterization of Red Jarvis. By the end of *The Knights of the Golden Horse-shoe* Jarvis so threatened Spotswood's supremacy that Caruthers could reestablish it only by the most arbitrary and artificial of means.

There is an obvious and striking similarity between the conclusions of *Knights of the Golden Horse-shoe* and of *Horse-Shoe Robinson*. In both novels the yeoman character who has come to dominate the action is pushed into the background while the final scene is given to the aristocratic characters. Caruthers' conclusion is even more flamboyantly romantic than Kennedy's. Both narratives, after having displayed the strength and the effectiveness of the yeoman, return in the end to the Cavalier figure and insist on asserting his dominance, even though the vigorous yeomen they have created call into question the validity of the Cavalier concept.

The Knights of the Golden Horse-shoe is a romance that exalts the

Cavalier and seeks to assure for him a prominent position in America's mythological pantheon. Yet as enamored as he is of this ideal, Caruthers, like John Pendleton Kennedy, is too intimately acquainted with the middle-class realities of life as it is lived in the Shenandoah Valley not to recognize at least obliquely the weaknesses and the limitations of the Cavalier ideal. These limitations become more obvious with each mile the governor's exploring party travels away from Williamsburg into the wilderness. Try as he might, Caruthers cannot avoid linking the frontier with the difficulties and hardships that are a natural part of the world of reality. Frank Lee is alien to this world but Red Jarvis is not. Here he is transformed from a buffoon into a man. A return to Williamsburg is essential if the Cavalier is to be restored to his full stature, for only in the realm of romance can he operate freely without the limitations of pragmatic circumstance.

The problem Caruthers faced in *The Knights of the Golden Horse-shoe* was one which all of the South's romance writers had to deal with in their fiction. William R. Taylor has discerned that during the years from 1830 to 1860 the South was forced to choose between living with the values of the nation at large or inventing alternative ideals "which had even less relevance to the Southern situation."[25] The South chose the latter course. In response to attacks from the North, southern writers created a mythical figure who embodied what were supposedly the highest ideals of their culture. Virginia writers dubbed him Cavalier. Yet this ideal character was created with the implicit understanding that the values for which he stood were incompatible with the modern doctrine of progress. As late as 1824 George Tucker openly recognized in his melodrama of the Grayson family the doom which surrounded the Cavalier in the modern world. Significantly, Caruthers was not capable of pronouncing the same verdict seventeen years later. Implicit in *The Knights of the Golden Horse-shoe* is the realization of the Cavalier's ineffectuality. But in spite of this understanding, Caruthers arbitrarily celebrates his mythical heroes as triumphant bearers of the nation's manifest destiny into the wilderness.

25. Taylor, *Cavalier and Yankee*, 17.

JOHN ESTEN COOKE

John Esten Cooke, like William Alexander Caruthers, was a native of the Old Dominion. He too translated Virginia's mythical past into the pages of his historical romances. However, the past he celebrated was not the early period of Virginia's settlement and initial expansion. Instead he focused primarily on what he termed the Dominion's golden age, the years immediately before the Revolutionary War when the planter aristocracy attained the height of its wealth and power. Cooke's biographer, John O. Beaty, claims for his subject the preeminence in the realm of the antebellum Virginia historical romance that Curtis Carroll Davis has also claimed for Caruthers. Cooke, Beaty contends, is primarily responsible for the idea of colonial Virginia held by residents of the Old Dominion in the twentieth century, an assessment supported by Francis Pendleton Gaines, who calls Cooke "the most notable figure between Kennedy and the postbellum masters."[26] Judged by Cooke's considerable literary output, one can safely declare that this Virginian continued in the tradition of his predecessor Caruthers and popularized even more widely and thoroughly a romantic, rose-colored view of Virginia's past. At the same time he enshrined the figure of the Cavalier more firmly in the minds of both southerners and northerners.

Cooke's ancestral roots struck more firmly into Virginia soil than Caruthers'. Through his mother's side he was related to the distinguished Pendleton family and included among his cousins the well-known writer John Pendleton Kennedy. His elder brother, Philip Pendleton Cooke, was a poet, particularly esteemed in Virginia. John Esten was born in 1830 in Winchester, and he spent his boyhood years in the valley. At the age of ten he moved with his family to Richmond, where he attended school, studied law, and later practiced under his father's tutelage. As a young man Cooke was drawn toward creative writing, but financial considerations forced him for many years to divide his time between literature and the profession of law.

26. John Owen Beaty, *John Esten Cooke, Virginian* (New York, 1922), 160; Gaines, *The Southern Plantation*, 54.

In spite of his limited time, Cooke was a prolific though frequently careless writer, addicted to clichés and to large statements of little substance. Nevertheless, his skillful use of the historical romance genre, his flair for colorful detail, and his command of dramatic incident paid off with an early success in 1854, *The Virginia Comedians*. This two-volume novel was followed in 1859 by *Henry St. John, Gentleman*. Together these novels constitute a loose trilogy and represent what most critics consider to be Cooke's most successful fictional effort.

Cooke fought throughout the Civil War, serving much of the time on the staff of General J. E. B. Stuart. Out of his war experiences came seven books, including adulatory biographies of Generals Jackson and Lee. The best known work of this period, however, was a novel, *Surry of Eagle's Nest*, published in 1866. After the war Cooke married the daughter of another distinguished Virginia family, Mary Frances Page, and retired to her estate, The Briars. Here he farmed and continued writing until his death in 1886. Notable among the works of this postwar period were *The Heir of Gaymount* (1870) and *My Lady Pokahontas* (1885). However, Cooke never reattained in his later writing the vigor of the Revolutionary War romances of the 1850s.

Cooke's romances of the Old Dominion reflect a historical perspective which accepts as essentially true Virginia's cherished notions of its aristocratic past. This subjective approach to his state's history was clearly present in Cooke's popular work *Virginia: A History of the People*. Here the writer's interpretation of the past was based on three major convictions. The first was a belief that Virginia's culture had been predominantly and profoundly influenced by large numbers of immigrants of Cavalier ancestry. "One of the highest authorities in American history," he observed, "has described the Cavalier element in Virginia as only 'perceptible.' It was really so strong as to control all things,—the forms of society, of religion, and the direction of public affairs. The fact was so plain that he who ran might read it."[27]

Cooke's second conviction was that the years from 1700 to 1775 had

27. Cooke, *Virginia: A History of the People*, 230, hereinafter cited in the text by page number only.

constituted Virginia's golden age. The years before this period had been years of formation; those that followed would be years of transition, and even of chaos. But during the golden age, he believed, the colony's society had remained a stationary "democratic aristocracy." In this period slaves and white servants had been contented, and the class of middling yeoman farmers had willingly deferred to the directives of the dominant planter class. "The planter in his manor-house, surrounded by his family and retainers," he concluded, "was a feudal patriarch mildly ruling everybody . . . and everybody, high and low, seemed to be happy" (365–71).

Cooke's sympathetic view of eighteenth-century Virginia formed the foundation of his third conviction. This conviction, though not directly expressed, is implicit in the final few pages of his history which deal with post–Revolutionary War Virginia. In these pages the reader clearly perceives that for Cooke the "Republican Ascendency" and the declining influence of the ancient aristocratic families had produced a new society which, if more egalitarian, was duller, less picturesque, and less distinguished than the society that had preceded it. "Democratic equality had become the watchword and controlled society," he observed in a passage redolent of the wistful nostalgia that is the special province of the Virginia romance writer. With democracy, he lamented, had come a "brusque address" which had rudely supplanted "the old ceremonious courtesy"(478).

It is essentially this romantic and nostalgic view of Virginia's golden age which Cooke expresses in his second and most popular novel, *The Virginia Comedians*. In this novel the writer sketches Old Dominion society during the period immediately before the outbreak of the Revolution, with dashes of romantic coloring that exceed even the productions of Caruthers. It is therefore startling as well as interesting to note that Cooke personally interpreted his novel as an attack on aristocracy. In a letter to writer and publisher Rufus Griswold dated May 28, 1855, he asserted that his novel was "profoundly democratic and American—the aristocracy, whom I don't like, getting the worst of it."[28]

28. Quoted in Hubbell, *The South in American Literature*, 514.

A close reading of *The Virginia Comedians* partially substantiates Cooke's interpretation, for in some respects the aristocrats do indeed seem to get the worst of things in the novel. The character who comes under most critical observation is Champ Effingham, a young Virginia Cavalier fresh home from Oxford and a grand tour of the Continent. The reader is first introduced to Champ as he lounges indolently in the well-furnished library of his father's James River estate. Cooke describes him in this manner: "His head is covered with a long flowing peruke, heavy with powder, and the drop curls hang down on his cheeks ambrosially: his cheeks are delicately rouged, and two patches, arranged with matchless art, complete the distinguished *tout ensemble* of the handsome face."[29] In short, Champ is a fop and a dandy, and he is exceedingly bored with rural Virginia life.

In the course of the first volume of the novel Champ becomes infatuated with a beautiful actress, Beatrice Hallam, one of the Virginia Company of Actors. Rejecting his childhood sweetheart, the lovely, charming, aristocratic Clare Lee, he pursues Beatrice with a vengeance. But Beatrice is a woman of noble mind, if not of noble birth. She rejects Effingham's slightly contemptuous advances and gives her love to Charlie Waters, son of a humble fisherman and leader of radical democratic sentiment in Williamsburg. At the end of the first volume Champ gravely wounds Charlie in an abortive attempt to abduct Miss Hallam. With Charlie lying near death, Champ catches an outward-bound ship for Europe.

Throughout the first part of his novel Cooke explicitly draws and develops the contrast between the Virginia aristocrats, represented mainly by Champ Effingham, and vigorous enterprising characters of more humble origin, such as Charlie Waters and the mysterious man in the red cloak, later identified as Patrick Henry. The political sentiments of the Virginia gentry are concisely expressed by Squire Effingham early in the novel: "*Educate* the lower classes! *Educate* my indentured servant, and the common tradesman and farmer, and have the knave

29. John Esten Cooke, *The Virginia Comedians; or, Old Days in the Old Dominion* (1854; rpr. Ridgewood, N.J., 1968), I, 18, hereinafter cited in the text by volume and page number.

talking to me of the 'rights of men,' and all the wretched stuff and foolery of Utopian castlebuilders" (I, 34). Charlie Waters, however, defiantly opposes these aristocratic sentiments with a democratic creed imbued with the ideals of Jefferson. "No sir!" he cries. "Men are not by nature destitute of truth and love, nobility and purity" (I, 13). He acknowledges that men have fallen and sinned, "but what is equally true is this—that everywhere the instincts of humanity, planted by God in it, have revolted against this abnormal state; love has effaced hatred, justice the spirit of wrong; heaven has opened and the abyss has closed!" (I, 13). Man can improve his condition. The masses, with the help of education, can learn to rule themselves wisely. In the character of Charlie Waters, Cooke presents the most sanguine hopes of democratic idealism.

The contrast between conservative and liberal, aristocratic and plebeian, which underlines the plot of the first volume is most vividly demonstrated in the scene in which Champ, for the first and only time in the novel, meets Patrick Henry: "The young gentleman . . . was clad with his usual elegance and richness, and for a moment his eye dwelt on the coarsely-dressed stranger. . . . The man in the red cloak surveyed him with great calmness, and some curiosity. An imaginative spectator might have fancied them the representatives of the old world and the new—the past and the future—the court and the backwoods" (I, 136). In scenes such as these Cooke draws the lines firmly between two opposing points of view. And in the final explosive scene of the novel there can be no doubt as to where the novelist, at least at this point, stands. In this scene Patrick Henry and Charlie Waters whip up the crowd's resentment against the Stamp Act into a frenzy of revolt. The aristocratic order seems doomed to destruction as Henry utters his final words: "Good! . . . The Revolution is begun!" (II, 279).

Considering that John Esten Cooke wrote his novel shortly before the Civil War, at a time when sectional sentiment ran high, his critical treatment of the Virginia aristocracy is little short of amazing. Indeed, if Cooke had consistently developed the contrast between Champ and Charlie, if he had emphasized the weaknesses within the aristocratic framework that had brought its destruction, he would probably still be read today. But Cooke was above all else a Virginian, and democratic sentiments to the contrary, he was hopelessly entangled in the romance of the myth, in the very charm and grace of those people that he said he did not like. Because of these warring sentiments it is not completely surprising to discover that Cooke has abandoned the Champ-Charlie conflict in the second volume of his novel. Charlie recovers from his wound and withdraws with Beatrice to live in the mountains. Beatrice dies there of consumption, and Charlie reappears again only in the last scene, inflaming the Williamsburg mob. Onto the stage vacated by Charlie and Beatrice returns Champ, chastened by experience, a wiser and stronger man. The remainder of the novel deals with the progress of several romances, including the heartwarming reconciliation of Champ and Clare Lee. In fine fashion worthy of the noble Cavalier tradition, several gentlemen win their beloved mistresses. *The Virginia Comedians* ends with multiple nuptials and profuse happiness.

In volume two Champ Effingham steadily improves in character until, by the end of the novel, it is clear that Cooke intends him to be the major object of the reader's sympathy. Those admirable qualities which Champ possesses in the first part of the novel—courage and a strong sense of honor—are augmented by a humility born of a sense of past iniquity and, above all, by his noble and purified passion for Clare. Champ's love for Clare finds consummate expression in his personal confession to her. Here Clare assumes the proper position in relation to the Cavalier's passion; she becomes his goddess. In youth, says Champ, "you were my ideal, all my world was full of you. I dreamed, and sang, and thought of you alone" (II, 175). Although he was led astray by his passion for Beatrice, he now realizes that Clare is the only woman he could ever love. "I ask God to bless you, Clare, and thank you for the small share of purity I have left, and say to you, 'I will love you and cherish your memory always, as that of the tenderest soul, the warmest, purest heart that ever was in human bosom'" (II, 177). The pure sentiment, the religious and devotional tone of praise, represent the most refined aspects of the Cavalier love code. It becomes quite clear that in the final portion of his novel Cooke intends for his readers to sympathize with Champ and to rejoice in the final consummation of his love.

One cannot read *The Virginia Comedians* without feeling that Cooke is essentially confused in his attitudes towards his characters. He claims to be giving his aristocrats the worst of things, but in the final portion of the novel he allows his aristocratic characters to dominate the action. Charlie and Beatrice Waters are forgotten as one views with increasing sympathy the exquisitely high-minded sentiments of Champ Effingham and his fellows among the first families of Virginia. This confusion is not lessened by the return of Charlie and Patrick Henry at the end of the book. The storm of revolution contrasts sharply with the happy conclusion of the romantic affairs. Yet the juxtaposition is not effective for the simple reason that Cooke makes no attempt to relate or draw the two parts together. In short, he is not able to bring his yeomen and his Cavaliers together to produce an effective statement or theme.

The ambiguity of Cooke's treatment of character is paralleled by an equally confusing treatment of Virginia society. Cooke may have been hostile to the aristocratic attitude, but he was decidedly sympathetic toward the aristocratic way of life. In his scenes of this life—the plantation homes with lush parks sloping gently to the river, the hall hung with numerous portraits of noble English ancestors—there is nothing to indicate that Cooke did not ardently embrace the legend of Old Virginia. He speaks with delight of Squire Effingham's ball in which the "noble mansion blazed from top to bottom with a thousand lights" and "chariots constantly rolled up, and deposited beautiful dames and gallant cavaliers" who "dined in state, and danced and feasted and made merry" (II, 106–107). Yet there is an element of wistful sadness in the description, for Cooke reflects that such high revelry only occasionally occurs in present-day Virginia. The nostalgic and romantic tone of the novel is most apparent in Cooke's description of racing day in old Williamsburg. "Where are they now, those stalwart cavaliers and lovely dames who filled that former time with so much light, and merriment, and joyous laughter? Where are those good coursers, Selim, Fair Anna, and Sir Archy; where are black and white, old and young, all the sporting men and women of the swaying crowd? What do we care for them today? . . . What do we care for all those happy maiden faces—gallant inclinations—graceful courtesies—everything connected with the cavaliers and dames of that old, brilliant, pompous, honest, worthy race" (II, 148). Cooke's sensibility, like that of John Pendleton Kennedy, seems to have been truly divided. One part of him was strongly attracted to the romantic vision of Virginia's splendidly colorful aristocratic past. Another part responded to the democratic ideal of the equality of all men, an ideal propounded by Charlie Waters and Patrick Henry. In *The Virginia Comedians* the aristocratic vision prevails in the end.

In 1859 Cooke returned to the Old Dominion's golden age with a sequel to *The Virginia Comedians*. The action of *Henry St. John, Gentleman* takes place ten years after that of *The Virginia Comedians*, on the eve of the Revolution. Henry St. John, Cooke's hero, represents the epitome of the Virginia Cavalier, graced with both a large estate and an ancestry that combines aristocratic English with royal Indian blood. Henry is the great-grandson of the Indian princess revered by all Virginians, Pocahontas. The noble-minded Henry stands opposed to two villains—the scheming, egotistical, authoritarian royal governor, Lord Dunmore, and Dunmore's proud, selfish, and cruel royalist supporter, Mr. Lindon, who treacherously seeks to undermine the romance between the handsome St. John and the beautiful Bonnybel Vane.

Henry St. John recaptures with equal force the colorful descriptions of the Virginia aristocracy which had characterized *The Virginia Comedians*. The most venerable of Cooke's new characters is Henry's uncle, friend, and financial advisor Colonel Vane. The old Cavalier closely resembles Champ Effingham's father. He is a powdered-haired, gouty old gentleman who lives in a splendid plantation home stocked with pictures of distinguished English ancestors. He combines an amusingly tempestuous humor with a fond indulgence of his lovely daughters, particularly his sprightly younger daughter, Bonnybel. In short, he is a figure who displays the clear influence of Addison's English squire, Sir Roger de Coverley.

Colonel Vane's estate is matched by Henry St. John's neighboring Flower of Hundreds. Cooke describes St. John's home as "a big old house, full of deer antlers, fine furniture, tall mirrors, portraits of old fellows in periwigs, and dames in odd-looking dresses."[30] Behind the house stand the slave quarters and a stable housing the finest collection of thoroughbreds in the Old Dominion. Vane and St. John's world is thus characterized by a luxuriousness and a suggestion of indolence and ease that easily calls to mind the world of the Effinghams in *The Virginia Comedians*.

Henry St. John inevitably finds a suitable object for adoration in Bonnybel Vane. Unlike Champ Effingham's placid Clare, Bonnybel is "a sparkling, mischievous little maiden of about seventeen" with a finely molded oval face "of that pure-blooded Norman type which fascinated the kings and princes of the middle ages, and led to so many bitter feuds and bloody wars" (59). She is a delightful coquette who leads her worshipful lover a merry chase. Henry serves his lady as a true Cavalier should. On two occasions he saves Bonnybel's life, rescuing her from a river and killing a rattlesnake poised to strike her. She, in turn, indirectly saves her lover in admirably romantic fashion. For it is her *billet-doux*, carried reverently in St. John's breastpocket, that saves the hero from the sword thrust of the villain, Lindon.

Henry St. John is a much more uniformly admirable and appealing character than the erratic Champ Effingham. The Cavalier ideal presents itself with even more concentrated force in this concluding portion of Cooke's trilogy. Henry remains a perfect gentleman from beginning to end. In the concluding chapters, for example, he pursues his adversary, Lindon, who has unsuccessfully sought to abduct Bonnybel. Tracking Lindon to the governor's palace, Henry finds that he has been accidentally shot dead. Inside the palace cowers Lindon's hateful ally, Lord Dunmore, and outside seethes a revolutionary mob ready to break down the palace doors. Henry feels only scorn for Dunmore, but his refined Cavalier sentiments dictate pity for Dunmore's wife, Lady Augusta. "Fear nothing, madam," he assures the frightened woman, "the men of Virginia do not make war on women" (481). He quickly brings

30. John Esten Cooke, *Henry St. John, Gentleman, of "Flower of Hundreds," in the County of Prince George, Virginia: A Tale of 1774–'75* (New York, 1859), 41, hereinafter cited in the text by page number only.

a carriage to the rear of the palace and ushers both Lord Dunmore and his wife away from the threatened building. Lady Augusta leaves, but not before dropping a glove at Henry's foot as a token of her appreciation. Henry in turn chivalrously places the token at his breast and lowers his head "with a low bow of thanks and farewell" (482).

As he had done in *The Virginia Comedians*, Cooke develops a dramatic contrast to his lavishly drawn Cavaliers by reintroducing into his narrative the plebeian democrat, Charlie Waters. Charlie has been working feverishly for independence during the nearly ten years that have elapsed since his beloved wife's death. Henry St. John first meets this dedicated revolutionary in historic Saint John's Church, the building that will later provide the setting for Patrick Henry's famous liberty-or-death speech. St. John has taken refuge in the church to escape from the violence of a summer thunderstorm. Inside, a flash of lightning reveals the towering figure of Waters, a man whose tempestuous passions are obviously reflected by the storm outside.

Henry is immediately drawn to this powerfully magnetic figure. Waters, after years of careful work, has become the head of a complex network of vigilance committees. Although neither rich nor well known, he stands as one of the most powerful leaders of the independence movement in Virginia. He is the archetypal revolutionary, "a machine of iron, with but one eternal idea burning like fire in his soul" (153), to liberate the human spirit. Like all true rebels he views political upheaval as divine necessity. "Revolution is logical, mathematical," he avows, "but it is the logic, the mathematics of God!" (204).

Charlie Waters is not merely a fiercely idealistic revolutionary; he is also a shrewdly pragmatic observer of society. He recognizes that the true strength of the independence party lies among the small yeoman farmers and frontiersmen. These men, he explains to St. John, are basically hostile to the notion of aristocracy and social gradations. It is they who will soon flood the streets of Williamsburg like "Goths and Huns in the streets of Rome." Waters recognizes, however, that these plebeian hordes are essentially powerless unless they are joined by the wealthy and more politically powerful planter aristocracy. Ordinarily such gentlemen would cling devotedly to England and its venerable traditions and repudiate the concept of majority rule. Yet, as Waters astutely observes, though they love England, like true Englishmen, they "love their personal liberty more. They are afraid of Democracy, but they are more afraid of Parliament" (403–404). With prophetic vision Waters sees that the shortsighted policies and the political depredations of the English government eventually will unite yeoman and Cavalier into a formidable force for independence.

Waters, with the insight informed by his democratic convictions, foresees that the coming revolution will bring profound and sweeping changes to the aristocratic order of Virginia society. He also perceives that the wealthy planters will become an ironic instrument of the very political changes they oppose. Henry St. John, himself an aristocrat, recognizes clearly enough that "as the palace, and the king in his royal trappings, are the incarnation of privilege and prerogative," Charlie Waters is the dramatic embodiment "of liberty, disenthrallment—of that freedom of thought and soul which the new world must inaugurate" (205). By the end of the novel Waters' prophesies have come true. The flood of revolution has finally been unleashed, and Waters, armed and sitting astride his plunging steed, stands poised on the crest of the wave. His final words to Henry express the fruition of his long-held dream: "Look friend . . . see the banner of England trodden down and torn to pieces! See the beginning of the end! The advent of war and revolution! The hour has struck! The day dawned! The old world has passed away—behold all things from henceforth become new!" (485).

Waters' analysis of the shifting allegiance of the aristocratic planter seems substantiated by the actions of the novel's Cavalier figures. Upon learning of the British blockade of Boston harbor, Colonel Vane—himself the richest characterization of the highborn Anglophile in the book—denounces British tyranny. "Whatever touches her [Boston]," he believes, "touches Virginia, nay, touches all the colonies, for this tyrannical edict is but the entering wedge! . . . I'll buckle on my sword and fight for the cause in the ranks, as a common soldier, before I'll forget that I'm a Virginia gentleman" (91). Henry St. John, the noblest manifestation of the aristocratic Cavalier in all of Cooke's novels, willingly joins the struggle for independence at the end of the book. "If the struggle's here in Virginia," he declares, "I'll myself cheerfully brace on my sword, and strike as hard blows as I'm able in the contest against this detestable tyranny!" (92).

Through his characterization of Charlie Waters, Cooke has already pointed to the irony of Virginia aristocrats fighting for independence in union with middle-class yeomen with whom they have little in common politically. Waters sees that by repudiating the mother country the planters are committing themselves to profound historical and institutional changes that implicitly threaten their social supremacy. And yet, curiously enough, Cooke introduces not a shred of irony in those scenes in which his Cavaliers repudiate British tyranny. Indeed, in these passages he seems to have forgotten that in supporting revolution his aristocratic characters are sowing the seeds of their own decline.

The final chapter seems less to repudiate Waters' theories than to ignore them. Henry marries the lovely Bonnybel and, after serving with distinction under General Washington himself, returns to Flower of Hundreds and hangs up his sword on his ancestral walls. To paraphrase Cooke's words, he sinks back into the role of Virginia planter. On the last page of the novel the reader takes leave of the handsome Cavalier hero and his beautiful belle; he leaves them as he found them at the beginning of the novel, just as James Ewell Heath and William Alexander Caruthers leave their characters, securely established and smiling. It is hard to imagine that a revolution has occurred. The status quo seems to stand as securely as it did before the war. In his final chapter Cooke is ignoring not only the prophecies of his democratic spokesman, Charlie Waters, but the facts of history as he himself interpreted them in his Prologue to *Henry St. John*. There he describes the Revolution as a gulf, separating "the colonial *regime* of ease and tranquility—the slow rolling coach, the aristocratic dignity, the machinery of class, and courtly ceremony" of the old order from "the mortal struggle of the new era, the leveling republicanism" of post-Revolution American society (x–xi).

Cooke saw clearly enough that the Revolution marked the beginning of the end of the wealth and the political and cultural supremacy of Virginia's planter-aristocrats. He embodied this force for change and political leveling in Charlie Waters, presented through Charlie's viewpoint an astute analysis of the political forces behind the Revolution, and set up a dramatic contrast in his novel between Cavalier and yeoman. But he was no more successful in resolving this tension and carrying through the implications of this conflict in *Henry St. John* than he had been in *The Virginia Comedians*. Cooke again found it impossible to administer the coup de grace to his Cavalier aristocrats. Thus he found it necessary to impose an ending on his narrative that, in providing a happy and secure future for his Cavalier hero, flew in the face of the historical realities expressed through his democratic spokesman.

John Esten Cooke's historical romances bear an obvious and strong resemblance to the novels of Walter Scott; yet they possess none of the appeal of the original master's work. Cooke's inferiority cannot be explained simply as a lack of technical proficiency. Truly this Virginia writer possessed a felicitous style that was well adapted to the presentation of romantic action and colorful detail. Scott's vast superiority over Cooke primarily resides in his profound and objective interpretation of historical forces. Georg Lukács has brilliantly analyzed the tension between past and present out of which Scott's art arises. Lukács perceives that Scott was torn between the affirmation of progress and the realization that such change was necessarily attended by social waste, broken human hopes, and cultural disintegration. The writer effectively reconciled these opposing attitudes, Lukács believes, by giving the collapse of the antiquated social order something of the dimension of a heroic tragedy. "It is precisely because of his character that Scott did not become a Romantic, a glorifier or elegist of past ages. And it was for this reason that he was able to portray objectively the ruination of past social formations, despite all his human sympathy for, and artistic sensitivity to the splendid, heroic qualities which they contained. Objectively, in a large historical and artistic sense, he saw at one and the same time their outstanding qualities and the historical necessity of their decline."[31]

The key to great historical novels is an approach toward the conflict of past and present that is basically objective, an attitude capable of celebrating the past while at the same time affirming the necessity of its

31. Lukács, *The Historical Novel*, 54–55.

destruction. The best writers of historical novels thus achieve a perilous but an artistically necessary synthesis of antithetical tensions. Scott achieved this synthesis. So too on the American scene did James Fenimore Cooper in his description of the tragic collision between white and Indian cultures.

Unfortunately Cooke was incapable of achieving a similar kind of synthesis. His novels lack the tragic tension, the depth, and the encompassing vision of the conflict between old and new cultures because he skirted the issue of the obsolescence of Cavalier society. Cooke speaks wistfully in his prologues and epilogues and in his history of Virginia of the passing away of the old order, but he is simply not able to dramatize this collapse in his narratives. He carries us to the edge of historical revelation, but he cannot complete the themes inherent in his plots. The past held Cooke too strongly. He was not able to achieve the objectivity necessary for the creation of significant historical fiction because, in the last analysis, he was not willing to turn his back on the lure of Virginia's romantic and legendary past.

VIRGINIA FICTION AND THE COMING OF CIVIL WAR

Jay Hubbell has observed that "the idealization of Virginia is the work of time and the imagination of a people. It is not the creation of the novelist's brain; for the novelist can only use it as it comes to him, giving it literary expression."[32] It would be foolish to claim that William Alexander Caruthers and John Esten Cooke created Virginia's romantic past. That, as Hubbell has noted, is the product of the collective imagination. Neither can it be asserted that these Virginia novelists deliberately or chauvinistically romanticized antebellum Virginia. For in fact neither writer made any references to the present, except to lament the decline of culture in the Old Dominion from its eighteenth-century height. Yet there can be little doubt that their romantic novels helped to promote a highly distorted view of pre–Civil War Virginia society and, indirectly, of all southern society.

32. Hubbell, *Virginia Life in Fiction*, 18.

Caruthers' and Cooke's narratives, even though set in the seventeenth and eighteenth centuries, depicted a society dominated by wealthy and aristocratic plantation owners. Theirs was the vision of Virginia that came to be accepted by northerners—most of whom were acquainted with this strange and exotic land only through the pages of romance novels—as representative not only of the Old Dominion but also of the entire South. Daniel Hundley, an Alabama native descended from Virginians, described a vigorous southern middle class and complained that, contrary to fact, northerners seemed "totally unconscious that [the South's] citizens were ever divided into other than three classes—Cavaliers, Poor Whites, and Slaves."[33] What Hundley did not perhaps understand was that southern romance writers, with Caruthers and Cooke preeminent among them, had done as much if not more than Yankee "honey-tongued libellers" to assure the popular acceptance of this distorted view.

Contemporary historical investigation has confirmed Hundley's description of a diverse southern social structure dominated by a broadly based middle class. Today we know that out of eight million whites fewer than four hundred thousand owned slaves and that only 4 percent of these slaveholders held more than one hundred.[34] We know that through the first six decades of the nineteenth century progressive forces steadily broadened the base of democracy in the South, producing a vigorous two-party system marked by citizen participation comparable to that exercised by citizens in the North.[35] Yet sectional discourse in 1860 was scarcely influenced by such realities. Americans of all sections responded much more readily to the aristocratic visions of novels such as *The Cavaliers of Virginia* and *The Virginia Comedians* than to the clear-eyed observations of Daniel Hundley. The historical romances of Caruthers and Cooke contributed to the widely held impression that the North and the South were fundamentally incompat-

33. Daniel R. Hundley, *Social Relations in Our Southern States* (New York, 1860), 10.

34. Howard R. Floan, *The South in Northern Eyes, 1831–1861* (New York, 1958), viii.

35. Fletcher M. Green, "Democracy in the Old South," *Journal of Southern History*, XII (1946), 3–23.

ible cultures. William R. Taylor succinctly describes these popular misconceptions:

> By 1860 most Americans had come to look upon their society and culture as divided between a North and a South, a democratic, commercial civilization and an aristocratic, agrarian one. Each section of the country, so it was believed, possessed its own ethic, its own historical traditions and even, by common agreement, a distinctive racial heritage. Each was governed by different values and animated by a different spirit. . . . Under the stimulus of this divided heritage the North had developed a leveling, go-getting utilitarian society and the South had developed a society based on the values of the English country gentry.[36]

Strangely enough, the aristocratic description of southern society penned by writers such as Caruthers and Cooke was confirmed by abolitionists. The dominant figure for William Lloyd Garrison as well as for John Esten Cooke was the privileged landholder. However, Garrison transformed Cooke's paragon into an irresponsible tyrant, a heartless sadist, a woman beater and infant stealer, who refused to bring the word of God to those whom he held in bondage.[37] Ironically, romancers like Caruthers and Cooke may have done their state and their region an unknowing disservice. For it is probably easier for a propagandist to work with stereotypes than with complex and fully developed human characters, even though the stereotypes might have originally been created to represent moral perfection.

By 1861 the plantation aristocrat had become the dominant symbol of southern culture, both in the North and in the South. Dixie adamantly embraced the myth, even though the noble planter-aristocrat was still in the process of being created by southern writers and even though he obviously stood at variance with the realities of contemporary southern society. As the intensity of verbal dueling increased between North and South, Marshall Fishwick has accurately discerned,

36. Taylor, *Cavalier and Yankee*, 15.
37. Floan, *The South in Northern Eyes*, 7–8.

southern apologists tended more and more to appeal to the myth of southern aristocracy. Southerners "defined and refined the image in the mirror of thousands of articles, orations, poems, and novels."[38]

The spiritually destructive and mentally debilitating results of blind allegiance to the Cavalier myth are clearly evident in an article contrasting the northern and southern "races," written for the *Southern Literary Messenger* in 1860. The author of this essay contends that northerners are primarily descended from the Puritans, who "constituted, as a class, the common people of England . . . and were descended of the ancient Britons and Saxons." These Saxon-descended Puritans are consequently people of vigorous intellects but no notion of honor—fanatics, incapable of controlling their passions. "Being devotional, they push their piety to the extremes of fanaticism,—being contentious withal, they are led to attack the interests of others, merely because those interests do not comport with *their* ideas of right."[39]

In contrast to this land of inbred extremists, the writer describes a "Southron" race descending from the English Norman aristocracy and manifesting that culture's generous, honorable, aristocratic nature. The southern states, and most significantly Virginia, were settled, by and large, by Cavaliers "directly descended from the Norman Barons of William the Conqueror, a race distinguished, in its earliest history, for its warlike and fearless character, a race, in all time since, renowned for its gallantry, its chivalry, its gentleness and its intellect."[40] For the writer of this essay, southerners obviously represent a type of master race divinely ordained by its heritage and blood lineage to rule and best qualified to control black slaves.

Of course it is possible to explain such a racial analysis as a type of overblown and exaggerated political propaganda. Yet many southerners appear to have eventually accepted as true attitudes such as those presented in the *Southern Literary Messenger*. William Russell, war corre-

38. Marshall W. Fishwick, *Virginia: A New Look at the Old Dominion* (New York, 1959), 199.
39. "The Difference of Race Between the Northern and Southern People," *Southern Literary Messenger*, XXX (June, 1860), 404–405.
40. *Ibid.*, 407.

spondent for the London *Times*, described a Virginian named Major Garnett, returning from England in 1861 to take up arms for his native state, as "an accomplished, well-read man; reserved, and rather gloomy; full of the doctrine of States' Rights, and animated with a considerable feeling of contempt for the New Englanders, and with the strongest prejudices in favor of the institution of slavery. He laughed to scorn the doctrine that all men are born equal in the sense of all men having equal rights. Some were born to be slaves—some to be labourers in the lower strata above the slaves—others to follow useful mechanical arts—the rest were born to rule and to own their fellow man."[41] Major Garnett was an American, but he was an American impelled by concepts and values radically opposed to the predominant national ideal of political and social equality. He was a southern American who proudly rose to the defense of his state and who justified his act of rebellion by appealing to the myth of southern aristocracy. The Cavalier figure was, of course, an integral part of this southern aristocratic myth, a romantic stereotype celebrated in novels of the antebellum period written most notably by Virginians. And his remarkable ascendancy in the popular imagination within a period of sixty years resulted in men like Major Garnett, men who were as alienated from the liberal principles of fellow Virginians of previous generations, such as Jefferson and Henry, as they were alienated from northern abolitionists.

The bitter, reactionary spirit of Major Garnett, a spirit which had been expressed in Virginia in the early decades of the nineteenth century by men such as John Randolph, had by 1860 become such a commonplace attitude that one does not have to look hard among the Old Dominion's writers to see it expressed. George Fitzhugh, in his influential defense of slavery, glibly agreed with Jefferson that all men were created equal and then offered this astonishing and perverted explanation of the concept: "The order and subordination observable in the physical, animal and human world, show that some are formed for higher, others for lower stations—the few to command, the many to

41. William Howard Russell, *My Diary North and South*, ed. Fletcher Pratt (1863; rpr. New York 1954), 1.

obey. We conclude that about nineteen out of every twenty individuals have 'a natural and inalienable right' to be taken care of and protected; to have guardians, trustees, husbands, or masters; in other words, they have a natural and inalienable right to be slaves."[42] Fitzhugh's use of the ideal of aristocratic paternalism to defend slavery suggests that the romantic fictional portraits of Cavaliers were not innocuous creations. Whether or not writers like Caruthers and Cooke were aware of it, a defense of the status quo and of a social system increasingly judged by outsiders as outmoded and inhumane was implicit in the romantic characterization of the southern planter-aristocrat.

The Cavalier myth ultimately bequeathed Virginia and the South a destructive legacy which survived the holocaust of war and helped to justify the postbellum southerners' attitude of proud and defiant bitterness. Forty years after the Civil War, Petersburg physician John Claiborne gave an assessment of southern history which undoubtedly reflected the views of millions of his fellow southerners. "The F.F.V's, descendants of the Cavalier elements which had settled that State and wrested it from the savage by their prowess . . . bred the six millions of Southrons who for four long years maintained an unequal war with thirty millions of Northern hybrids, backed by a hireling soldiery brought from the whole world to put down constitutional liberty—a war waged to free four million of servile blacks and to enslave six million of proud and cultivated whites."[43]

Caruthers and Cooke would probably have been shocked had they been told that their antebellum novels would indirectly contribute to the caustic xenophobia of Dr. Claiborne. Certainly neither writer saw himself as a sectional apologist or as an advocate of disunion. Caruthers was pledged to the ideal of the nation's manifest destiny, and Cooke was convinced that at least one of his novels was a critique of Virginia's aristocracy. Yet despite their professed aims neither writer was able to achieve an adequate perspective from which to interpret the Old Do-

42. George Fitzhugh, *Cannibals All! or, Slaves Without Masters* (Richmond, 1857), 102–103.

43. Quoted in Davis, *Chronicler of the Cavaliers*, 136.

minion's past. Their depiction of Virginia life and manners was consequently even less realistic than the productions of George Tucker and John Pendleton Kennedy. Both Tucker and Kennedy set their narratives in the near past, in the Virginia of the early nineteenth century. And although both of these earlier writers in the end succumbed to the legendary vision of the Old Dominion, each in his own way managed to retain a partial degree of objective control over his subject. Thanks to this control, readers can still respond to the homely and slightly flawed charms of Swallow Barn Plantation, and they can still mark with interest Tucker's analysis of the decay of Virginia's landed aristocracy. The near contemporaneity of Tucker's and Kennedy's settings serve as a partial check to undisciplined flights of romantic fantasy.

Caruthers and Cooke, in contrast to their predecessors, moved their settings further back in time to the prerevolutionary "golden age" of the colony. Unhampered by facts, they proceeded to create an ideal fictional society. Responding to increasingly bitter attacks on southern values and traditions from the North, Caruthers and Cooke apotheosized the Cavalier figure in their fiction and helped to provide for Virginia and for the entire South an ideal to carry into battle. In spite of their professed aims they served the myth more completely in their novels than either Tucker or Kennedy had done.

Ultimately, however, despite their glorification of the Cavalier figure, Caruthers and Cooke implicitly share with Tucker and Kennedy an understanding of the limitations imposed on him by the dominant national ideals of liberty and equality. We have seen how in the works of George Tucker and John Pendleton Kennedy the Cavalier character is viewed in part from a realistic perspective as an anachronism, doomed by the progressive forces of history. Caruthers and Cooke, of course, do not confront the issue of their aristocratic characters' social viability so directly. In *Knights of the Golden Horse-shoe* and *The Virginia Comedians* the question of the relevance of the role of the Cavalier in American society is raised, but both writers draw back from a serious examination of the conflict between Cavalier and yeoman ideals. Neither is capable of admitting that these two traditions may be incompatible or that the yeoman ideal may be more germane to the American experience. Yet the very presence of strongly conceived yeoman characters in their aristocratic romances indicates that they implicitly understand the limitations of the character type they are apotheosizing. Behind Governor Spotswood and Champ Effingham loom Red Jarvis and Charlie Waters. Felicitous endings dominated by aristocratic characters do not altogether dispel their presence in the novels or the challenge they give to the old order. The sense of the Cavalier as doomed aristocrat is not as strong in the novels of Caruthers and Cooke as it is in the earlier work of Tucker and Kennedy, but it is present nonetheless. Even as the Cavalier is being most glorified in antebellum Virginia fiction, a faint voice persistently whispers his doom. Red Jarvis and Charlie Waters prophesy the destruction of the Cavalier and of the way of life he represents, a destruction which came to pass with the Civil War.

FIVE

The Cavalier and the Lost Cause

PAGE AND JOHNSTON

RECONCILIATION AND LITERARY REBIRTH

Literary activity in Virginia from 1865 to 1900, as in the rest of the South, was strongly influenced by the realities of bitter defeat, humiliating occupation, and economic depression. One of the chief battle arenas, the Old Dominion had sustained more than its share of devastation. Richmond, Abingdon, Wytheville, Bristol, Fredericksburg, and Petersburg had been heavily damaged by fire and bombardment; and the countryside was even more ravaged. Virginius Dabney paints a vivid picture of rural Virginia after the war. "In huge areas," he writes, "bridges were down, roads cut up, homes severely damaged, barns and fences were burned or otherwise wrecked, crops trampled and cattle driven off."[1]

Because of the economic dislocations brought on by defeat, the value

---

1. Virginius Dabney, *Virginia, the New Dominion* (Garden City, N.Y., 1971), 353.

of land in Virginia plummeted. Holdings worth $150 an acre before the war sold for as little as $2 an acre shortly after. Confederate bonds, in which many Virginians had loyally invested, were worthless. The total financial loss to Virginians during the Civil War–Reconstruction period was estimated in 1877 at $457 million—a huge sum at that time for a state that contained only 700,000 white citizens.[2] Under these adverse economic conditions the plantation system, which had slowly declined through the decades preceeding 1860, collapsed. The number of farms in Virginia of one thousand or more acres dropped precipitously, from 641 in 1860 to 317 in 1870.[3]

With such economic catastrophe and cultural trauma, it is not surprising that during the immediate postwar years literary activity in Virginia and in all the southern states virtually ceased. The scarcity of ink and paper had forced the closing of the venerable *Southern Literary Messenger* in 1864, and after the war subscriptions to belletristic magazines became a luxury for most southerners. Publishing nearly disappeared in the South, even as it was flourishing remarkably in the economically prosperous North. There, improved printing techniques released floods of cheaply printed books to the markets, and the number of magazines multiplied rapidly, swelling from approximately 200 in 1860 to over 1,800 by 1900.[4] A number of these new magazines achieved a mass circulation that dwarfed prewar distribution. The larger publications offered lucrative rates for contributors that, not surprisingly, attracted the attention and envy of the impoverished southern writer.

By 1870 literary publication was taking place almost exclusively north of the Mason-Dixon Line. The South had become as much a literary as an economic and political adjunct of the northern states. This reality was not ignored by those southerners who aspired to literary success. Paul Buck notes that southern writers were more than ever before aware that they could not survive on local patronage alone and that

2. Louis D. Rubin, *Virginia: A Bicentennial History* (New York, 1977), 137.
3. Dabney, *Virginia, the New Dominion*, 357.
4. Jay Herbert Martin, *Harvests of Change: American Literature, 1865–1914* (Englewood Cliffs, N.J., 1967), 16–17.

"unless Southern literature became sufficiently American in tone to appeal to Northern readers there would be no Southern literature."[5]

Faced with harsh economic realities, the tone of belligerence and the impassioned defense of the South's peculiar institution which had characterized much prewar southern writing largely vanished. Unrepentant southerners of the old school might fervently agree with the sentiments of Virginian Edmund Ruffin, who, in a testament he penned before committing suicide soon after Appomattox, willingly proclaimed his "unmitigated hatred to Yankee rule—to all political, social and business connections with Yankees, and the perfidious, malignant and vile Yankee race."[6] However, for the postwar generation of younger southern writers intent on securing national reputations, reconciliation necessarily became the prevailing attitude. Thomas Nelson Page was one writer who thought he had discovered a surefire formula for appealing to northern magazine editors, a formula which, many years afterward, he communicated to fellow southerner Grace King: "Now I will tell you what to do; for I did it! It is the easiest thing to do in the world. Get a pretty girl and name her Jeanne. That name always takes! Make her fall in love with a Federal Officer and your story will be printed at once!"[7]

The fanatical spirit of Edmund Ruffin, though it had precipitated the Civil War, would not be the spirit embraced by Dixie's writers after 1865. The conciliatory attitude of the South's postbellum writers toward the North did not signify, however, that they were willing to abandon the stereotypes of the plantation myth which had been created and romantically exalted before the war. The planter aristocrat remained a key element in southern romanticism after the Civil War. But he was not associated with hatred and unreconciled sectional bitterness. The postbellum Cavalier figure, tied though he was to the South's military defeat, transcended that defeat and continued to represent the highest standards of courage and nobility of character.

5. Paul H. Buck, *The Road to Reunion, 1865–1900* (Boston, 1937), 199.

6. Avery Craven, *Edmund Ruffin, Southerner: A Study in Secession* (New York, 1932), 259.

7. Quoted in Edmund Wilson, *Patriotic Gore: Studies in the Literature of the American Civil War* (New York, 1962), 606.

In reconstructing the Cavalier ideal the South's writers were blessed with the noble example of a remarkable Confederate leader, an example to which they easily could refer as an inspiration for their fictional creations. This man was Robert E. Lee. Lee had risen to the defense of the South, not because he supported slavery or advocated rebellion, but because he felt his duty to his native state of Virginia demanded his course of action. As he simply expressed it: "I could have taken no other course without dishonor." Lee's calm graciousness, his dignity of manner, and his sense of family and tradition combined with his self-denial, his abstinence, and his Christian piety to make him "the patriarch and oracle of the shattered South."[8] Even after the Civil War he continued to exhibit those aristocratic but humane qualities which set him off in vivid contrast to the political and social corruption of the Gilded Age. Refusing $10,000 a year in return for the use of his name as titular president of an insurance company, Lee instead accepted the presidency of an impoverished Virginia college, and he was among the first to apply to the federal government for a pardon.

It is difficult to overestimate the importance of Lee for the defeated South. Dixie might labor in poverty and humiliation but, as Douglas Freeman observes, southerners had one distinction: "Their stock had produced Lee; they had seen him, had known him, had obeyed his orders and, at his behest, had challenged Cemetery Ridge and had starved in the Petersburg trenches. Association with him was the glory of their generation."[9] Perhaps most significantly, Lee's example gave southerners hope that the chivalric attitudes for which they believed they had fought had not been destroyed. In the words of Dixon Wecter, Lee "was the last and most perfect flower of that culture—which reclaimed her chivalry from bombast, and made into poetry the fact of her defeat."[10]

No southern writer did more to glorify the memory of Lee and those Virginia military gentlemen of nearly equal luster—Stonewall Jackson and Jeb Stuart—than John Esten Cooke, a writer who had served with

8. Dixon Wecter, *The Hero in America: A Chronicle of Hero Worship* (New York, 1941), 281.
9. Douglas Southall Freeman, *The South to Posterity: An Introduction to the Writings of Confederate History* (New York, 1951), 59.
10. Wecter, *The Hero in America*, 284.

distinction throughout the Civil War and who had been a member of Stuart's staff. In *Hammer and Rapier*, an account of the major battles of the Virginia campaign published in 1870, Cooke concluded that "history nowhere exhibit[ed] a more obstinate combativeness, a more inexorable will, a more trained and daring courage than that of Lee." For Cooke, Lee was a symbol of the highest and most noble characteristics of the plantation culture of the Old Dominion. Both the great general and the great state which produced him had entered into the struggle with genuine reluctance. Yet, in spite of their initial misgivings, both Lee and Virginia had "dared all, risked all, suffered all—and to-day . . . lost all." But though as a result of this daring all else had been lost, neither Lee nor his native state had surrendered its most cherished possession. "Her stainless escutcheon is still left to her—and her broken sword, which no taint of bad faith or dishonor ever tarnished."[11]

In *Surry of Eagle's Nest*, published immediately after the War in 1866, and in *Mohun*, a sequel narrative published in 1869, Cooke used the historical novel to embellish the reputations of Virginia's greatest military commanders—Lee, Jackson, and Stuart. The novels are linked by a common protagonist, Surry of Eagle's Nest, a Virginia gentleman of unblemished aristocratic credentials. Surry's ancestral Rappahannock River plantation is the legacy of the first Surry, a "gay gallant" who had served with valor under Prince Rupert and who had repaired to the Old Dominion after his defeat. Both *Surry of Eagle's Nest* and *Mohun* juxtapose realistic and factual descriptions of Civil War battles against the labyrinthine and highly melodramatic action of Cooke's fictional plot.

In *Surry of Eagle's Nest* the protagonist serves under General Stonewall Jackson. Although turning this plain and pious Presbyterian soldier into a Cavalier figure presented Cooke with difficulties, he did the best he could with the material at hand. For example, before his death on the eve of the battle at Chancellorsville, Jackson utters sentiments which identify his personal honor with that of his native state in a way

11. John Esten Cooke, *Hammer and Rapier* (New York, 1870), 292, 307.

that strongly suggests the nobility of character of the more aristocratic Lee: "It was duty no less than pleasure to fight for the land I loved. . . . There is not a foot of Virginia soil that is not dear to me—not a river, a stream, or a mountain that is not sacred."[12]

Cooke found more promising material available in the person of General Turner Ashby, "the Knight of the Valley," a valiant cavalryman who served under Jackson in the early Shenandoah Valley campaigns. When Ashby encounters northern ladies stranded in the town of Winchester, they claim they have no contraband and that he is welcome to search them. Ashby's reply is typical of a knightly Confederate hero: "I am a Virginia gentleman; we do not search the trunks or persons of ladies here, madame." A sample of the diction lavished on Ashby within the space of a single page after his death in battle gives a good indication of the assiduousness with which Cooke maintained the Cavalier stereotype in his Civil War novels. Ashby, the narrator opines, was "heroic," a "dauntless cavalier," a "noble gentleman," and a "splendid chevalier." He was the "perfect flower of chivalry," the "perfect chevalier."[13]

In *Mohun* Cooke's focus shifts from Stonewall Jackson to Jeb Stuart, whose staff Surry joins after the death of Jackson. Cooke's sequel is characterized, like *Surry of Eagle's Nest*, by a blatantly apotheosizing tone. The objects associated with these legendary military heroes become objects of veneration. "The great tree on the grassy knoll" of a northern Virginia plantation, "under which Stuart erected his own tent," is known ever after as Stuart's Oak. "To this day," the narrator observes, "no axe will ever harm it, I hope; gold could not purchase it; for tender hearts cherish the gnarled trunk and huge boughs, as a souvenir of the great soldier whom it sheltered." The death of Stuart at Yellow Tavern combines with the death of Jackson in the Wilderness to prefigure the ultimate destruction of the Old South, a land comparable in its perfection to Arthur's Camelot. "These two kings of battle," the narrator ruminates, "had gone down in the storm, and, like the knights

<hr />

12. John Esten Cooke, *Surry of Eagle's Nest; or, The Memoirs of a Staff Officer Serving in Virginia* (1866; rpr. New York, 1894), 458.

13. *Ibid.*, 223.

of Arthur, I looked around me with vacant and inquiring eyes. . . . Jackson! Stuart!—who could replace them?"[14] No one can, of course, and the action of *Mohun* proceeds, despite the heroic struggles of Lee, inexorably to its conclusion at Appomattox.

John Esten Cooke's Civil War novels gave an early indication that the South's literary surrender, unlike its military surrender, was to be only a partial one. Though avoiding an excessively bitter tone, Dixie's writers would continue to present their region and its inhabitants, both past and present, lovingly, with an attitude of deference and loyalty. As Frank E. Vandiver has observed, southern writers immediately began to create new myths to replace those which had been destroyed. One of the most potent of these was the myth of the Lost Cause. The articles of faith of the Lost Cause myth included the beliefs that all southerners had been states' righters, that the South's soldiers and civilians had demonstrated uniformly dauntless courage and loyalty throughout the conflict, and that southerners had fought primarily to defend their racial integrity.[15] The Civil War had failed to destroy the Cavalier figure. The southern aristocrat, in fact, had merely become enshrined in the new myth of the Lost Cause. The noble but doomed cause for which the South's chivalric, gray-clad knights had bravely fought was celebrated in the postbellum South in thousands of stories, poems, essays, and editorials.

It is not surprising that the South refused to abandon its cherished illusions of itself. But it does seem odd that northerners did not massively object to the tone of muted apologia coming from southern pens. Indeed, not only were northern readers receptive soon after the war to sympathetic portrayals of the South by southern writers, but northern writers also demonstrated in a number of popular novels published as early as the late 1860s what Joyce Appleby has described as "an amazing readiness to let bygones be bygones. Southern postwar characters are depicted as contrite, forgiving, and rededicated to the old Union." These early popular novels, she concludes, "supplied the Northern

---

14. John Esten Cooke, *Mohun, a Novel* (1868; rpr. New York, 1896), 100, 216.

15. Frank E. Vandiver, "The Confederate Myth," in Gerster and Cords (eds.), *Myth and Southern History*, 147–53.

reader with a striking alternative to the angry political rhetoric emanating from Congress, the lecture platform, and the press."[16]

By the 1870s and 1880s the receptivity of northern writers to the South had taken on a deeper significance. A number of America's most distinguished literary figures were using southerners and southern attitudes as moral references by which the failures of American society might be better judged. In *The Burden of Southern History* C. Vann Woodward details this use of southern characters in Herman Melville's philosophical poem *Clarel* (1876), in Henry Adams' *Democracy* (1880), and in Henry James's *The Bostonians* (1886). In each of these works, Woodward observes, "a Southerner, a veteran of the Confederate Army, is introduced in a sympathetic role. His importance varies with the work concerned, but in each of the three works the Southerner serves as the mouthpiece of the severest strictures upon American society or, by his actions or character, exposes the worst faults in that society."[17]

The surprising degree of sympathy of both the North's readers and her writers toward the South was indirectly attributable to the enormous and unsettling changes that were transforming social institutions above the Potomac. Jay Martin describes the rise of new wealth, the extraordinary growth of cities, and the astonishing triumphs of science and technology that marked the latter half of the nineteenth century in America. Yet rapid change brought concomitant anxieties to millions of Americans. Industrialization carried with it new and more complex social problems, such as the creation of large urban slums and the dehumanization and alienation of workers. To many, the price of progress seemed too great. As Martin has observed, Americans "longed for simpler conditions, and made a mythical past embody collective fantasies."[18] Northerners accepted the South's assessment of its own culture in part because southern culture seemed to represent the simplicity and purity which the North had abandoned. Against the materialism and

16. Joyce Appleby, "Reconciliation and the Northern Novelist, 1865–1880," *Civil War History*, X (1964), 120, 129.

17. Woodward, *The Burden of Southern History*, 110–11.

18. Martin, *Harvests of Change*, 83.

the crass commercial values of the triumphant North, the South held forth a pastoral life whose values were rooted in the land and centered in the family. The central symbol of this pastoral Eden was the planter aristocrat who was associated, in the words of Rollin Osterweis, with "honor, courage, orthodox religion, respect for women, noblesse oblige to inferiors, and white supremacy."[19]

The thoroughness with which northerners were converted to a sympathetic view of southern life is no more clearly manifested than in *Colonel Carter of Cartersville*, published in 1891 and written by Francis Hopkinson Smith, a native Baltimorean turned New Yorker. The central character of Smith's narrative is Colonel George Fairfax Carter of Carter Hall, Cartersville, Virginia—a "frank, generous, tender-hearted" gentleman, "hospitable to the verge of beggary." The colonel is a Virginian "of good birth, fair education, and limited knowledge of the world and of men, proud of his ancestry, proud of his state, and proud of himself; believing in states' rights, slavery, and the Confederacy; and away down deep in the bottom of his soul still clinging to the belief that the poor white trash of the earth includes about everybody outside of Fairfax County."[20]

Colonel Carter is a character who exhibits the mythical Cavalier's disdain for money and for commercial pursuits. He always buys his groceries on account, a procedure which eliminates the need for what the Colonel calls "vulgar bargainin!" But when he is asked by an acquaintance when he is expected to pay his bill, he gives this astonished reply: "I have never inquired, suh, and would not hurt the gentleman's feelin's by doin' so for the world" (29).

As the novel opens Carter is living a threadbare existence in New York City, purveying his dream of the Cartersville and Warrentown Air Line Railroad, which will link his town with the "broad Atlantic" fifty miles away. Carter's scheme is the product of a mind that has no understanding of practical business considerations. The rail line has no con-

---

19. Rollin G. Osterweis, *The Myth of the Lost Cause, 1865–1900* (Hamden, Conn., 1973), 152.

20. Francis Hopkinson Smith, *Colonel Carter of Cartersville* (1891; rpr. Saddle River, N.J., 1970), 10, hereinafter cited in the text by page number only.

necting links with other lines, and when prospective investors question the need for running the railroad twelve extra miles to reach Carter Hall, Colonel Carter gives this rationale: "A place settled mo' than one hundred years ago, belongin' to one of the very fust fam'lies of Virginia. . . . Why, suh, it will give an air of respectability to the whole thing that nothin' else could ever do" (34).

In the end Carter is saved from his own Cavalier impracticality by the discovery of a rich vein of coal on his plantation. It is very clear, however, that his salvation is the result of blind luck. Colonel Carter is a Virginia Cavalier hopelessly ill-adapted to surviving in an age of mercantile capitalism. The tone of Smith's novel reminds one of *Swallow Barn*, another Marylander's work. Like Frank Meriwether, the squire of Swallow Barn Plantation, Colonel Carter is an amusing anachronism. Yet in his boundless though ill-advised hospitality and in his imperviousness to practical considerations there is a quixotic element that evokes a mixed tone of condescension and admiration. Foolish and blind though he may be, Smith leaves no doubt that as a gentleman Carter is superior to his northern acquaintances.

Nothing illustrates more clearly the progress of conciliatory attitudes in the North toward the South than the humorous tale told by Colonel Carter about Colonel Talcott of Talcottville in Virginia, who, because he is not carrying any money, is refused a three-cent stamp by a Reconstruction postmaster, a "low-lived Yankee, who had never known a gentleman in his life." "Well suh," says Carter, "what was there left for a high-toned Southern gentleman to do? Colonel Talcott drew his revolver and shot that Yankee scoundrel through the heart, and killed him on the spot" (23). Carter tells the story with a completely straight face while his northern friends can barely stifle their amusement. It is hard to imagine that such a story, told at the expense of a "low-lived Yankee," would have been amusing to northern readers in 1871. Twenty years later, however, such humor was apparently acceptable to a northern audience, as the popularity of Smith's novel attests.[21]

21. See Wayne Mixon, *Southern Writers and the New South Movement, 1865–1913* (Chapel Hill, 1980), 32.

Colonel Carter of Cartersville gives a valuable indication of the sympathetic and approving, if also distinctly condescending, attitude with which northern readers and writers were inclined to view the South. This forgiving tone was linked to the predilection of northern readers for stories emphasizing regional characteristics and customs, stories which provided a rapidly industrializing and urbanizing nation with attractive and suitably picturesque visions of its past. Within a few years of the conclusion of the Civil War the intellectual climate had become remarkably favorable for a resurgence of southern writing, for the southern writer was admirably equipped for the writing of local color sketches and stories. His region was in many respects different from the rest of the country, and he was blessed with a generous fund of provincial customs and lore which came from cultures as diverse in texture as Tidewater Virginia plantations and Tennessee mountain cabins. The northern reader forgot old animosities and delightedly perused the colorful descriptions of old-time southern customs. "Having devastated the feudal South," Edmund Wilson ironically writes, "the Northerners wanted to be told of its glamor, of its old-time courtesy and grace. . . . They took over the Southern myth and themselves began to revel in it."[22]

The spirit of reconciliation combined with northern interest in southern local color to produce a strong market for Dixie's writers in northern magazines. *Scribner's Monthly*, later renamed *Century Magazine*, pioneered the era of literary reconciliation in 1873–1874 with its "Great South" series. This series was written by Edward King, who, on a trip to New Orleans, discovered and encouraged the young writer George Washington Cable. Within ten years *Lippincott's Magazine*, *Harper's Monthly*, *Atlantic*, *Cosmopolitan*, *Munsey's*, and *McClure's* were all accepting contributions from below the Mason-Dixon Line.[23] The major southern writers of this period—Cable, Joel Chandler Harris, Mary Murfree, and Thomas Nelson Page—owed their success to generous reception from these magazines and their publishing affiliates. Just beginning to recover from the economic devastation of the Civil

22. Wilson, *Patriotic Gore*, 605.
23. Buck, *The Road to Reunion*, 220–35.

War, the South in the 1880s could claim a surprisingly large number of successful writers. Though dependent on northern publishing outlets, these writers commanded a much larger readership than their antebellum predecessors.

The South had lost the war, but by 1890 its writers had unquestionably captured the hearts and imaginations of northern readers. Albion Tourgée ironically observed in an essay written in 1888 that American literature had become distinctly southern in sympathy. Even the war was being viewed through southern eyes. "The federal or Union soldier," Tourgee noted, "is not exactly depreciated, but subordinated; the Northern type is not decried, but the Southern is preferred." The southern soldier, he went on to complain, is always an aristocratic Cavalier. "So far as our fiction is concerned there does not appear to have been any Confederate infantry."[24]

The South's attempt to leave the Union had failed, but for many decades its writers continued to look back with nostalgia and affection to the period immediately preceding secession, a period that rapidly assumed the dimensions of a mythical golden age. Sympathetically received by northern audiences, southern apologists achieved prominence in American literature and profoundly altered attitudes toward their region.

Virginia had played a dominant role in the development of antebellum southern letters, and she continued to exert a strong influence during the postwar literary renascence. Indeed, her writers were particularly favored. The Old Dominion had been the setting of many of the most dramatic and decisive battles of the war, and Virginia had provided the Confederacy with its most illustrious military leaders. Moreover, the popularity of a novel like *Colonel Carter of Cartersville* suggests that for postbellum audiences Virginia remained the southern state most evocative of the aristocratic Cavalier ideal.

The Old Dominion produced a large number of writers during the last decades of the nineteenth century; the best and most successful of them were Thomas Nelson Page and Mary Johnston. Both writers

24. Albion W. Tourgée, "The South as a Field for Fiction," *Forum*, VI (1888), 405, 408.

were to a significant degree concerned with presenting an apology for their state and their region, and both celebrated the Cavalier figure as the embodiment of the most sublime aspects of southern culture. Johnston returned to seventeenth-century Virginia in her earlier romantic works, while Page placed his heroes in Civil War and Reconstruction Virginia. Whatever the milieu, their male characters reflected essentially the same exalted characteristics as Caruthers' and Cooke's dashing Cavaliers. Later Johnston moved from the rather shallow romances of her early period into a more interesting examination of human history, but her most popular and influential works were these first novels. The romantic novels and short stories of Page and Johnston successfully delineated the romantic Cavalier and escorted him to the threshold of the twentieth century.

THOMAS NELSON PAGE

Thomas Nelson Page was a fitting literary spokesman for the aristocratic Cavalier ideal. Indeed, it is unlikely that any fellow Virginian could have claimed a more venerable ancestry. His mother was the former Elizabeth Burwell Nelson, who numbered among her illustrious forebears a president of the Colonial Council of State, William Nelson, and a signer of the Declaration of Independence and governor of Virginia, Thomas Nelson. The Page family also claimed a governorship and possessed a Virginia family line that extended back well into the seventeenth century. Intermingled with Nelsons and Pages was the blood of Burwells, Lees, Carters, Berkeleys, and other first families. However, as Theodore Gross has noted, the Page pedigree was not matched by great wealth. Thomas Nelson Page's father was a respected Hanover County lawyer, but he was not remarkably prosperous. The family plantation, Oakland, though it was worked by sixty slaves, supported only a modest standard of living.[25]

Born in 1853, young Page received his grammar school education in Hanover County and subsequently attended Washington College

25. Theodore L. Gross, *Thomas Nelson Page* (New York, 1967), 17–18.

when General Lee was its president. A mediocre student, he left school without graduating. After tutoring for a year in Kentucky and saving his wages, Page went to Charlottesville and completed work for a law degree at the University of Virginia. For two years he practiced on the Hanover County Circuit, but the lure of a more lucrative practice with his cousin Henry Wickham drew him in 1876 to Richmond, where for seventeen years he practiced law.

Like most southern authors, Page for many years regarded his writing as an avocation and never attempted to live solely on the proceeds from his literary works. His first sketches and dialect poems were the natural outgrowth of his skill at telling good stories. They came at precisely the right moment, for local color works were in demand from northern magazines. His first published work was a dialect poem, "Uncle Gabe's White Folks," printed in *Scribner's Monthly* in 1877. In 1884 and 1886 the newly renamed *Century Magazine* published two of Page's most popular stories, "Marse Chan" and "Meh Lady." These were collected with other local color pieces and published in 1887 in a volume entitled *In Ole Virginia*, a work that sold briskly and remains Page's most popular work.

In spite of the success of his stories and poems and numerous requests to lecture, however, Page was not able to devote his resources fully to writing. But five years after the death of his first wife, Ann Bruce Page, he married a wealthy Chicago widow, Florence Lathrop, sister-in-law of Marshall Field. The new Mrs. Page's private fortune enabled Page to give up his law practice and to move from Richmond to Washington. There, a man of leisure as well as letters, he was able to complete his most successful novel, *Red Rock*, in 1898.

During his later Washington years Page was friend and confidant of high political figures, including Theodore Roosevelt and Woodrow Wilson. Wilson appointed him ambassador to Italy, a post in which he served from 1913 to 1919. Page died in 1922 after a distinguished career which brought him success as both writer and political figure and which carried him far from the rural Virginia of his boyhood days—a Virginia which he romantically immortalized in his best stories.

As we have seen in previous chapters, Virginians have commonly looked back on past periods of their history as embodying a perfection and a felicity which they have inevitably found absent in contemporary life. John Esten Cooke, writing in the 1850s, virtually ignored antebellum Virginia and focused instead on the Revolutionary period. But younger writers who had grown up during the difficult War and Reconstruction times became convinced that Cooke's age, the period immediately prior to the Civil War, had witnessed a paradisiacal social order that had been destroyed by the Yankee armies. Postwar writers thus conveniently advanced Virginia's golden age by seventy-five years. George Cary Eggleston, an adopted Virginian who originally hailed from Indiana, described the antebellum golden age in an article written for the *Atlantic Monthly* in 1875. Before Reconstruction had converted a "picturesque commonwealth into a commonplace modern state," Eggleston reflected, the Virginian had led "a soft, dreamy, deliciously quiet life, a life of repose, an old life, with all its sharp corners and rough surfaces long ago worn round and smooth."[26]

Page had been eight years old when the Civil War began, and he was only twelve when it ended. Not surprisingly, he too looked upon the Virginia of his boyhood days with reverence and cursed Reconstruction as a betrayal and destruction of all that had been good in the old civilization. Reconstruction had been for the young Virginian "a riot of rapine and rascality" that had destroyed a society which, with all its faults, represented "the purest, sweetest life ever lived." The Old South, in Page's eyes, had played the major share in founding the nation and had ruled a half-savage, servile race with temperance and justice. It was a culture which "partook of the philosophic tone of the Grecian, of the dominant spirit of the Roman, and of the guardfulness of individual rights of the Saxon civilization." "Over all," Page reflected, "brooded a softness and beauty, the joint product of Chivalry and Christianity."[27]

26. George Cary Eggleston, "The Old Regime in the Old Dominion," *Atlantic Monthly*, XXXVI (1875), 603.
27. Thomas Nelson Page, "The Southern People During Reconstruction," in his *The Old Dominion: Her Making and Her Manners* (New York, 1910), 272, Thomas Nelson Page, "Social Life in Old Virginia Before the War" and "The Old South," both in

With such a conception of Virginia before the war, Page's stories and sketches of the old days never approached objectivity. A reader will look in vain for representations of small farmers or unhappy slaves. Page's characterizations, like those of Caruthers and Cooke before him, are stereotypes representing the three main categories of southerners that the writer recognized: the aristocratic planter, the pure damsel or the dignified plantation matron, and the happy darky.

Page's Cavaliers, whether young or old, closely follow a strictly prescribed code. As Theodore L. Gross has noted, this code is founded on principles of heroism, honor and loyalty.[28] The Cavalier figure combines refined manners and courtesy with more vigorous and manly pursuits, such as fencing, riding, and hunting. He is always prepared to defend the honor of his family, his state, and most importantly, his lady. Like Caruthers' Nathaniel Bacon and Cooke's Henry St. John, the Page Cavalier is a moral paragon; and like them, he represents the highest ideals of his culture.

The Cavalier of Page's fiction inevitably finds a lady to worship and to make his life worth living. These young heroines are always creatures "of peach-blossom and snow; languid, delicate, saucy; now imperious, now melting, always bewitching." Yet this delicate exterior covers reserves of astounding inner fortitude, upon which the young lady draws in times of crisis. When the maiden marries, she transforms herself into a grave and decorous plantation mistress of endurance and competence, before whom her husband can only stand "in dumb, half-amazed admiration, as he might before the inscrutable vision of a superior being."[29]

This picture of aristocratic felicity is complemented by legions of loyal and contented Negroes. In Page's extended delineation of plantation life, "Social Life in Old Virginia," the writer spends many pages describing the house, the gardens, and the domestic servants. He gives,

---

his *The Old South: Essays Social and Political* (New York, 1906), 220, 5, Vols. XIII and XII of Page, *The Novels, Stories, Sketches, and Poems of Thomas Nelson Page.*

28. Gross, *Thomas Nelson Page,* 21–22.

29. Page, "Social Life in Old Virginia," 194, 185.

in contrast, only a brief glimpse of the fields, where gangs of blacks work in corn and tobacco. Here "loud shouts and peals of laughter, mellowed by the distance," float into the air, "telling that the heart was light and the toil not too heavy." Rosewell Page was convinced that his brother knew the Negro "as thoroughly as if he had been a scientist studying any subject in which he might be interested." Actually, Thomas Nelson Page seems to have seen only those characteristics which supported his view of Virginia's golden age. Writing in opposition to George Washington Cable in 1890, he explicitly stated his opinion of the black man. The Negro race, he contended, was an inferior one. It had never made substantial contributions to civilization, and it was incapable of governing itself. And in a slipshod application of Darwin's theory of evolution, Page benignly predicted that in the course of centuries the Negro race would disappear, "crowded out by a superior race more adapted to competition." It may be true, as Theodore Gross asserts, that Page's Negroes represent his only engaging and credible characters.[30] But this point should not obscure the fact that they serve as stereotyped complements to the world of Cavalier lords and ladies.

Page's vision of antebellum magnificence is most effectively fictionalized in the stories which make up *In Ole Virginia*. Here are presented the attitudes and themes which would characterize nearly all of this writers' subsequent fiction. Among the works in this collection, "Marse Chan" was and remains the most effective and powerfully moving story Page ever wrote. This popular tale is marked by an economy of purpose and a tightness of construction that is often notably lacking in his other writings.

The central story is framed by an anonymous but gentlemanly narrator who is traveling on an autumn afternoon through a Tidewater landscape of decaying mansions and overgrown fields and who is speculating about the former inhabitants of these abandoned estates. His re-

---

30. *Ibid.*, 180; Rosewell Page, *Thomas Nelson Page: A Memoir of a Virginia Gentleman* (New York, 1923), 137; Thomas Nelson Page, "The Negro Question," in his *The Old South: Essays Social and Political* (New York, 1892), 342; Gross, *Thomas Nelson Page*, 26.

flections are interrupted by the appearance in the road of an elderly Negro named Sam, who proceeds to tell the narrator the story of his old master. For this venerable darky the early days of his life when he was a slave "wuz good ole times, marster—de bes' Sam ever see!"[31] What he subsequently tells is the tragic love story, delivered in Tidewater Negro dialect, of Marse Chan and Anne Chamberlin.

The narrative-within-narrative technique enables Page to develop the love between Chan and Anne through the first person point of view of Chan's own faithful and loving body servant. Sam's love for Chan is easy for the reader to understand. The young master is a born Cavalier. He is loyal, brave, intelligent, and kind—marked by qualities of noblesse oblige toward his inferiors and of worshipful devotion toward pretty Anne Chamberlin. During the early years of their relationship he demonstrates his love by carrying her books to school, bringing her sweets and delicacies, and conveying her bravely across flooded streams. The enduring love of Marse Chan for his lovely damsel is threatened by a falling out of families. Bitter resentments arise when Chan publicly opposes secession, a cause that Anne's father fervently supports. The ill feeling eventually leads to a duel between Chan and the elderly Chamberlin, in which Chan magnanimously refuses to kill his opponent. The duel, however, forces Anne to reject her heartbroken lover.

Although opposed to secession, Chan enlists in the Confederate army as a private, fighting with reckless bravery and rising quickly to the rank of captain. Meanwhile, Anne has finally won her father's permission to marry Chan, and she writes him a letter of acceptance and love. But before he can return home he is mortally wounded, dying with flag in hand and with Anne's love letter in his breast pocket. Chan's death is quickly followed by those of his father and mother and, soon after, of Anne herself. Page implies that the unhappy maiden has gone to join in heaven the brave Cavalier that fate had denied her on earth.

31. Thomas Nelson Page, "Marse Chan: A Tale of Old Virginia," in his *In Ole Virginia; or, Marse Chan and Other Stories* (1887; rpr. Chapel Hill, 1969), 10. Unless otherwise noted, all citations are to this edition.

"Marse Chan" illustrates two of Page's most basic themes. One of these is the obedient attitude of the Cavalier gentleman toward his lady. As Theodore Gross points out, Chan passively accepts Anne's rejection after the duel. "The lover," he notes, "though morbidly melancholy, does not question her judgment—she is, after all, a moral arbiter, an absolute spiritual criterion against which he measures his own inadequate self."[32] In Page's stories the quality of the Cavalier's worship of his beloved is even more exquisitely submissive than that of Caruthers' or Cooke's heroes.

Kimball King has perceptively detected a second major theme in "Marse Chan." Here, as well as in subsequent stories, Page associates his heroes with grief, martyrdom, undeserved injury, and loss. Chan is the representative of an older order founded on ideals of loyalty and honor and courage. This order is destroyed by new social forces objectified in Page's fiction as the forces of war; the death of Chan and Anne is thus the symbolic death of the system for which they stand. King is correct when he says that there are tensions beneath the placid surface story of "Marse Chan."[33] Page's sympathy is obviously and unqualifiedly extended to the inhabitants of this vanished age. Yet he is realistic enough to be aware of the unsuitability of the values of this age in a more progressive era. He thus surrounds his sad tale with a tragic inevitability and a tone of stoic acceptance, skillfully conveyed through Negro Sam, that makes "Marse Chan" a very effective story. In Page's fictional world there is no room for the accommodation of past and present cultures. The past is destroyed, and only Sam survives to tell its story.

The destruction of the old order is combined with a third major theme in another of Page's most popular tales, "Meh Lady," a story of reconciliation between North and South. *Century Magazine* editor Robert Underwood suggested the idea for the story, the execution of which amply supports Page's assertion in his Introduction to the Plantation Edition of his writings that he had "never wittingly written a line

32. Gross, *Thomas Nelson Page*, 26.
33. Kimball King, Introduction to Thomas Nelson Page, *In Ole Virginia*, xvii, xxviii.

which he did not hope might tend to bring about a better understanding between the North and the South."[34]

"Meh Lady," like "Marse Chan," is told by a faithful Negro servant, Old Billy, to an anonymous framework narrator. The old servant fondly remembers Marse Phil and his younger sister, Meh Lady. Billy's Phil is a carbon copy of Sam's Marse Chan—brave, noble, selfless, pure of heart and mind, and ever respectful toward his sister and his mother. But the idyllic plantation life of Phil and Meh Lady is disrupted forever by the Civil War. Phil, like Chan, enlists, fights bravely, and dies a hero's death. Billy, who follows his master to battle, describes him in his final charge "in de lead cheerin', wid bullets an' shells hailin' all round' him; an he wuz de fust man in de redoubt. An' he fall jes' as he jump he horse over." Phil dies but not before imparting these last words to his mother, a sentiment worthy of the patriarchal Robert E. Lee: "He tole he ma when he wuz dyin' dat he had try to do he duty."[35]

The Old Mistress is devastated by her son's loss, and the responsibility of holding the plantation together falls on the fragile shoulders of Meh Lady. She strives courageously with the help of Old Billy, but the Yankee hosts descend like Goths and Vandals. Only the intervention of a young Federal officer, Captain Wilton, saves the plantation from total ruin. Wilton's good breeding and sense of honor are soon explained; his father is a native Virginian, and he is even distantly related to Meh Lady's own family.

The Yankee Wilton turns out to be as dashing a Cavalier as the departed Phil had been, risking his life to carry a personal letter from General McClellan providing protection for Meh Lady's plantation. He is eventually wounded on a nearby battlefield, leading, like Phil, a cavalry charge. Because he is a distant relative, courtesy enjoins the Old Mistress to bring the gravely wounded Wilton into her home. Here love between the young Yankee and Meh Lady predictably flowers, but the

34. Thomas Nelson Page, Introduction to the Plantation Edition, *In Ole Virginia* (New York, 1908), xi, Vol. I of Page, *The Novels, Stories, Sketches, and Poems of Thomas Nelson Page*.
35. Thomas Nelson Page, "Meh Lady: A Story of the War," in his *In Ole Virginia*, 84.

lovers are saddened by the conviction that, because of their divided loyalties, their love can never be fulfilled. With Meh Lady's sad rejection ringing in his ears, Wilton returns to the war.

The war's end brings ruin to Meh Lady's plantation. She continues to struggle with the help of Billy and even teaches a school for young darkies to help support herself. But unpaid taxes mount, the Old Mistress dies, and the exhausted Meh Lady seems, like Anne Chamberlin, doomed to follow. Just at the last moment, however, the knight of the North returns, his love undimmed by the intervening years. With Old Mistress dead, the only barrier to Meh Lady's love has been removed. She finally consents to be Wilton's bride, and the ceremony is performed in the family parlor beneath the portrait of one whom Wilton resembles so closely in character, Marse Phil.

The major theme of "Meh Lady" is reconciliation between North and South, but it is clearly reconciliation of a special kind. The *rapprochement* is achieved on southern terms. Wilton, whom one would logically assume to be the representative of the new order, is actually a thinly disguised copy of the Cavalier representative of the old order, Marse Phil. Page was willing enough to accept the fact that the South had lost the war. But he was evidently not willing to believe that the northern culture which had victoriously imposed itself upon the South could have any true values apart from those borrowed from the Cavalier ideal. Clothing the ideal in the uniform of a Federal officer and having that officer fall in love with a southern belle does not really reconcile opposing sectional viewpoints in a meaningful way. But, happily for Page, his northern readers seemed not to mind.

The unresolved tensions that are a part of "Marse Chan" and "Meh Lady"—the opposing pull of past and present, North and South—are even more interestingly apparent in Page's most successful novel, *Red Rock*. This novel is a highly biased chronicle of Reconstruction Virginia. In the narrative Jacquelin Gray and his cousin, Steven Allen of Red Rock Plantation, and Dr. Cary and his daughter, Blair, of Birdwood, strive unsuccessfully to maintain their property and their way of life against the insidious designs of the carpetbagger Leech and his scalawag confederate Hiram Still, once the trusted overseer of Red Rock Plantation.

Page's novel is primarily a sympathetic study of the residents of the Red Rock country. His characters represent the finest products of the golden age that flourished before the war. They are a people of courtesy, grace, and charm, of dignity, courage, and humor. Yet it becomes plain in the process of reading the novel that these very qualities are ineffectual and even a hindrance in the struggle against Leech and Hiram Still. In a battle against unjust federal and state laws courage and honor and honesty are not enough. Mrs. Welch, wife of a northern businessman who has retired to the South for his health, feels a qualified admiration for the Red Rock people. Judging them from her practical Yankee point of view, she finds them charming but anachronistic survivals of a dead civilization. "She was charmed with Miss Thomasia and the General. The former reminded her of her grandmother, whom she remembered as a white-haired old lady knitting in her armchair, and the General was an old French field marshal, of the time of Bayard or Sidney, who had strayed into this century, and who would not surprise her by appearing in armour with a sleeve around his helmet, 'funny dear, old fossil that he is.'" [36] No matter how sympathetically Page presents them, the reader must agree with Mrs. Welch's practical judgment of the Red Rock folk. They are indeed an antique race that has somehow stumbled into the nineteenth century, tragically unequipped to survive in a newer age.

Dr. Cary of Birdwood embodies all the best qualities of his society. He is a man of keen insight who originally opposes secession. When Virginia finally breaks away, he realizes that her citizens have not chosen to fight merely the North. "We are at war now," he says, "with the greatest power on earth: the power of universal progress. It is not the North that we shall have to fight, but the world. Go home and make ready. If we have talked like fools, we shall at least fight like men" (41). After the war Cary and his defeated countrymen seek to pick up the

36. Thomas Nelson Page, *Red Rock: A Chronicle of Reconstruction* (New York, 1899), 332, hereinafter cited in the text by page number only.

broken threads of their lives, to live as much as possible in the old way. In the course of the novel the rueful lesson they all learn is that a return to the shelter of the past is impossible.

Dr. Cary fights a losing battle for survival in the brutal world of the Reconstruction South. In this battle his system of values is of no help to him. He is not a good businessman. He cannot cheat his creditors, and he cannot collect debts from patients who are as destitute as himself. Like the fine Cavalier that he is, he is not really interested in making money. Indeed, he often gives away more to needy friends than he earns. Finally he must confess to Senator Rockford, a wealthy and successful northern friend, that he is destitute. He has lost Birdwood and all his property to the carpetbagger Leech. Yet he is content. For as he observes, "I have learned that a quiet mind is richer than a crown" (246).

Dr. Cary is a man of courage who quietly and within the law resists the depredations of Leech. Toward the end of the novel, however, Leech imprisons him along with most of the leading citizens of the community, charging him with a crime that he has not committed. Cary can fight no more. At this point he must seek the aid of his powerful friend in the North, Senator Rockford. The energy and forcefulness with which Rockford obtains the release of his friends contrasts with Cary's own noble and good-intentioned but fruitless actions. Unlike Dr. Cary, Senator Rockford has power. Moreover, his power is combined with a practical shrewdness, with an instinct for applying pressure in the right places to attain desired results. Senator Rockford suggests a certain crude strength; he combines the qualities of forthrightness and justice with a pragmatic Yankee temperament. Dr. Cary impresses the reader as a more noble embodiment of courage and honor. Yet Senator Rockford is one of the few characters who acts and acts successfully for the right cause.

Toward the end of the novel Dr. Cary sacrifices his life in a manner that is both foolish and highly admirable. Weakened by his imprisonment and by ceaseless rounds of house calls, the doctor, against the pleas of his wife and daughter, travels through a cold, windy night to minister to the gravely ill Leech. Leech survives, but the doctor lives only long enough to return home. His death marks the symbolic passing away of the old order. To Jacquelin Gray he represents the finest and noblest qualities of the Red Rock community. "He seemed to be a part of the old life—in all the country, its best and most enduring type; and, now that he had gone, Jacquelin felt as though the foundations were falling out—as though the old life had passed away with him" (557). In his characterization of Dr. Cary, Page effectively creates a Cavalier of the old order, a man who lives by a code that is both heroic and impractical, both noble and foolish.

The older members of the Red Rock community, represented by Dr. Cary, fail to defend their culture against the forces of Reconstruction and change. The problem is handed on to a younger generation, but this generation too is limited in its effectiveness to the extent that it follows the code of the Cavalier. Steve Allen is the acknowledged leader of the white community, the man whom Leech fears most. Yet ironically, he too is rescued from a hopeless situation by the practical ingenuity of a northerner. Steve is in love with Ruth Welch and he casually tells her of his brief involvement with the Ku Klux Klan. Leech learns about Steve's illegal association and plots to use Ruth's forced testimony to convict Allen of Klan membership and to punish him to the full extent of the law. Ruth, who fully returns Steve's love, decides to save him by marrying him on the eve of his trial. Steve, however, reacts in the noble and impractical manner which has been characteristic of the older generation of Cavaliers throughout the novel. He tells Mrs. Welch that "while he had loved her daughter better than his life, ever since the day he had met her, and while the knowledge that she cared for him had changed the world for him . . . he would not allow her to sacrifice herself by marrying him when under a criminal charge, and with a sentence staring him in the face" (571). The shrewd Mrs. Welch saves the situation by assuring Allen that the marriage is necessary to "prevent the horror of her daughter's having to appear, and give testimony against him, in open court" (571). Steve, who has not been swayed by considerations of expediency, is finally subdued by considerations of honor.

One of the unifying images of Page's novel is the portrait of the Old Indian Fighter, the founder who had carved Red Rock Plantation out of the wilderness and whose portrait hangs in the central hall of the old house. The powerful and brooding figure in the painting seems to watch the struggles of his descendants, struggles which result in only a partial victory for the Grays and the Carys. The Indian fighter had won his battles with savage foes, but Steve Allen and Jacquelin Gray must fight a more elusive adversary. They must combat institutional hypocrisy and trickery, lies and deceit. In such a battle the virtues that made the Indian fighter successful may count for little or nothing at all.

At the end of the novel Red Rock has survived the onslaught of carpetbaggers and scalawags. Leech has not been destroyed, but his power has begun to wane. Birdwood remains in his hands, but Steve and Jacquelin manage to win back Red Rock Plantation with part of their original lands. Here spinster Aunt Thomasia returns, the last remnant of a dying era, and spends her final days "knitting silently and looking around her with softened eyes and lips that moved constantly, though they uttered no sound" (584).

In *Red Rock* Thomas Nelson Page lovingly surveys Virginia's past. Yet his unqualified sympathy for his Cavaliers and their ladies is shadowed by the realization that such people are unsuited to follow the march of time and progress and that they are thus fated to wither away. Assessed as a whole, *Red Rock*'s perspective is not exclusively parochial, and it is not entirely oriented toward the past. It represents something of an advance over the simplistic tone of the early stories. Page anticipates a future in which a unified nation is destined to expand and strengthen. Thus the theme of reconciliation is important in the novel; it is projected through the sympathetic treatment of several northerners—Major Welch and Senator Rockford, for example—as well as through the fortunate marriage of Steve Allen and Ruth Welch.

It is significant that Major Welch and Senator Rockford, unlike Captain Wilton in "Meh Lady," are not merely copies of Virginia Cavalier originals. Roughly sketched as they are, Welch and particularly Rockford are distinguishable from their Red Rock friends by a more pragmatic approach toward solving problems. This slightly more complex approach toward the characterization of his northerners may possibly be a result of Page's greater acquaintance with northern temperament as a result of his extensive lecture tours and of his residence in Washington. Whatever the explanation, it is clear that in the eleven years between *In Ole Virginia* and the publication of *Red Rock*, Page's nationalistic sentiments had become more pronounced. Jacquelin Gray becomes Page's spokesman for reconciliation and for the reunified nation's manifest destiny. "He had begun to realize the idea of a great nation that should be known and respected wherever a ship could sail or a traveller could penetrate; of a re-unified country in which the people of both sides, retaining all the best of both sides, should vie with each other in building up the nation" (257).

Red Rock does not represent a revolutionary departure from Page's previously published fiction. In spite of Jacquelin's occasional visions of a glorious future for the United States, the book remains predominantly elegiac in tone. The conflict between the chivalric code of the past and the expediency of the modern world remains unresolved, as it did in "Marse Chan" and "Meh Lady." Page was clearly more aware in *Red Rock* than he had been in his earlier stories of the necessity of somehow moving past this tension and toward a more forward-looking viewpoint that transcended sectional perspectives. With the exception of a few passages, however, he was not able to transcend his sectional limitations. *Red Rock* remains preeminently a highly partisan denunciation of Reconstruction and an emotional defense of the southern way of life as Page believed it to have existed before the war.

Among the reviewers of the novel, Thomas Wentworth Higginson took sharp exception to Page's bias. Higginson argued that Negro suffrage had been necessary to prevent the southern states from returning blacks to near slavery and noted that many honest and honorable "carpetbaggers" had settled in the South, only to be frozen out of southern life by bitter and senseless hostility to all northerners. Other reviews of *Red Rock*, however, unequivocally accepted Page's interpretation of the period. The *Nation* called the book an "impartial" picture "of what was going on all over the South for several years after the war." And the *Atlantic* bemoaned "the contemptible persecution of the vanquished, which went on, under the name of Reconstruction."[37] Regardless of how much literary tastes change, *Red Rock* will probably remain in the eyes of the literary historian a deft and skillful accomplishment—a popular American novel in which a southern writer celebrates both national unity and the sectional culture that had sought less than fifty years before to destroy that unity.

Red Rock was the last unqualifiedly successful work of fiction that Page wrote. *Gordon Keith*, published five years later in 1903, is set partly in Virginia and, like *Red Rock*, deals with antebellum greatness and Reconstruction depredations and with the struggle of a new generation of southerners to move successfully into the twentieth century. Yet this novel lacks the vigor and sustaining interest of its predecessor. It was a financial but not a critical success.[38] The major difference between *Red Rock* and *Gordon Keith* is that in his new novel Page concentrated more on the manner in which contemporary southerners bring their old code of conduct into contact with new social problems. In the course of the novel, Page conducts his title character to New York and exposes him to the vices and temptations of wealthy, urban society. The novelist's purpose has changed significantly since *Red Rock*. His Cavalier hero has now been deliberately placed in an alien setting, far from Virginia. Significantly *Gordon Keith* becomes poorer fiction as its hero moves farther from his original plantation environment.

The fictional difficulties incurred in removing the traditional Page hero from his native environment are even more apparent in the last novel Page completed. In *John Marvel, Assistant*, published in 1909, the Old Dominion is conspicuously absent. Obviously seeking to forge new directions for himself, Page does not once mention Virginia by name in this novel, although he has clearly placed the opening setting in his home state.

The reader is immediately introduced to the main character, Henry Glave, the only offspring of an aristocratic family reduced to near pov-

---

37. Thomas Wentworth Higginson, "The Case of the Carpet-baggers," Review of Page, *Red Rock*, both in *Nation*, March 2, 1899, pp. 163, 167; Review of Page, *Red Rock*, in *Atlantic Monthly*, LXXXIII (1899), 520.

38. Hubbell, *The South in American Literature*, 799.

erty by the Civil War. His father is a gentleman of the old school who wisely teaches him that, though a king can make a nobleman, "it takes Jehovah to make a gentleman."[39] Yet combined with Henry's respect for his father's wisdom is a certain contempt for the older man's inability to live successfully with the present. Armed with his youthful expectations and his ambitions, Henry enrolls in a small but academically respectable college near his home. Here he distinguishes himself more for his glib tongue and poker playing skills than for his application to scholarship.

The college years are important for Henry because they introduce him to two good friends. One of these is John Marvel, a kind-natured and idealistic divinity student who has dedicated his life to God and who faithfully awaits the future coming of universal brotherhood and freedom. The second friend is a Jew named Leo Wolffert, a serious-minded and brilliant student who in later years rejects his father's wealth and becomes a socialist, crusading for the rights of workers. Henry is not initially influenced by his high-minded friends, and after college he drifts toward the largest city in his state (Richmond), where he hopes a successful law career awaits him.

In Richmond, Henry continues living an aimless, unguided life. He wastes away a promising law practice, accumulates a large debt speculating in stocks, and woos a shallow and selfish heiress named Lilian Poole. A sharp reverse in the stock market plunges him into bankruptcy. Left alone by the deaths of his mother and father, deserted by the opportunistic Miss Poole, Glave is driven from his home state in disgrace. He eventually arrives in a large midwestern city and seeks to begin a new practice, a penniless but wiser man.

Isolated in an impersonal urban environment, Henry Glave begins to display the thoughtful and honorable standards that are the only surviving gifts of his aristocratic father. All around him he sees frauds and cheats: Dr. Capon, the worldly minister of pious platitudes whose desk is littered with stock quotations; Coll McSheen and James Canter, railroad

---

39. Thomas Nelson Page, *John Marvel, Assistant* (New York, 1909), XV, 6, Vols. XV and XVI of Page, *The Novels, Stories, Sketches, and Poems of Thomas Nelson Page*, hereinafter cited in the text by volume and page number.

magnates who charge all the traffic will bear and force their workers to slave under inhuman conditions; Wringman, the corrupt labor chief, in secret alliance with wealthy industrialists. Surrounded by such men, Glave feels that the principles upon which he was reared have been scrapped by society and replaced by a brutal, dog-eat-dog attitude. He feels lost in an "inextinguishingly common" mass.

Reunited with Marvel and Wolffert, who are both working in the city to aid the oppressed working classes, Glave becomes increasingly aware of the enormous gap between the rich and the poor. "Often," he observes, "but a block or even but a wall divides the reeking slum where [men] creep and fester and rot, from the broad, well-lighted, smooth-paved avenue where irresponsible wealth goes clattering by in its wild orgy of extravagance and reckless mirth" (XV, 248). He disdains the *nouveaux riches*, who know "no standard but wealth and possess no ability to display it but through parade" (XV, 245). Soon after arriving in the city Glave witnesses an event that completely opens his eyes to social injustice and enables him to identify with the lower classes. A child's funeral is proceeding down a city steet at the same moment that a wealthy woman steps to the curb for a carriage. She insolently orders a policeman to move the mourners and steps unconcernedly into the carriage, ordering the driver to pass through the procession. Glave sees the glint of hatred in the eyes of the policeman and the cabby and understands. "I suddenly felt drawn to them both," he says, "and the old fight between the People and the Bourgeoisie suddenly took shape before me, and I found where my sympathy lay" (XV, 218).

The reader who is acquainted with *In Ole Virginia* and *Red Rock* cannot fail to realize that Page is charting a significantly different course in *John Marvel, Assistant.* The difference, however, does not lie in the characterization of the hero, Henry Glave. Henry, by the middle of the novel, exhibits essentially the same Cavalier qualities as Marse Phil and Steve Allen. He possesses innate good breeding. He is kind and courteous to those below him on the social scale. Even during his most frivolous years, he retains a strong sense of honesty and honor, and after his bankruptcy he cultivates the Cavalier's traditional disdain for money and vulgar display. Last but not least, he finds in the city a worthy young lady to worship, the wealthy Eleanor Leigh. In suitably extravagant terms Glave declares that since he has met his love the whole world has become "the home and enshrinement of one being" (XVI, 126). Marse Chan could not have expressed the sentiment more appropriately.

What distinguishes *John Marvel, Assistant* from Page's earlier work is not, therefore, characterization of his Cavalier hero, but the placing of that hero in an urban environment and the identification of his sympathies with the downtrodden poor. In *Gorden Keith*, of course, the Cavalier had been introduced to the city. Yet the engagement of Henry Glave in the actual fighting of privilege and corruption and his close association with John Marvel, advocate of the social gospel, and Leo Wolffert, advocate of socialism, clearly represents a further advance of the Cavalier into the modern arena of class conflict. Glave dedicates his practice to helping the poor and engages in long conversations with Wolffert concerning the advantages of socialist reform. Indeed, at one point in the novel, Henry seems almost ready to join Wolffert's cause.

In his last novel Page has abandoned romance and turned toward the creation of a work in the style of a William Dean Howells problem novel. He is experimenting with what for him is new and daring material—socialism, urban corruption, and anti-Semitism. But his attempt at social realism is doomed from the beginning by the old fashioned Cavalier code with which he equips his hero. The code of the Virginia gentleman, as Page and as all the Virginia novelists of the nineteenth century have defined it, is founded most basically on the ideal of the social stability associated with a rural culture dominated by large landowners. The Cavalier cannot live compatibly with revolutionary social theories that promulgate or prophesy profound social change. A Virginia aristocrat's sense of justice and honor may enable him to recognize the excesses of laissez-faire capitalism, but the code, founded as it is on the aristocratic and paternalistic rural ideal, cannot address itself in a meaningful way to the solution of complex urban problems.

Henry Glave is the traditional Page beau ideal. He belongs on a James River plantation, not in a midwestern city slum. Yet Page has placed him here and involved him in an embarrassing flirtation with Wolffert's socialism. Page must have recognized the awkward position of his gentleman hero. For toward the end of his novel he provides Henry with a convenient excuse for dissociating himself from political radicalism and removing himself from the ghetto to a social condition more compatible with his good breeding. Henry's escape arrives in the form of a long and bloody strike, secretly cooked up by the corrupt capitalist McSheen with the aid of the labor agitator Wringman. The strike has not been brought to improve the lot of the laborers, but to destroy an honest and principled competitor, the father of lovely Eleanor Leigh. The basic honesty of this industrialist, Page implies, is connected with his origin, which, not surprisingly, is the same as that of Henry Glave—Virginia.

The ease with which the working classes' hatreds are whipped up and the burning, looting, and anarchy which accompany the strike cause Glave to reject abstractions about the dignity and rights of the common man and to turn his back on Wolffert's socialist dogma. The validity of Glave's decision is presumably affirmed when Wolffert, who is trying to pacify a mob, is killed by the very men he has devoted his life to help. Through his efforts to mediate in the strike, Henry is recognized as a responsible citizen and a capable lawyer. He is consequently given a position in one of the city's prestigious law firms. He marries Eleanor and goes to live in her father's modest but tasteful mansion. Leo Wolffert is dead and John Marvel, for whom the novel is inappropriately named, remains in his slum church, faithfully serving the poor.

At the end of the novel Henry concludes that through his friendships with Marvel and with Wolffert and through his experiences in the city he has learned a valuable lesson: "that the fundamental law is to do good to mankind" (XVI, 330). If that is the lesson which Page would impart to the reader, it is surely an inadequate one. Restoring Henry to relative wealth and happiness, killing off Wolffert, and ending with a general admonition to do good to others does not begin to provide a satisfactory resolution for the serious social problems that have been described somewhat effectively earlier in the novel. The grinding poverty and the filthy slums still exist; the shocking disparity between rich and poor still exists. One cannot feel that Henry Glave has achieved any understanding of the crises he has struggled through. Glave's failure is, as Theodore Gross has perceived, "Page's unintended admission that the code of heroism which served so well for his ante-bellum Southern heroes is not suited to a changing world."[40]

John Marvel, Assistant is a poor novel with many weaknesses. The point of view fluctuates between first and third person; the narrative is much too long and rambling and is moved by too many coincidences. But even if Page had avoided these flaws, his novel would not have been a success. The fundamental weakness of the book is that neither Page nor his spokesman Henry Glave can carry through the social investigation that he has begun, because the possible solutions to the problems analyzed would be in violent opposition to the spirit of the aristocratic code for which he stands. Appearances are preserved by the imposition of an arbitrary conclusion, but the reader cannot help but feel in the end that the author has disposed of the social tensions that were the prime movers of the plot much as a magician disposes of his rabbit. The audience knows it should be there, even though it is not.

Page's failure with *John Marvel* is linked significantly with the failures of his Virginia predecessors. His inability to make his Cavalier hero an effective spokesman for social reform echoes the failure of William Alexander Caruthers seventy-five years earlier in *Knights of the Golden Horse-shoe* to transform Governor Spotswood into an effective symbol of America's manifest destiny. Like Caruthers, Page failed to understand the limitations of his character stereotype. The Cavalier was an effective figure only within the domain of the legendary plantation.

Ultimately, Thomas Nelson Page will be remembered, not for his later novels in which he tries halfheartedly to move his Virginia gentleman into the twentieth century, but for his early stories in which the romantic Cavalier is expertly melded with the Lost Cause myth. It is

40. Gross, *Thomas Nelson Page*, 136.

heavily ironic that this celebrator of the Old Dominion's antebellum golden age was also one of the leading spokesmen of the New South movement, advocating industrialization, the expansion of mining, and improved transportation in Virginia and in all of Dixie. However, as Wayne Mixon has perceptively observed, Page believed that the industrialization of the New South would be accomplished within the region's antebellum social framework. He was confident that the old order would continue to direct the South's destiny and that there would be an abundance of material progress but a minimum of social change. The New South, in Page's view, was to be put to the service of sustaining the Old South.[41]

In Page's fiction we see how this Old South–New South equation is subtly and neatly worked out. The Old South celebrated in his romantic stories becomes an indirect vindication of the reassertion of authority in the New South by the old aristocratic order. Though the agricultural base of the old order was to be supplemented and perhaps finally replaced by a new industrial structure, conservatives like Page envisioned that this new order would be controlled by the same people—the right people—the old planter aristocracy.

Because Page was a talented storyteller his celebration of the Cavalier stereotype and the Lost Cause myth was appealing and popular with northern readers. As a result, he may have been the most insidiously influential Virginia writer of the nineteenth century. Certainly he was as responsible as any Virginia writer for the pernicious effects of Lost Causism which Frank Vandiver describes. "While post–Civil War southerners were pushing as fast as they could into the New South, were grasping Yankee dollars with enthusiasm, they purified their motives in the well of Lost Causism. . . . Lost Causism came to fulfill a role similar to that of the pro-slavery argument in antebellum times. It offered justification for resistance to the leveling tendencies continued by harsh Reconstruction measures. It cloaked the lawless Klansman and lent license to the segregating Christian. It was, finally, the cornerstone of the New South."[42]

41. Mixon, *Southern Writers and the New South Movement*, 410.
42. Vandiver, "The Confederate Myth," 149.

FROM PEDESTAL TO PEN: VIRGINIA WOMEN WRITERS

As Anne Firor Scott has observed, one of the effects of the Civil War was to project southern women into professions that had heretofore been closed to them or that had been considered inappropriate occupations. Change was dictated by necessity. Many women in the South discovered after the war that the survival of their families depended on their making money. The scarcity of able-bodied men turned significant numbers of women into farmers and planters, and large numbers also became schoolteachers, journalists, and writers. The assumption of writing careers by southern women was a particularly significant phenomenon. "Not only did a large number of women see themselves as literary artists," Scott writes, "but many women active in other fields—farming, temperance, teaching—wrote poems and stories on the side. What southern literature lacked in quality it made up in quantity."[43]

Postbellum Virginia writing clearly illustrates the movement of southern women from pedestal to pen. Indeed, Virginia's women writers dominated the literary production of romantic Cavalier figures in the last decades of the nineteenth century. It might have been hoped that these women would have approached the Old Dominion's mythic past with a more critical eye or at least with a slightly different perspective. Such, alas, was not the case. Women writers of this period embraced the Lost Cause myth and apotheosized the Cavalier with the same enthusiasm as their male counterparts. But for the name on the title page, a reader is given few clues to suggest the sex of the writer.

Mary Tucker Magill was among the first of the South's female authors to use her pen to vindicate antebellum society. Magill dedicated *The Holcombes: A Story of Virginia Home Life* to her native state. Her expressed purpose was "to present to the world a faithful picture of a Virginia home as it was before the late war." Her idea of fidelity was to introduce her readers to the lavish plantation life of the Holcombes of Rose Hill, an opulent mansion which, in the narrator's words, might pass "for some olden castle, with its white walls gleaming." Here on this

43. Scott, *The Southern Lady*, 118.

Albemarle County estate one is regaled with a jousting tournament, lavish holiday feasting, and a poignant Christmas Day trip to the slave quarters to visit the family's faithful and loving mammy. *The Holcombes* also comes complete with a malicious Yankee suitor, who schemes for the hand of the lovely plantation belle and who is determined to prove "that a Massachusetts Yankee is more than a match for a Virginia aristocrat."[44] In the end, of course, the palms go to the noble Cavalier suitor.

One is impressed by Mary Tucker Magill's absolute commitment to the plantation ideal. Even after the issue has been decided, she allows her Cavaliers a spirited defense of slavery. Mr. Holcombe, the master of Rose Hill, argues that "there would not be nearly so many bad masters if there had been less legislation on the subject of slavery; if the feeling of irritation and bitterness were not kept up by the interference which is continually going on with our domestic concerns by the fanatics of the North."[45]

Magill's fundamentally unreconstructed point of view is confirmed in *Women; or, Chronicles of the Late War*, a "story of the 'Lost Cause'" dedicated to "the women of the South." In this novel, which focuses on the Randolph family of Winchester and the Holcombes of Rose Hill, the ladies of the Old Dominion are as cognizant of their duty to their native state as are their Virginia gentlemen, and they send their knights into battle with their blessings. "You bear it!" one lady observes. "Oh, yes! Cover over your heart-wounds and smile as you writhe, because this much you sacrifice for the liberty of your country!" The fanatical devotion of Virginia's women to the South's holy cause is illustrated by the reaction of a young belle to her fiancé after she learns that, having been captured by Union forces, he has been persuaded by his ailing parents, who have moved to the North, to leave the Confederate army. When he returns South to beg her to forgive him and to marry him, she recoils in horror. "What madness," she cries, "possessed you to think that I could ever link myself with dishonor?"[46]

44. Mary Tucker Magill, *The Holcombes: A Story of Virginia Home Life* (Philadelphia, 1871), 1, 25.

45. *Ibid.*, 248–49.

46. Mary Tucker Magill, *Women; or, Chronicles of the Late War* (Baltimore, 1871), 41, 176.

Two decades after Mary Tucker Magill's paeans to Virginia's planter-aristocracy and to the Lost Cause, the Old Dominion's women writers continued to play on the same romantic chords and to evoke the same mythic stereotypes. In *Broadoaks* (1893) Mary Greenway Mc-Clelland juxtaposes Cavalier Geoffrey Bruce, a Confederate veteran who has made enough money in the West after the war to save his father's plantation, with Yankee Stuart Redwood, a mining engineer who has come to the Blue Ridge foothills to find commercial deposits of gold. During his stay in Virginia some of Redwood's prejudices against southerners are altered. For example, he comes to share the Virginian's view of the Negro as "stupid and unreliable." Other of his prejudices, however, are confirmed. He believes that Virginia's aristocrats are "un-businesslike and helpless" and insists that a Yankee makes just as fine a gentleman as a Virginian. "I know that you Virginians come from swashbuckling younger sons and we New Englanders from religious fanatics," Redwood concedes. But, he goes on to argue, "for myself I don't see, in point of discretion and respectability, a pin to chose [*sic*] between the antecedents of the two sections."[47]

Although Redwood recognizes no superiority of Cavalier over Yankee, McClelland clearly does. As Geoffrey Bruce and Redwood battle for the love of a Virginia belle named Rebie Kennedy, the author makes it plain that Bruce is the suitor to be preferred. Geoffrey Bruce woos like a proper Cavalier. For Rebie he would "'fight for love, or die,' if there were occasion" (150). His single wish, as he expresses it, is "to hold a woman apart, as in a sure fortress; to guard, cherish and protect her through life" (151). In contrast to Bruce, Redwood is a man, according to the narrator, for whom money is "the prime factor of existence." It is the pushing, striving, dissatisfied materialism in him to which Rebie responds, and McClelland stresses that Redwood's attraction for Rebie is "a malign fascination such as Indian hemp is said to possess for its votaries" (95).

Throughout her novel McClelland draws the sharp distinction between Yankees like Redwood, who are identified with pragmatism, in-

---

47. Mary Greenway McClelland, *Broadoaks* (St. Paul, 1893), 53, hereinafter cited in the text by page number only.

tellect, and ravening materialism, and Cavaliers like Geoffrey Bruce, who are motivated more by concerns for feeling than by pragmatism. Redwood discovers a rich vein of gold on the ancestral Kennedy burying ground. It is ironic but appropriate, given the terms in which the two characters have been presented, that while Geoffrey cannot conceive of violating the burial site of one's ancestors to mine for gold, Redwood can. Indeed, his love for Rebie becomes closely bound with his lust for the gold on her family's property. Finally, it is this lust for gold which destroys him. He is killed by a Negro while unearthing a grave at night, looking for his cherished vein of gold.

At the novel's end Redwood is dead and Rebie seems destined to marry Geoffrey Bruce. Now that Redwood is gone, she has been restored to good sense. The unnatural excitement, which the Yankee's presence precipitated and of which McClelland so obviously disapproves, has vanished. McClelland seems to ask her readers to share her relief for Rebie's narrow escape from the coils of the Yankee serpent and to share the satisfaction of knowing that her belle has made the only choice that she could have made—she has chosen a Virginia Cavalier.

The struggle between Yankee and Cavalier suitors for the affections of a charming Virginia belle is presented in a much lighter vein by Julia Magruder in "Miss Ayr of Virginia," included in a collection entitled *Miss Ayr of Virginia and Other Stories* (1896). In this rather charming short story a rustic Virginia maiden travels North and, armed with innocence, simplicity, and charm, wins a social triumph over her haughty and wealthy New York cousins. For Julia Magruder, however, Miss Ayr's supreme triumph is her rejection of the sincere love of a Yankee multimillionaire for the equally sincere love of the noble but impoverished Cavalier who waits for her at home. Implicit in the story is the idea that there is a quality of character which makes the Virginia gentleman superior to his northern competitor, even though the Cavalier is poor and the Yankee is astonishingly rich.

During the last decades of the nineteenth century some of the most popular depictions of the romantic Cavalier were penned by Constance Cary Harrison, who lived her formative years in Virginia. She is known today chiefly for her interesting account of Civil War Richmond under siege, *Recollections Grave and Gay* (1911). She moved with her husband after the war to New York and subsequently established a solid literary reputation there. Some of Harrison's works, such as *The Anglomaniacs* (1890), were in a broadly realistic vein and were set in contemporary New York. However, she also wrote a number of popular historical romances set in Virginia. In *A Son of the Old Dominion* (1897), whose action takes place on the eve of the Revolution, the novelist contrasts episodes of Indian warfare on the Virginia frontier with scenes of the magnificent plantation life of Vue de l'Eau, the Potomac River estate of Colonel Hugh Poythress. Colonel Poythress' "manor house" reproduces "as nearly as might be, his ancestral home in a southern shire of England."[48]

Like Virginia writers before her, Constance Cary Harrison stresses the close links between the English and the Virginia aristocracy. For example, Rolfe Poythress, the handsome, brave, and virile representative of the family's frontier branch, is revealed toward the novel's end as the fifth Earl of Avenal, heir to the family's vast estates in England. Harrison also insists on the rigid social distinction in Tidewater Virginia between planter aristocrat and common farmer. At a neighborhood barbecue we catch brief glimpses of the more modest social orders, whom Harrison lumps together under the common rubric "rustics." These types obediently turn aside in the crowd to let their betters through. The author observes that it would no more occur to these people "to wish to pass the dividing line between them and their superiors in fortune, than it would have done to a similar class in the mother country."[49]

In *Flower de Hundred: The Story of a Virginia Plantation* (1890) Constance Cary Harrison focuses on antebellum Virginia, weaving a romantic tale of the Throckmorton family, whose ancient James River plantation gives the novel its title. Like so many fictional first families of Virginia before them, the Throckmortons trace their ancestral line back to the seventeenth-century immigration of Cavalier exiles. *Flower de Hundred* is replete with holiday plantation festivities, fox hunts, happy

48. Constance Cary Harrison, *A Son of the Old Dominion* (Boston, 1897), 12.
49. *Ibid.*, 63.

and loyal darkies, and kind and indulgent masters—the traditional staples of plantation fiction. Though she observed northern society with a distinctly sharper eye, Harrison viewed the prewar Old Dominion as a land of enchantment and near perfection. "Here," she proclaimed, "was a race of conscientious men full of a high sense of personal honor and responsibility to God; here were unselfish and helpful women; a minority of intelligence and capacity, surrounded and isolated by masses of ignorant peasants. The blacks, whatever their external polish, were ready at a hint to relapse into the barbarous habits and beliefs of their African ancestors."[50]

Even as late as 1890 Constance Cary Harrison could not disguise the bitterness she felt toward the predatory Yankee who had destroyed Virginia's felicitous social system. This bitterness is clearly conveyed in the scene describing the despoliation of Flower de Hundred by Federal troops. "Soldiers mad with excitement overran the rooms and, dragging whatever they could lay hands on out upon the lawn, made merry with their spoil. Furniture, pictures, mirrors, carpets, books, saddles, fire-irons strewed the grass; and when to these were added the unfortunate discovery of a cask of buried whiskey, an orgy followed in which all semblance of restraint was thrown aside."[51] *Flower de Hundred* suggests that, almost twenty years after Mary Tucker Magill's account of the Civil War in Virginia, the Old Dominion's women writers were as determinedly unreconstructed as ever in their view of the conflict.

Of the considerable number of Virginia women writers who published novels and short story collections between 1870 and 1900, only one, Mary Spear Tiernan, depicted the Old Dominion in less than idealized terms. A native of Virginia, she married Charles Tiernan of Baltimore and lived most of her life in Maryland; nevertheless, she used her native state as the setting for her fiction. In *Suzette* (1885) a conventional love story is developed in antebellum Richmond. However, in a novel entitled *Homoselle* (1881) Tiernan takes a less conventional approach to Virginia's past which, considering the predilection of post-

50. Constance Cary Harrison, *Flower de Hundred: The Story of a Virginia Plantation* (New York, 1890), 42–43.
51. *Ibid.*, 245.

bellum writers for abjectly worshiping the Old Dominion's standard myths, is comparatively daring.

Homoselle is set at Dunmore, the James River plantation of the Despard family, built with brick brought from England in colonial days. The main plot is a conventional love story in which the plantation belle, Homoselle Despard, must choose between two suitors, an English gentleman who is visiting Virginia and a local Cavalier. Of considerably more interest to the contemporary reader is the thoughtful treatment of the question of slavery, which provides an interesting background to action that is otherwise entirely predictable. The English visitor disapproves of slavery and cordially but seriously debates with his hosts over the moral and practical problems associated with such a system. Unlike her contemporaries, Tiernan allows her English character's arguments to be as forceful as the rebuttals of her Virginia planters. Even more extraordinary than the discussion of slavery in the novel are Mary Tiernan's depiction of the acute yearning for freedom of her Virginia slaves and her dramatization of an actual slave rebellion which has otherwise been completely ignored by Virginia's writers—Gabriel's Insurrection of 1800.

In *Homoselle* Gabriel leads hundreds of his fellow slaves in a night march to seize the arsenal at Richmond. Mr. Despard is utterly shocked that many of his own slaves, whom, the narrator informs us, the master "had believed too contented and too timid to strike for freedom," have joined Gabriel's army. But Tiernan, by turning Gabriel into a roughly individualized character, indicates why Despard's slaves are willing to take the risks he never imagined they would take. Gabriel speaks humbly but eloquently in the novel of the slaves' yearning for freedom. "You mus' do right, you mus' be brave an' perseverin'," Gabriel admonishes his followers. "An' when de day of freedom come, you'll know how to use de liberty de Lord is gwine to help you to win. For de Lord is on our side. He is always on de side of de po', de miserable, an' de oppressed."[52] Gabriel's charismatic appeal and his vision of a divinely sanctioned insurrection loosely but provocatively suggests the divinely

52. Mary Spear Tiernan, *Homoselle* (Boston, 1881), 286, 188.

inspired madness of William Styron's Nat Turner, another fictional slave drawn loosely from fact who would appear nearly ninety years later.

Of course, it would be a mistake to overestimate Mary Spear Tiernan's achievement. She is limited in her treatment of the slave revolt by her commitment to a conventional romantic plot. She takes fictional liberties with the factual rebellion, creating a loyal slave who risks her life to warn the Despard plantation of the revolt and allowing her English hero to alert the city of Richmond before the slaves arrive. In the end she even gives us a contrite Gabriel, who confesses in his prison cell to a white minister and acknowledges "his transgressions" and "his need for pardon," freely forgiving the judges who have sentenced him to death. Nevertheless, neither Gabriel's sentimental final confession nor Homoselle's marriage to her English gentleman can quite dispel the serious social questions Tiernan's novel has raised or entirely cancel out her disturbing revelation of the depth of the slaves' desire for freedom.

Virginius Dabney, in his account of Gabriel's Insurrection, contends that "the dimensions of the conspiracy were truly staggering" and that the rebellion "had a powerful impact on the minds of the whites in Virginia."[53] Perhaps the profound fear it aroused accounts for the fact that there were no fictional treatments of the event in the state's antebellum fiction. Gabriel's Insurrection, like Nat Turner's Rebellion, gave the lie to the idealized stereotype of the happy and contented plantation darky. G. P. R. James, English consul to Norfolk and Richmond from 1852 to 1858, had written a novel entitled *The Old Dominion; or, The Southhampton Massacre* (1856) which incorporated a number of factual incidents as well as a briefly sketched characterization of Nat Turner into its highly melodramatic love plot.[54] No Virginia writer, however, had been willing to tackle Turner's bloody revolt, and no writer, either inside or outside the state, had been drawn to Gabriel's earlier rebellion.

53. Dabney, *Virginia, the New Dominion*, 186.
54. For a detailed description of G. P. R. James's life and career, including the years he spent in Virginia, see James Meehan, "The Solitary Horseman in Virginia: Novelist G. P. R. James as British Consul, 1852–1858," *Virginia Cavalcade*, XXVII (Autumn, 1977), 58–67.

Only in 1936 would Arna Bontemps test the subject from a Black American perspective in *Black Thunder*. Mary Spear Tiernan's inclusion of Gabriel's Insurrection in her novel is thus both surprising and gratifying, for it indicates that she was willing to confront, at least obliquely, the cancer which festered at the core of the Edenic vision of plantation Virginia and which neither her predecessors nor her contemporaries had the integrity of vision to recognize.

Homoselle contains few strongly realized scenes, but the reader is likely to remember one episode in which a slave named Michael, fleeing after the collapse of Gabriel's army, holds off an entire party of white pursuers with his fists until one of the men returns with a gun. Michael has been depicted throughout the narrative as a brutal and animalistic character, but at this point, spurred by his instinctive desire for survival, he attains a kind of nobility. "With one last, mighty effort," Tiernan writes, "he sprang, like some splendid animal, from among his captors, and was fleeing for his life, when he was brought to the ground by a rifle-shot."[55] At the instant of Michael's death both the narrator and the reader identify completely with the Negro slave. It is not an overstatement to call this instant a historic moment in Virginia fiction.

The publication of Tiernan's third and last novel, *Jack Horner* (1890), shows that the comparatively unorthodox approach to her state's past exhibited in *Homoselle* is not a mere fluke. Although burdened with a melodramatic plot that is even more contrived than that of *Homoselle*, *Jack Horner*, like her first novel, presents revealing glimpses of black characters and develops out of its Civil War setting a conflict between Yankee and Cavalier, the resolution of which is unique in nineteenth-century Virginia fiction.

Jack Horner is a Civil War novel set mainly in Richmond. The novel's title is drawn from the name given to an unidentified orphan who is left at the door of the wealthy Pritchard family at the beginning of the conflict. The Pritchards adopt the unfortunate child, assuming that he is the offspring of some valiant Confederate soldier. However, through

55. Tiernan, *Homoselle*, 300.

convoluted movement of plot, Jack Horner turns out to be the son of a northern officer named Dorset whose wife has died behind southern lines. This officer, though an enemy, is presented as a loving father who goes so far as to disguise himself as a wounded Rebel soldier in order to spend time in the Pritchard household and gain glimpses of his precious son.

In spite of its wildly improbable plot, *Jack Horner*, like *Homoselle*, contains interesting elements, including the characterization of a Negro slave named Afra. With her colorful costumes and her warm and loyal nature, Afra seems through most of the novel to be little more than a variation on Thomas Nelson Page's happy darkie stereotype. Toward the novel's end, however, she is depicted in a manner that would have been inconceivable to Page. On a warm April Sunday morning in 1865 Afra is the first to bring news to the Pritchard household of the imminent fall of Richmond. But far from being distressed by the news, "the jolly, good-humored cook was like a creature possessed." Before the "dazed sight" of her owners she "seemed to be Afra, and yet not Afra." Tiernan makes it very clear in this scene that Afra is moved by emotions and feelings of which her white masters had never dreamed her capable. Though Tiernan's white characters may not comprehend Afra's joy, her readers understand why the slave hugs herself: "Yes, I mus' hug dis nigger 'cos she's free. She never been free befo'. But she free now, glory be to God."[56] Like *Homoselle*, *Jack Horner* conveys an authentic and powerful sense of the black man's desire for freedom; and as in *Homoselle*, the brief scenes in which this yearning is dramatized are all the more vivid because they contrast with the sterile romanticism of the novel's plot.

In addition to black characterization which departs significantly from conventional stereotypes, *Jack Horner* contains an interesting conflict between Cavalier and Yankee characters. This conflict is not one of martial arms, but is centered in the heart of Madelaine Key, niece to the Pritchards and a member of their household. She must choose between

56. Mary Spear Tiernan, *Jack Horner* (Boston, 1890), 332, 333, hereinafter cited in the text by page number only.

Major Hugh Dallas, who serves valiantly under Stonewall Jackson in defense of the Old Dominion, and Yankee Major John Dorset, whom Madelaine nurses to health before she realizes that he is not a southern officer but a detested Yankee who, nevertheless, loves his son enough to risk his life to be near him.

As we have seen, there was nothing unique about presenting a love affair between Yankee and southern belle in postbellum Virginia fiction. Thomas Nelson Page had skillfully developed the theme in "Meh Lady." But though Yankee officer had won Virginia belle, Page had been careful not to bring his northern beau up against a Cavalier rival. What is unique about Tiernan's presentation is that Cavalier struggles with Yankee for the heart of a southern belle and loses the battle.

Wounded, maimed, captured, and languishing in a prison in Washington toward the novel's end, Cavalier Hugh Dallas still seems destined to win Madelaine's affections. For she is his fiancée, and she cannot begin to think of giving her heart to a Yankee. Armed with this resolve, she makes the difficult and dangerous passage through enemy lines to Washington to nurse Dallas back to health. In this endeavor she is aided by Dorset, who, though he loves her, respects her decision to faithfully attend Dallas. After Madelaine arrives in Washington, however, Dallas accidentally learns of Dorset's deep love for his fiancée and of her equally strong, though largely unacknowledged, attraction toward Dorset. In a scene worthy of Henry Mackenzie's *Man of Feeling*, Dallas literally dies for love, giving up a woman who he knows respects him but can never completely give her heart to him.

The death of the Cavalier major leaves the field open for Dorset. The reader is not entirely surprised that the handsome Federal officer wins the Virginia belle's heart, for Tiernan has prepared her readers in a faintly sensual passage in which the strength of Dorset's physical magnetism for Madelaine is revealed. Though the temptation of "his beauty" remains "the innermost secret of her soul," the Yankee's appeal cannot be entirely denied. In rather typical Victorian fashion Tiernan calls her heroine's passion an "involuntary weakness," but she also frankly acknowledges the sway over Madelaine of "all the sweet human influences of companionship and youth in the blood" (311). It is this youthful blood urge for the enemy which must be hidden deep in her soul.

Ultimately, however, Madelaine acknowledges what had once seemed to her to be unthinkable—she acknowledges her love for a Yankee. In the final scene Dorset comes to war-scarred Richmond to claim his son. In the Pritchard mansion, a former citadel of rebel sentiments, little Jack Horner seizes the hands of both his father and Madelaine, symbolically reuniting North and South. "As his little hands touched the hand of each," Tiernan writes, "he completed a chain through which shot a thrill that made Dorset and Madelaine tremble" (347). The cause of true love prevails over sectional bitterness, and in terms distinctly favorable to the Yankee suitor.

Endowing a young northern gentleman with romantic appeal and placing him in opposition to a Cavalier foil was not unheard of among Virginia's postbellum romancers. In *Broadoaks*, one recalls, Mary Greenway McClelland had juxtaposed a Confederate veteran with a Yankee mining engineer. But in this novel the heroine's fascination for the ambitious and aggressive northerner was labeled a "malign fascination," and the Yankee was unceremoniously killed off so that the novel's Cavalier hero could claim undisputed possession of his belle. We will never know the influences which directed Tiernan to do the opposite, to kill off her Cavalier and give the victory to his Yankee rival, but the result is a surprising and unprecedented inversion of the traditional Cavalier-Yankee fictional equation.

Jack Horner confirms the unorthodox attitudes implicit in *Homoselle* and establishes Mary Spear Tiernan's unique position in postbellum Virginia fiction. Of a number of women writers who appeared in the decades after the Civil War, she was the only one to depart significantly from the male-created vision of Virginia as a patriarchal Eden. Tiernan was not so skillful a writer as Thomas Nelson Page or Constance Cary Harrison. Still, the iconoclasm of her novels, though it is tentative and obscured by the conventional fictional clichés of the period, deserves recognition. No other writer of her generation dared to depart as far as

Mary Spear Tiernan from the rigidly established patterns of the Virginia plantation romance.

MARY JOHNSTON

By 1900 the popularity of local color fiction had greatly decreased, but realistic writers such as Henry James and William Dean Howells were forced to share their reading public with a new crop of historical romance novelists. The turn-of-the-century vogue for this familiar genre is amply demonstrated by publishing statistics. Between 1895 and 1912 approximately four hundred new historical novels were published. Southern writers, including Virginia writers such as Constance Cary Harrison, responded swiftly to the changing preference in fiction and wrote a surprisingly large portion of these works. Thirty-four of the seventy-two best-selling historical novels of this period were penned by southerners, and of the seven which sold 500,000 copies or more, Dixie's writers claimed four.[57]

Mary Johnston was a Virginia-born writer whose early historical novels mirrored the popular taste of the day and brought her substantial financial and critical success. She was a member of a turn-of-the-century generation of Virginia writers which included Ellen Glasgow, James Branch Cabell, and Amélie Rives. She was born in Buchanan, Virginia, at the southern tip of the Shenandoah Valley, in 1870. Her father, Major John William Johnston, was a lawyer, a member of the Virginia legislature from Botetourt County, and a veteran of the Civil War. Her uncle was the Confederate hero, Joseph E. Johnston. Poor health, which plagued her most of her life, necessitated home instruction, and consequently she received little formal education. At fifteen she moved with her family to Birmingham, Alabama. Two years later her mother died and she took over the management of her father's house. In her twenties she moved with her father to New York City, where she wrote her earliest novels of the Old Dominion.

57. C. Vann Woodward, *Origins of the New South, 1877–1913* (Baton Rouge, 1951), 431.

Her first two works—*Prisoners of Hope* (1898) and *To Have and to Hold* (1900)—were immediate successes. *To Have and to Hold* was one of the seven historical novels of the period which sold over 500,000 copies. The royalties from these and subsequent novels enabled her to travel widely in Europe and the Middle East. But after the death of her father she returned to her native state, which was the locale of most of her fiction. She lived in Richmond and later at her cottage at Warm Springs, Virginia, where she had retired for her health. She died there in 1936.

Although Johnston set her narratives in widely differing locales and periods, ranging from Renaissance England to Medieval France, fifteen of her twenty-three works are Virginia novels. Some of these novels deal with earlier periods of Virginia history. *Lewis Rand*, for example, is placed in the age of Jefferson. The action of *Hagar*, on the other hand, is contemporary. Her most popular Virginia narratives, however, were her colonial romances, *Prisoners of Hope* and *To Have and to Hold*.

Prisoners of Hope is set in colonial Virginia immediately after the Restoration of Charles II, the period that had been well cultivated by William Alexander Caruthers in *The Cavaliers of Virginia*. *Prisoners of Hope*, however, is an even more colorful and effective period piece than its predecessor.

The opening scene presents the heroine, Patricia Verney, lounging on the porch of her father's plantation in a gown of green dimity decorated with pink roses and yellow lace, "made according to the latest Paris mode, as described in a year-old letter from the court of Charles the Second." Sitting beside her is her admiring cousin, Sir Charles Carew. He too is dressed in the peak of fashion, complete with scented periwig and rapier with jeweled hilt, and he is singing a Cavalier love song to the fair Patricia. The young cousins are joined by the lord of the manor, Colonel Verney, "trader, planter, magistrate, member of the council of state, soldier, author on occasion, and fine gentleman all rolled into one." With him is his sister, Mistress Lettice Verney, who compensates with elegant clothing for what she lacks in youth. The opulence of Johnston's character descriptions amply supports Patricia's contention, "We *are* a little bit of England set down here in the wilderness."[58]

A reader of nineteenth-century Virginia romances will be immediately familiar with the novel's opening scene. It closely resembles Cooke's description of Champ Effingham's estate and Caruthers' presentation of Governor Spotswood's plantation. As in the earlier novels, the small farmer and the hardworking planter are absent. Colonel Verney and his ladies are linked by Sir Charles Carew with an aristocratic English ancestry, and Johnston suggests that those early Virginians have ample leisure time for lounging away summer afternoons on the great porch. Yet as the narrative progresses, the reader is introduced to characters who stand in opposition to fundamental values of the plantation system and who give Johnston's portrait of early Virginia society a more subtle and complex texture than either Caruthers' or Cooke's. There is Miles Carrington, Puritan surveyor general to the colony, a secret supporter of the doctrines of self-rule, self-taxation, free trade, and religious toleration. His daughter, Betty, opposes the importation of savage African slaves and an indentured labor system which, in her words, leaves the laborer "bowed and broken" before his freedom comes.

Though the Carringtons sound but a minor note of discord, the voice of freedom finds a more impressive spokesman in Godfrey Landless. Landless is a white slave, a Newgate felon who has been banished to a life of servitude in Virginia. Yet he is also a gentleman of noble bearing and good manners, and his punishment is obviously linked in some way to his Puritan loyalties. Johnston immediately concentrates her attention on Landless, and the reader is soon aware that he will be a central character in the unfolding drama.

The alternating focus on the convict Landless and the Verney family creates an interesting juxtaposition of scenes. Johnston describes not only the banquet of the aristocrats—the sideboard laden with delicacies and shining with silver—but also the humble meal of the slaves and

58. Mary Johnston, *Prisoners of Hope: A Tale of Colonial Virginia* (1898; rpr. Boston, 1926), 1, 16, 3, hereinafter cited in the text by page number only.

indentured servants. The reader is present at the simple corn bread and fish suppers prepared communally around an open fire. He sees the cabins—rude and windowless, with mud chimneys—and the pillory and whipping post, which dominate the quarters and are constant reminders of the punishment which attends disobedience or attempted escape. Johnston uses a character named Win-Grace Porringer to gruesomely objectify the punitive nature of the forced labor system. Porringer is a religious fanatic whose servitude is imposed as punishment for his nonconformity. His constant attempts to escape cause Colonel Verney to whip him, to brand him on the cheek, to shave his head and shackle him, and to nail him by his ears to the pillory.

As Jay B. Hubbell has noted, Johnston is the first Virginia novelist to use the indentured servant as a character in her fiction.[59] Actually, she accomplishes considerably more in *Prisoners of Hope*. She describes carefully and in considerable detail the different kinds of laborers who make up the plantation work force. There are redemptioners, or indentured servants, who, in return for passage to the New World, work for seven years for the planter. Below these men are the white criminals who, as punishment for serious crimes, are sent to Virginia as slaves. Godfrey Landless is one of these. Even lower in the scale of humanity, however, are the black slaves who have just begun to pour into the Colony from the holds of New England trading schooners. Mary Johnston has not simply presented the reader with the traditional scenery of the typical plantation novel. Her work is, in part, a serious examination of the origin and the degrees of enforced servitude in the Old Dominion.

Among Verney's laborers Godfrey Landless is most to be pitied. He is clearly a gentleman who has known better days, and he most keenly feels the humiliation of slavery. He loves Patricia Verney; yet she shrinks from him in horror. He suffers from the gibes of Carew, who seems unconsciously to fear him as a rival for his cousin's affections. He is whipped by the hard overseer, Woodson, as a result of a fancied insult. This whipping drives him to join and to take the leadership of a group of slaves seeking to overthrow their masters. The plot is masterminded

59. Jay Broadus Hubbell, "Cavalier and Indentured Servant in Virginia Fiction," *South Atlantic Quarterly*, XXVI (1927), 35–36.

by Puritan elements, followers of Cromwell who have been condemned to servitude in Virginia and who seek to use their baser allies to win their freedom. Godfrey, like his Puritan compatriots, joins the conspiracy reluctantly and pledges himself to avoid as much violence as possible.

Handling the slave revolt is difficult for Johnston. She sympathizes with Godfrey's desire for freedom, a desire which he eloquently defends before the disdainful Patricia. "Is it of choice, do you think," he asks her, "that men lie rotting in prison, in the noisome holds of ships, are bought and sold like oxen, are chained to the oar, to the tobacco field, are herded with the refuse of the earth, are obedient to the finger, to the whip? We—they who are known as Oliverians, and they who are felons, and I who am, if you choose, of both parties, were haled here with ropes. What allegiance did we owe to them who had cast us out, or to them who bought us as they buy dumb beasts? As God lives, none!" (312). Yet even though the Puritan position is effectively stated, Johnston seems to draw back from giving full sympathy to the Africans and Newgate felons. These men are depicted as savages who are easily controlled by the sly and malevolent mulatto, Luiz Sebastian. The author's position regarding the conflict between aristocrat and slave is made more cloudy by the admiration and sympathy with which she describes the Verneys. They are, indeed, proud and snobbish. They do not understand the humiliation and degradation of slavery. But they are also brave and spirited, governed by a strong sense of honor. The Verneys are representatives of a way of life that combines true hospitality with graceful living. Neither the colonel nor Sir Charles Carew is a villain.

Johnston resolves her divided loyalties by crushing the revolt before it erupts, on the one hand, and assuring pardon for the Puritan leaders, on the other. Following the discovery of the conspiracy, the Puritans are imprisoned, but Luiz Sebastian has meanwhile made an alliance between the Blacks and discontented Indian tribes. In the face of an even more dangerous uprising, Cavalier and Puritan unite at Landless' urging to defend the plantation. The attack is successfully repelled, though with great loss of life. All the surviving Puritans, except their leader, Landless, are pardoned. The manner in which Miss Johnston resolves her conflict reminds one of the contrived and ineffective conclusion of Page's *John Marvel, Assistant*. The Negroes are beaten down and the Puritans conveniently pardoned, but the question of the morality of slave labor, which underlies the conflict, is not satisfactorily answered. At the end of this portion of her novel, both noble-minded Puritans and Africans remain enslaved.

Johnston has clearly dropped the broader implications of her freedom-versus-slavery and Puritan-versus-Cavalier conflicts. In the final third of her novel, however, she is much more effective in dealing with these conflicts on a person-to-person level. In this concluding section, Landless escapes from prison and, aided by his Indian friend, Monakatocka, successfully finds and rescues Patricia, who has been abducted by enemy Indians during the attack on her father's plantation. In the wilderness, far from corrupt human institutions and their associated prejudices, Patricia is forced to assess Landless as a human being, not as a Puritan or a slave. Dependence changes to gratitude and gratitude, finally, into love.

Johnston's ending is an honest and effective one. The love between Landless and Patricia is more powerful than all the fear and mistrust that human misunderstanding can devise. Yet such a love can only flourish in the wide forest, far from Jamestown. When the lovers finally make contact with the forces of Governor Berkeley, Colonel Verney, grateful to Landless for saving his daughter's life, offers him the choice of returning to Jamestown for execution or remaining behind alone in a hostile wilderness. With winter setting in, the colonel leads the heart-stricken Patricia back to civilization, leaving Landless alone to face near-certain death. The spiritual reunion of these lovers, Johnston implies, can only be gained through death.

Prisoners of Hope furnishes an interesting contrast with *The Cavaliers of Virginia*. Both novels are structured around the conflict between Cavalier and Puritan. In Caruthers' novel the conflict is illusory because the Roundhead hero, Nathaniel Bacon, is in reality a Cavalier figure. Such is not the case in Johnston's novel. Godfrey Landless does illustrate some of the Cavalier principles, notably his reverential worship of Patricia. In the wilderness, Johnston remarks, he "cared for her, tended her, guarded her, served her as if he had been a knight-errant out of a romance, and she a distressed princess" (337). Yet in spite of this Cavalier devotion, Landless consistently exhibits other traits, such as seriousness and piety, which definitely set him off from pure Cavalier types such as Sir Charles Carew. Indeed, the tragic and emotional ending of the novel depends on Landless' remaining an anti-Cavalier spokesman throughout the novel. The effectiveness of Johnston's conclusion testifies to Landless' consistency as a spokesman for liberty and for the dignity of the human spirit.

Mary Johnston's first novel is a curious work. It fails to provide a complete analysis of the conflict between Cavalier and Puritan, aristocrat and slave. Yet through the love of Landless and Patricia it makes an effective statement about the limitations and dehumanization of social institutions. It contains an important Cavalier element that is colorfully and sympathetically projected. Yet its hero is not a Cavalier. Mary Johnston, in this early novel, clearly had not developed the detachment necessary to view Virginia's past with complete objectivity. But she seems to be moving beyond the simple stereotypes that Caruthers, Cooke, and Page had employed before her. One cannot completely agree with Lawrence Nelson that her early novels successfully convey "a sense of actual and meaningful history."[60] But even at this early point in her career, she was depicting Virginia's past more meaningfully than any Virginia writer since George Tucker.

In 1900, two years after *Prisoners of Hope*, Mary Johnston published her most popular historical romance, *To Have and to Hold*. This novel's enormous appeal was undoubtedly due to Miss Johnston's skillful blending of romantic characterization with a highly melodramatic plot. Yet it was decidedly more realistic in its presentation of scenic detail than *Prisoners of Hope* had been. Set in 1621 during the difficult early years of Virginia's settlement, *The Have and to Hold* clearly conveys the rude, semicivilized nature of the colony in the early seventeenth century. Jamestown, for the first time in Virginia romance fic-

60. Lawrence G. Nelson, "Mary Johnston and the Historical Imagination," in Rinaldo Simonini, Jr. (ed.), *Southern Writers: Appraisals in Our Time* (Charlottesville, 1964), 76.

tion, is simply described as a haphazard collection of small cottages, protected from Indian attack by a frail wooden palisade. There are no palaces, and no carriages roll through its streets. Unlike Caruthers, Johnston does not seek to transform the colonial capital into a minia-ture replica of London. In a similarly realistic manner she describes the typical plantation home as a roughly hewn wooden structure, contain-ing only a few small windows and separated from the surrounding for-ests by a log wall.

Even more significant than her descriptions of Jamestown and of the river plantations is Johnston's account of the colony's early settlement. In *To Have and to Hold* Virginia is not simply a haven for Cavaliers; it is a melting pot, combining all types of people from all walks of life. In-cluded among its population are "ancient planters, Smith's men, Dale's men, tenants and servants . . . negroes, Paspaheghs, French vignerons, Dutch sawmill men, Italian glassworkers." On such a rough and dan-gerous frontier women are in short supply and in great demand. The novel opens with the arrival of a cargo of young women, imported to provide brides for the hundreds of lonely bachelor planters. The young women are not, it is true, of noble birth. But as John Rolfe observes, "Beggars must not be choosers. The land is new and must be peopled, nor will those who come after us look too curiously into the lineage of those to whom a nation owes its birth."[61]

Nevertheless, in spite of these interesting touches of scenic realism, the tone of *To Have and to Hold* is as romantic as that of *Prisoners of Hope*. The aristocratic ideal is quickly established through the main characters. The novel's hero, Ralph Percy, is a member of the ancient and noble Percy family and is a cousin of the powerful Earl of Northum-berland. Memories of England carry Ralph back to "the old grey manor house" with the "imperious elder brother" who strode "to and fro among his hounds." Percy travels to Jamestown to choose a bride from among the newly arrived ship's collection of women. He falls immediately in love with and marries on the spot a young girl who, though her enroll-ment in that company of women proclaims her "meanly born," carries

61. Mary Johnston, *To Have and to Hold* (New York, 1900), 58, 5.

herself "as of blood royal." This haughty beauty later reveals herself to her new husband as Jocelyn Leigh, a ward of King James who had fled to Virginia to escape the vile attentions of the king's current favorite, Lord Carnel. Percy's instinctive attraction toward the highborn Jocelyn indicates that Johnston subscribed to the Virginia romancer's traditional belief in the mystic affinity of refined bloods.

The remainder of *To Have and to Hold* chronicles Jocelyn's slowly developing love for Ralph and his heroic efforts to prevent Lord Carnel from taking the object of his passion back to England. The reader is carried from Jamestown to the Spanish Main and back to a Virginia beset by murderous Indian attacks. By the end of this breathtaking action, Ralph has successfully defended his love from the wicked Carnel, upholding in the process the highest truths of chivalric love. At one point in the narrative, Jocelyn, obsessed with guilt for having married Percy and for having exposed him to the rage of both Carnel and the Crown, begs Ralph to despise her. "What is mine is yours," he answers. "It's little beside my sword and my name. The one is naturally at my wife's service; for the other, I have had some pride in keeping it untarnished. It is now in your keeping as well as my own. I do not fear to leave it there, madam." [62]

To Have and to Hold is in many ways a less interesting novel than *Prisoners of Hope*. In spite of its greater surface realism, it does not provide the thought-provoking analysis of slavery and of indentured servitude. There is no real tension between aristocratic and nonaristocratic perspectives because the main characters uniformly represent and uphold the aristocratic code. The happy ending is conventional, without the complexity of the ending of *Prisoners of Hope*. American readers in 1900, however, obviously preferred a more conventional romantic history.

Mary Johnston followed *To Have and to Hold* with other successful historical romances, including *Audrey* (1902), *Sir Mortimer* (1904), and *Lewis Rand* (1908). It was in her two-volume novelistic history of the Civil War, however, that she revealed her highest creative energy.

62. *Ibid.,* 81.

The Long Roll (1911) centers on the military career of Stonewall Jackson, beginning with the general's earliest campaigns—battles which earned him the epithet of "fool Tom" Jackson—and ending with his accidental death in the Wilderness and his hero's burial in Richmond. *Cease Firing* (1912) surveys the fighting in the Deep South, beginning with the siege of Vicksburg and continuing through General Joseph Johnston's retreat to Atlanta and Sherman's destructive march to the sea. The panoramic action ends in the spring of 1865 in the trenches of Petersburg. Against this sweeping scenic background of battles, sieges, and retreats, Johnston presents the individual dramas of the southern people gripped by the forces of war. She focuses on the Cleave family of Three Oaks Plantation in Botetourt County and the Cary family of Greenwood Plantation in Albemarle County.

Lawrence G. Nelson has called these two novels Johnston's finest achievement, "the completest and most authentic embodiment of the Southern Myth."[63] Few contemporary readers of her novels would dispute this assessment. But *The Long Roll* and *Cease Firing* are not simply subjective defenses of the South's attempted secession. Indeed, the author, speaking through her characters, frequently judges the war as folly, folly for both the North and the South. As Fauquier Cary observes near the end of the conflict in *Cease Firing*, war is never a realistic way to settle disputes. "It is not, and it never was, and it never will be. And that despite the glamour and the cry of 'Necessity!'"[64]

Johnston's tendency to judge the Civil War as a pathetic product of man's spiritual limitations is counterbalanced, however, by the opposing urge toward a nostalgic "if." "If" Jackson had moved forward more resolutely in the Seven Days Campaign, "if" Lee had kept Stuart closer to him when he invaded Pennsylvania, the South, she implies, might have won the war. "It is not overdone," writes Sheldon Van Auken, "it never obtrudes itself, but the little nostalgic theme of 'what might have been' runs through the books, particularly *Cease Firing*."[65]

63. Nelson, "Mary Johnston and the Historical Imagination," 89.
64. Mary Johnston, *Cease Firing* (Boston, 1912), 448.
65. Sheldon Van Auken, "The Southern Historical Novel in the Early Twentieth Century," *Journal of Southern History*, XIV (1948), 181.

In the final analysis, nostalgia dominates the tone of Johnston's account of the destruction of antebellum southern culture. The nostalgia is, indeed, muted. And the defense of the southern way of life is not presented without certain critical qualifications. Yet the author clearly venerates the Old South of vanished splendor. More important, she identifies its most basic values with the aristocratic tradition. Johnston's Confederates, it is true, are not all planters. Included among her cast of characters are Billy Maydew, a small farmer; Allan Gold, a country schoolteacher; and Steve Dagg, a poor-white scoundrel who runs away from battle and complains more than he fights. The major roles in this Civil War drama, however, are reserved for the planter-aristocrats. The men of this upper class—the Cleaves and Carys, the Pages, Carters, and Lees—lead the South into battle and demonstrate by the high courage and nobility of character they display under stress of battle the ideals for which the South is fighting.

In *The Long Roll* and *Cease Firing*, Johnston combines the chivalric Cavalier code with realistic descriptions of an essentially modern war. Cooke and Page had identified the Cavalier ideal with the Confederate war hero, but neither writer had managed to convey the solid texture of a war in which men suffer painfully and die horribly. Death does not always come cleanly and neatly with the thrust of a sword or the impact of a bullet for Johnston's soldiers. This is how she describes in *The Long Roll* the decimation of the Confederate batteries at the bloody battle of Malvern Hill: "At the first gun gunner No. 1, ramming home a charge, was blown into fragments; at the second the arm holding the sponge staff was severed from gunner No. 3's shoulder. A great shell, bursting directly over the third, killed two men and horribly mangled others." Johnston takes the reader into the desperately overcrowded hospitals in Richmond, detailing the reeking heat, the "strong smell of human effluvia, of sweat-dampened clothing, of blood and powder grime."[66]

In Johnston's novels war is indeed hell. Yet this brutal reality does

---

66. Mary Johnston, *The Long Roll* (New York, 1911), 520, 445, hereinafter cited in the text by page number only.

not undermine the credibility of the author's chivalric heroes. The Cleaves and the Carys prove convincingly through their actions that the Cavalier qualities of courage, honor, and *noblesse oblige* are as essential to nineteenth-century infantry charges and trench warfare as they had been in eighteenth-century duels and Indian fights.

Johnston's Cavalier Confederates are both brave and self-sacrificing. During Jackson's 1861 winter march into the Alleghenies, Will Cleave, whose sister has given him a thick comforter to sleep under, notices a fellow soldier limping along the frozen road with no shoes. Will promptly cuts his comforter into two pieces and gives it to his unfortunate comrade to wrap around his feet. The author underscores the social significance of Will's action by drawing a pointed contrast between his station in life and that of the recipient of the gift, who is a store clerk. Edward Cary is the central character of *Cease Firing*, who demonstrates his nobility of character by rejecting a commission and enlisting in the army as a private. His Uncle Fauquier discovers him one day behind the lines cutting firewood. Fauquier asks Edward why he does not have his body servant, Jeames, do such menial chores. "Why, you see," the young aristocrat answers, "it hurts his pride—and, beside, some one must cook. Jeames cooks" (75). Imagine, his uncle later comments, "Phoebus Apollo swincking for Mars!" (75). Mary Johnston clearly believed that the master-slave relationship, at least in Virginia, was primarily characterized by the kindness and the sensitivity of refined masters.

As in the novels of her nineteenth-century predecessors, Johnston's Cavaliers are supported by the high-minded and pure plantation lady. The heroines of these novels, like those of Thomas Nelson Page's stories, are transformed by the war from tender and appealingly flirtatious belles into women with courage and wills of iron. Margaret Cleave in *The Long Roll* most effectively expresses the wartime creed of the Virginia lady. "War is war," she says, "and we must all stand it. We must stand it with just as high and exquisite a courage as we can muster. If we can add a gaiety that isn't thoughtless, so much the better! We've got to do it for Virginia and for the South" (101).

In each of these novels, the love affair between the Cavalier hero and his maiden is a major element of the plot. In *The Long Roll* the battle-grounds of the Shenandoah Valley, Richmond, and Fredericksburg provide a dramatic setting for the development of the romance between Richard Cleave and Judith Cary. The complications which threaten to destroy this relationship are not resolved until the end of *Cease Firing*. Meanwhile in this second novel Johnston develops and brings to a tragic conclusion a love affair between Edward Cary and his lovely Creole bride from Belle Island Plantation, Désirée Gaillard. In both of these love stories the lady resides in the realms of the ideal, and her Cavalier lover approaches her like a worshipful suppliant. Richard Cleave expresses precisely the traditional devotional tone of the aristocratic suitor. "Judith, Judith, how lovely are you!" he declares. "I have seen you always, always! . . . Only I called it 'vision,' 'ideal.' At the top of every deed I have your eyes; from the height of every thought you have beckoned further!" (219). The pronouncements of Johnston's hero sound remarkably like those of Caruthers', Cooke's, and Page's beau ideals.

The larger-than-life dimensions of Johnston's Cavalier heroes are most evident in the author's characterization of the man whose military genius impels the South to victory after victory in *The Long Roll*— General Stonewall Jackson. In many ways General Jackson would seem a strange choice of heroes. An unostentatious, pietistic, and rigidly Presbyterian man who hails from the Valley, Jackson appears at first glance to be more plebeian than patrician, more Puritan than Cavalier. Yet, as in John Esten Cooke's *Surry of Eagle's Nest*, beneath the homespun exterior the reader eventually discovers the heart of a pure Virginia gentleman. Stonewall is actuated by an instinctive courtesy and a profound veneration for individual honor. His code is clearly the code of the Cavalier.

Specific plot incidents bring Jackson's chivalric code into focus. Marching his army toward a second meeting with Federal troops at Manassas, the general bivouacs his troops near the Wilson house, a country home surrounded by an ornamental fence. In spite of torrential rains during the night, Jackson orders that not one pale of the fence be touched for firewood. The next morning, however, he discovers one panel missing. He consequently orders the arrest of all six of his regimental colonels, until they agree to pay for the cost of the entire fence in gold dollars.

It is hard to reconcile Jackson, the coldly efficient battle strategist, with Jackson, the idealistic general who entertains such an acutely refined notion of honor and of respect for private property. Yet Stonewall is both pragmatist and idealist. He is a man capable both of marching his men until they drop from exhaustion and of halting an entire army to allow a mother to find her son and give him a basket of food and clothing. He is a military genius, but he is also a Cavalier, capable of making noble but impractical decisions. The faintly quixotic *noblesse oblige* which he occasionally exhibits recalls Thomas Nelson Page's Confederate heroes.

In the course of this first novel Jackson is transfigured by war. "The awkward figure," writes Johnston in *The Long Roll*, "took on a stalwart grace. . . . The inner came outward, the atmosphere altered, and the man was seen as he rode in the plane above" (84). Jackson becomes a resident of the southern pantheon of mythical heroes and a representative of all the best values that Johnston associates with the South's antebellum golden age. Like John Esten Cooke, Mary Johnston believes that the tragic death of this great man points toward the inevitable destruction of that prewar culture, a destruction that is pathetically and effectively delineated in *Cease Firing*. The sad words of old Aunt Lucy Cary provide an effective obituary for the Old South: "I have lived out of a gold world into an iron one." [67]

With the publication of her war novels, Mary Johnston proved herself a strongly imaginative, as well as a skillful and competent creator of historical romance; yet by 1912 she seems to have been undergoing many inner spiritual changes—changes which dictated a new direction for her fiction. In 1913 her reading public received with surprise and puzzlement a new novel, entitled *Hagar*, which indicated the new form her fiction would take. Unlike her previous novels, the action of *Hagar* was placed in the contemporary period. It was not a romance. It dealt

67. Johnston, *Cease Firing*, 111.

instead with the very practical problem of how a turn-of-the-century woman fights to resist society's limited definition of what a lady should be and to win the right to choose her own destiny.

Hagar is an interesting novel, but it is not a good one. The question of the proper role for contemporary women dominates the novel, but it is discussed and verbalized more than it is effectively embodied in a swiftly moving and interesting plot. However, even though it is not an engrossing novel, *Hagar*'s emphasis on the primacy of inner growth indicates a movement toward what Edward Wagenknecht and Lawrence Nelson have called Johnston's mystical transcendentalism. Johnston seemed to believe that man's spiritual growth depended on his discovery of the Godhead within him and of the unity of this inner spirit with the spirit which dwelled within external nature. She further believed that this spiritual growth was inevitable and that in the future it would become a progressively greater factor in human actions. "We are growing," says Hagar; "we are changing—we feel a strange new life within us—we are passing out, we are coming in—we need a new word."[68] Unfortunately, as Hagar herself admits, the new word has not yet been coined. The world is still awaiting the time when a progressive growth of spiritual insight will transform man's corrupt and inadequate social institutions.

Transcendental spiritual meditations were not what Mary Johnston's readers wanted. They wanted more of the exciting and well-written historical novels that had made her famous. But Johnston was responding to her own inner muse. Her spiritualism reached its climax in three novels that appeared in successive years: *Foes* (1918), *Michael Forth* (1919), and *Sweet Rocket* (1920). In the twenties she returned to the historical novel, but as Lawrence Nelson clearly demonstrates, she had lost her large following.[69] Changing literary tastes and the poor reception of her mystical transcendental novels combined to deprive her of a substantial audience for later works, such as *The Great Valley* (1926).

A critical assessment of Mary Johnston's historical novels yields a

68. Mary Johnston, *Hagar* (Boston, 1913), 294.
69. Nelson, "Mary Johnston and the Historical Imagination," 86–88.

mixed judgment. They betray, on one hand, a pronounced tendency toward enshrining the Virginia Cavalier, thereby placing the author in the tradition of Cooke and Page. But they also reveal flashes of vivid realism and, in *Prisoners of Hope*, a provocatively developed, though unresolved conflict between Cavalier and Yankee traditions that projects Johnston's fiction beyond the romantic plantation genre. Johnston serves as a link in Virginia fiction between the essentially unreflective romanticism of those writers who preceded her and the more ironic and penetrating approach of a new generation of writers who were to follow her.

SIX

The Cavalier Enters the Twentieth Century

CABELL AND GLASGOW

In 1904, just six years after the publication of Thomas Nelson Page's *Red Rock*, a novel entitled *The Deliverance* by a young Virginia novelist named Ellen Glasgow appeared in bookstores across the country. In many ways reminiscent of *Red Rock*, *The Deliverance* was set in the poverty-stricken rural landscape of postbellum Virginia; it depended on melodramatic action to sustain the reader's interest; and its plot featured the fraudulent seizure of a large plantation from its aristocratic owners by an unscrupulous former overseer. Yet there were significant differences between the way Page and Glasgow handled their subjects. Unlike Page, Glasgow did not emphasize the wickedness and deceitfulness of carpetbaggers and scalawags. Instead, she analyzed the

213

way aristocratic Virginians responded to the destruction of their ante-bellum social and economic order.

The Deliverance focuses on the Blake family, a family that has lost nearly all of its great plantation during the hard Reconstruction years and that now lives in what was once the overseer's cabin. The family is presided over by the matriarchic Mrs. Blake, a blind and invalid widow whose eyesight failed just before the end of the Civil War. Fearful that the truth will crush their mother, the children weave a tapestry of lies and evasions for her, insulating her from the knowledge that the Civil War is over, that she no longer lives in the big house, and that her im-poverished family must stint and struggle to provide her with the port, the fresh chicken, and the other delicacies that she takes for granted.

Ellen Glasgow was clearly aware of the ironic symbolic implications of Mrs. Blake. In her Preface to the 1929 edition of the novel she wrote that the blind woman was emblematic of Virginia and of the South, "unaware of the changes about them, clinging with passionate fidelity to the empty ceremonial forms of tradition."[1] It is an added irony that the illusions of a woman who lives entirely in the past are sustained with tremendous sacrifice by children who have, at best, a hazy recol-lection both of the antebellum splendors that Mrs. Blake tirelessly evokes and of the war which destroyed this idyllic past.

The Deliverance is neither a major nor a minor masterpiece. Yet in spite of its melodramatic excesses and its absence of subtle characteriza-tion, it is a considerably more interesting novel than *Red Rock*. For the first time in Virginia fiction since *Swallow Barn*, irony is consciously employed to enforce a distance between writer and subject and to pro-vide the perspective for a critical examination of the bondage of Virgin-ians to their past. Compared with later southern writers, Glasgow's irony is not terribly harsh, and her critical attitude toward her native state seems rather qualified and tentative. Yet in 1904 ironic detach-ment of any kind was rare in southern writing, and Glasgow's deter-mined break with the romantic tradition of Cooke and Page was a sig-nificant moment in Virginia fiction and in southern fiction as well. It

1. Ellen Glasgow, *The Deliverance: A Romance of the Virginia Tobacco Fields* (1904; rpr. New York, 1929), vi.

should not be surprising that she was widely hailed in the opening decades of this century as the pathfinder of modern southern literature, a courageous writer who had dared to realistically examine her native state. Glasgow willingly accepted this role. She was determined, she wrote in a book of essays, to inject blood and irony into southern writing: "Blood it needed because Southern culture had strained too far away from its roots in the earth; it had grown thin and pale; it was satisfied to exist on borrowed ideas, to copy instead of create. And irony is an indispensable ingredient of the critical vision; it is the safest antidote to sentimental decay."[2]

Ellen Glasgow's determination to bring blood and irony to her analysis of Virginia indicates that significant changes of attitude toward the Old Dominion's legendary past and its sacrosanct traditions were taking place among many Virginians of intelligence and perception at the turn of the century. Glasgow's novels were the products of a penetrating mind which understood that important economic, social, and political changes had occurred in Virginia since the end of the Civil War and were continuing to occur. Perhaps the most significant of these changes was the profound shift in the attitude of the Old Dominion's conservative business and political leaders toward industrialization.

As Jack Maddex observes, Virginia conservatives—Confederate officers prominent among them—quickly learned the lesson of the Civil War. Humiliating defeat and Reconstruction taught them that their state would have to remodel itself along northern capitalist lines if it was to repair the ravages of war and reattain the prosperity it had known in the eighteenth century. For some of these men industrialization was viewed as a positive good; for others it was an inevitable and necessary evil. "However motivated," Maddex writes, "they co-operated to bring Virginia into the mainstream of Gilded Age America."[3]

Northern capital was badly needed to rebuild the Old Dominion, and by 1880 outside investments were flowing into Virginia in substan-

2. Ellen Glasgow, *A Certain Measure: An Interpretation of Prose Fiction* (New York, 1929), 28, hereinafter cited in the text by page number only.
3. Jack P. Maddex, Jr., *The Virginia Conservatives, 1867–1879: A Study in Reconstruction Politics* (Chapel Hill, 1970), 276.

tial amounts. Virginius Dabney notes that in response to this new economic northern invasion "impecunious local citizens . . . often welcomed [Northern investors] with open arms and loud hosannahs." Millions of dollars were poured into the coal mines of southwest Virginia, and soon coal trains of the Norfolk and Western Railroad were rumbling across the state to the expanding port of Norfolk. Norfolk and Richmond experienced substantial growth, and Roanoke became the state's newest metropolis, growing in six years from the hamlet of Big Lick into western Virginia's first small city. Tidewater Virginia's urban growth was stimulated by northern industrialist, Collis P. Huntington, who bought the Chesapeake and Ohio Railroad, extending it to the small town of Newport News and building coal and freight piers there. Huntington also established the Newport News Shipbuilding and Dry Dock Company, soon to be one of the state's major employers.[4]

Winds of change were sweeping through Virginia. The wealth of the state was more and more being concentrated in the mines of the southwest, in the ports of Hampton Roads, and in the factories and businesses of Richmond and Roanoke. This shift of economic power from plantation to city necessarily produced important social changes. As Douglas Freeman astutely observed, by 1900 a Confederate widow of the old school might still wear black and mourn the Lost Cause and its valiant dead alone in her upstairs bedroom, but downstairs her children and grandchildren were receiving new callers, the names of most of whom the widow could not recognize. This is the way Freeman described the shifting tone of Virginia social life at the beginning of the twentieth century:

> Names and blood still count in Virginia, but lack of them handicaps a man less in acquiring social position than possession of them aids him in preserving it. A few who have ancestry and no money keep their place; many who have money and no ancestry make their place. Even in Richmond, where the doors of the Monday German once were unlocked only for those who had as

4. Dabney, *Virginia, the New Dominion*, 405, 406.

many quarterings as an officer in the bodyguard of a Bourbon, the daughter of the rich newcomer always is invited after two or three years and, a little later, her mother and father. "He's rich" is now an apologia for many shortcomings.[5]

Yet though economic and social changes were beginning to reshape life in Virginia, the prevailing attitude of the state's ruling class toward the transformation of social structures that these changes heralded was one of denial. Well-bred Virginians thought it best to ignore the social implications of the advances of industry and commerce in their state. They resolutely insisted on the continued validity of the old moonlight-and-magnolia vision of the antebellum period, in spite of statistical evidence to the contrary. It was more comforting to believe that the Old Dominion's rigid social structure and its gracious manner of living had remained fundamentally unchanged.

As Paul Gaston has explained, there were definite advantages to be derived from this form of social and intellectual hypocrisy. The idea of the South as a stable and unchanging land governed by the noble principles of a landed aristocracy ironically encouraged industrial development and the influx of northern investment. The trappings of the Old South were thus used to legitimize the capitalistic ventures of the New South.[6] But in Virginia as in the rest of the South, if allegiance to the moonlight-and-magnolia myth had its advantages, it also forced southerners to ignore certain not-so-pleasing aspects of the Gilded Age. Virginians must have had a difficult time reconciling their exalted assessment of their commonwealth with the massive voting scandals which their newspapers headlined with depressing regularity during the last three decades of the nineteenth century and which persisted until the Constitution of 1902, promulgated by many high-principled Virginia gentlemen, effectively eliminated the need for voting fraud by disenfranchising nearly all black voters, as well as a substantial portion of

5. Douglas Southal Freeman, "Virginia: A Gentle Dominion," in Ernest Gruening (ed.), *The United States: A Symposium* (New York, 1924), 3–4.
6. Paul M. Gaston, *The New South Creed: A Study in Southern Mythmaking* (New York, 1970).

whites.[7] Residents of the state could not have been unaware of the speculative fever which periodically raged in booming western towns along the routes of the newly consolidated railroads. Lexington, Buena Vista, and Glasgow were the scenes of disastrous real estate busts that gave embarrassing testimony to the zeal with which many solid Virginia citizens pursued the fast buck. Fitzhugh Lee, nephew of sainted "Marse Robert," and other scions of the first families of Virginia lost or compromised their heretofore stainless reputations in such ventures.[8]

In spite of the fact that Virginia moved steadily during the postbellum period toward modeling its economy along northern lines, the gulf between myth and reality lay broader than ever at the turn of the century. By 1900, however, a new generation of writers had come of age. Removed in time from the passions of the Civil War and the bitterness of Reconstruction, they were able to measure the dimensions of this gulf with a more detached eye than their elders. James Branch Cabell, in a beautifully written essay included in *Let Me Lie*, suggests how Virginians of his and Ellen Glasgow's generation slowly became aware of the discrepancy between Edenic vision and mundane realities.

The Richmond of Cabell's youth remained the spiritual bastion of the Confederacy. On public occasions veterans of the war spoke "as to a paradise in which they had lived once upon a time, and in which there had been no imperfection, but only beauty and chivalry and contentment." Even for a small child, however, there were difficulties in matching the legend with the present-day reality. "Because," Cabell observed, "you lived in Richmond; and Richmond was not like Camelot. Richmond was a modern city, with sidewalks and plumbing and gas light and horse cars. . . . Damsels in green kirtles and fire-breathing dragons and champions in bright armor did not go up and down the streets of Richmond, but only some hacks and surreys, and oxcarts hauling tobacco." Moreover, as one grew older he slowly began to realize that his elders did not speak so enthusiastically about the Confederacy and its heroes "when they were just talking to one another in your father's

7. Allen W. Moger, *Virginia: Bourbonism to Byrd, 1870–1925* (Charlottesville, 1968), 181–202.

8. Dabney, *Virginia, the New Dominion*, 419–20.

drugstore, or in your mother's dining-room at Sunday night supper." Slowly the youth began to see that his elders were not really describing the real Confederacy or the real Richmond. They were molding a myth. "They were creating . . . in the same instant that they lamented the Old South's extinction, an Old South which had died proudly at Appomattox without ever having been smirched by the wear and tear of existence."[9]

Cabell's essay lucidly illustrates the unreconciled tension in Virginia at the turn of the century between dedication to progress and loyalty to the often stultifying traditions and myths of the past. Richard Gray describes this southern predicament, this pull-and-tug of past and present, as a kind of cultural schizophrenia. He goes on to observe that it ultimately provided the impetus for a literature concerned with the meaning and uses of history.[10] The profound shift of consciousness which occurred in the modern South and which enabled southern writers to exploit their region's internal tensions fictionally is examined by Allen Tate in a seminal essay called "A Southern Mode of Imagination." Tate interprets this shift as a movement from a traditional "rhetorical mode" of discourse, in which the virtues southerners cherished "were almost exclusively social and moral," to a "dialectical mode" of thinking, under the influence of which modern southern writers began to look beneath the surface of regional piety, to examine with a new kind of detachment both the South's complex present and its equally complex past.[11] However the change in southern mentality might be described or explained, it resulted in the first widespread expressions of serious southern literature.

It should not be surprising that Virginia produced the earliest writers of what was later to be termed the southern literary renascence. Cabell's and Glasgow's work preceded the post–World War I surge of southern writing by twenty years. There are two primary factors that

9. James Branch Cabell, "Almost Touching the Confederacy," in his *Let Me Lie: Being in the Main an Ethnological Account of the Remarkable Commonwealth of Virginia and the Making of Its History* (New York, 1947), 145, 147, 148–49, 153–54.

10. Gray, *The Literature of Memory*, 35–39.

11. Allen Tate, "A Southern Mode of the Imagination," in his *Collective Essays* (Denver, 1959), 554–68.

explain Virginia's significant early contributions to the southern renascence. First, more than any other southern state, the Old Dominion possessed an established literary tradition which the state's modern writers could use as a starting point, even if it was in their fiction a point of departure. Second, the economic changes that brought cultural trauma to the modern South came earliest to Virginia, which by 1900 was well embarked along the path of industrial and commercial development on the northern model. The deep discrepancy between myth and reality in the South was probably most in evidence in turn-of-the-century Richmond, the home of both Cabell and Glasgow.

Ellen Glasgow and James Branch Cabell were thus the first modern southern writers to examine their native state with an objectivity that would have been impossible for a previous generation. No doubt, this attitude of detachment was encouraged, in part, by the examples of the great realistic and naturalistic novelists of Europe and America. Glasgow placed herself firmly within the realistic tradition and saw herself as the champion of the principles of critical realism in the South. In *A Certain Measure* she described her struggle to educate herself as a young writer in a region dominated by sentimental literary tastes and for *The Voice of the People* (1900) claimed rather proudly, "So far as I am aware, this novel was the first work of genuine realism to appear in Southern fiction" (62).

In contrast to Ellen Glasgow, James Branch Cabell disdainfully rejected the prevailing spirit of realism and naturalism in the novel. In *Beyond Life* Cabell's fictional spokesman, John Charteris, defines realism as "the art of being superficial seriously"; and in *Smirt* naturalism is labeled "a very lusty bastard begotten upon realism with the phallus of agony." Cabell insisted on the right of the writer to omit, color, or even deny any facts that were not suitable to his purpose. Yet, as Arvin R. Wells has observed in his perceptive analysis, Cabell's romanticism has been widely misunderstood. He did not write in isolation from the contemporary literary context. His cynicism and his darker ironies reflect an understanding and a partial acceptance of the attitudes of Zola and Dreiser, and the background of his comedies is strongly formed by naturalistic assumptions.[12] Cabell's description of man in *Beyond Life* as a creature surrounded by an unceasingly gyrating and flowing universe, who adheres to the earth like a parasite to a "blown molecule," is a description with which neither Zola nor Dreiser would have quarreled. Both Glasgow and Cabell thus brought themselves into contact with the literary and philosophical theories of their day, and it is undeniable that their interaction with the contemporary intellectual milieu helped to shape their attitudes toward Virginia and its legendary past, even though in Cabell's case this interaction did not shape the form of the fiction.

But the desire of Glasgow and Cabell to treat Virginia's past with ironic detachment cannot entirely be explained by their willingness to open themselves to the perspectives of realism and naturalism. Realism had gained a foothold in this country shortly after the Civil War, some years before either Glasgow or Cabell was born. One might assume that young Virginia writers such as Thomas Nelson Page would have responded to the prevailingly realistic fictional currents of the 1870s and 1880s. Page's contemporaries, however, could never embrace these new modes. Born as they were before the Civil War, they remembered the agony of defeat and, more immediately, the humiliation and despair of Reconstruction. They could never free themselves from the compulsion to justify through the most effective means at their disposal the perfection of antebellum Virginia—of its plantation system, of its enslavement of the Negro, and of its ruling aristocracy. This justification was achieved in Page's novels and stories through character stereotypes and blatantly sentimental plots.

Unlike Page, Glasgow and Cabell had no personal memories of antebellum Virginia, the Civil War, or the grim days of Reconstruction. By the 1880s Virginia had accepted the fact of defeat and had begun its slow movement back into the Union. The movement away from the old agrarian plantation order to the new industrial-commercial order was nowhere more evident in the Old Dominion than in the Richmond of

12. Arvin R. Wells, *Jesting Moses: A Study in Cabellian Comedy* (Gainesville, Fla. 1962), 133.

Cabell and Glasgow's youth. As Cabell observed, Richmond was not Camelot but a modern city of gaslight, plumbing, and horsecars. Virginians of Cabell and Glasgow's generation were the first to find themselves free of the necessity of defending the old order because that order had been irredeemably destroyed before their births. The time was propitious for Virginia's writers to declare an imaginative declaration of independence, to cease simply enshrining the Old Dominion's past, and to use that mythical past as the basis of an examination of the relation between man and myth, of the nature, extent, and causes of human self-deception.

Ellen Glasgow and James Branch Cabell did declare their imaginative independence, but as we shall see, they were not entirely successful in removing themselves from the shadow of Virginia's legendary past. At the same time that they satirized the folly of blind submission to a dead tradition, their novels often tacitly affirmed the very articles of the code to which their characters blindly submitted themselves. This paradoxical attitude produced a thematic tension and an unresolved tone in the novels of both writers. Glasgow did not fully recognize the extent of her ambivalence toward the past, which, though it does not seriously weaken her best fiction, does suggest that she never completely committed herself to the implications of her realistic credo. One also detects in the tone of Cabell's contemporary Virginia novels an ironic understanding of the insufficiency of an antique social code counterbalanced by a deep repugnance for the modern attitudes which have supplanted it.

In the novels of both writers the tensions between present and past, myth and reality, are often focused with great intensity in the characterizations of their Cavaliers, or gentlemen, and an analysis of these gentlemen reveals much about the nature of the ambivalence of both writers.

JAMES BRANCH CABELL

Most of the works of James Branch Cabell seem to bear little relationship either to Virginia or to the South. Cabell is best known for a series of novels and stories collected in the eighteen-volume Storisende Edition entitled *The Biography of the Life of Manuel*. Four of these novels deal with the descendants of Manuel in turn-of-the-century Virginia. Most of them, however, take place in the imaginary land of Poictesme, a medieval kingdom vaguely situated in the southern part of France. In this highly fanciful setting Manuel and his descendants engage in fantastic exploits in which romance, magic, and supernatural elements figure prominently.

Of the Manuel series, *Jurgen* is the most famous, or infamous, its publication having aroused a national controversy over the issue of its obscenity. It was this novel that made Cabell the darling of the intelligentsia during the early twenties, attracting such disparate admirers as Joseph Hergesheimer, Carl Van Vechten, Sinclair Lewis, and H. L. Mencken. After a brief period of acclamation, however, his work suffered a severe loss of prestige. To the socially conscious critics of the 1930s, the novels seemed little more than meretricious romances, written primarily to appeal to whimsical tastes and escapist sentiments. Cabell's reputation has not been materially strengthened in the intervening decades. The efforts of Edward Wagenknecht, Edmund Wilson, and Louis D. Rubin have failed to reestablish a prominent place for him in modern American literature. Many teachers and critics would no doubt second the judgment of Oscar Cargill, delivered on Cabell back in 1941: "He is, beyond all shadow of a doubt, the most tedious person who has achieved high repute as a *literatus* in America."[13]

Today the consensus of those who continue to evaluate Cabell's work is that he is far from a tedious romancer. Among the more recent studies of his fiction, Arvin Wells's *Jesting Moses* has succeeded most convincingly in arguing Cabell's case as a serious writer with an encompassing world view.[14] According to Wells, Cabell's world view is predicated on the conviction that the universe is irrational and incomprehensible to man. In the face of the horrible chaos of matter man has no alternative but to dream and to create and worship his own fictions, which provide, if only for a short period of time, the illusion that the universe is meaningful and that man's existence is purposeful. Cabell's

13. Oscar Cargill, *Intellectual America: Ideas on the March* (New York, 1941), 495.
14. Wells, *Jesting Moses*, 9–23.

characters obstinately refuse to accept the ultimate reality of the natural world, and this obstinance exposes them to disillusionment when their dreams are inevitably smashed by reality or to failure when they understand that they can never completely realize their dreams. Yet the price man pays in shattered illusions is essential if he is to sustain that imaginative spark within him which is the quintessential mark of his humanness. No sooner has one network of illusions been ripped apart than man properly employs himself spinning another.

Cabell sees three attitudes variously dominating man's imagination through history. The chivalric attitude creates the illusion that man is God's special creature and that his purpose on earth consists of striving to accomplish his will. Manuel himself is such a chivalric figure. The gallant attitude accepts the fact that man can know nothing about the universe and offers the fiction that he can be happy on earth by avoiding speculations about his cosmic fate and concentrating exclusively on the pleasures of day-to-day living. The poetic attitude sees chaotic reality as the raw material for creative vision, to be shaped by the artist into lovely and harmonious fictions that can sustain the illusion of meaning and purpose.

All of these attitudes give man a sense of order and coherence; all of them come to dominate various periods of human history; and all of them eventually fail and are supplanted by newer visions. Yet momentarily they evoke the fullest expression of the human spirit. Cabell's world view is one of kindly and humane skepticism which understands the necessity for imaginative attitudes and for the myths which cluster around them at the same time as it realizes the ultimate inadequacy of these attitudes and myths. A passage from Cabell's novel, *The Cream of the Jest*, nicely captures this ambivalent attitude toward man, the dreamer:

> In short, to me this man seemed an inadequate kick-worthy creature, who had muddled away the only life he was quite certain of enjoying, in contemplation of a dream; and who had, moreover, despoiled the lives of others, too, for the dream's sake. To him the dream alone could matter—his proud assurance that life was not

a blind and aimless business, not all a hopeless waste and confusion; and that he, this gross weak animal, could be strong and excellent and wise, and his existence a pageant of beauty and nobility. To prove this dream was based on a delusion would be no doubt an enjoyable retaliation, for his being so unengaging to the eye and so stupid to talk to; but it would make the dream no whit less lively or less dear to him—or to the rest of us, either.[15]

Because he chose medieval Old World settings for most of his novels, Cabell's view of man as mythmaker and dreamer does not seem obviously connected to his being a Virginian growing up in late nineteenth-century Richmond. But as Louis D. Rubin has observed, Cabell's conception of his hero, Manuel, and of the myths which were attached to him after his death were directly related to his understanding of how the survivors of the Confederacy had created their own pantheon of demigods, including such heroes as Lee and Jackson. The myth of Manuel was made possible by Cabell's insights into the myth of the Confederacy.[16] Indeed, Cabell lived in an ideal place to observe the mythologizing of the Confederate heroes, for as he suggested in *Let Me Lie*, the process was pursued as intensely in the former Confederate capital as anywhere in the South.

Not only did Cabell come to understand the motives for the enshrinement of the South's heroes; he himself found it impossible to look at these men with complete objectivity. His essay on General Lee in *Let Me Lie* begins quietly and reasonably. Gradually, however, Cabell's admiration for Lee becomes more fervent as he praises Lee's refusal to capitalize his fame to make money, his choice of the presidency of a small Virginia college, and his decision not to write his memoirs. Finally, with a delicate mixture of reverence and irony, Cabell admits that he cannot describe Lee as he was, "as being a conscientious and somewhat ponderous, quiet-spoken and gray-bearded and stoop-shouldered

15. James Branch Cabell, *The Cream of the Jest: A Comedy of Evasions* (New York, 1917), 278–79.

16. Louis D. Rubin, *No Place on Earth: Ellen Glasgow, James Branch Cabell, and Richmond-in-Virginia* (Austin, 1973), 64–66.

Confederate veteran." Speaking directly to Lee, he confesses: "My blood warms to you, betrayingly; and reason, defeated by atavism, quits the field." [17]

Growing up in a defeated and impoverished region which had just struggled through the trauma of Reconstruction, Cabell was perceptive enough to understand and to sympathize with the deep need of southerners for order and coherence that the myths of the Confederacy satisfied. He translated this understanding into his *Life of Manuel* and gave it fullest expression in *The Silver Stallion*. Here Manuel becomes, after his death, the Christlike redeemer of Poictesme who, according to the eyewitness account of the young Jurgen, does not die, but ascends directly to heaven. Cabell observes in the Preface to his novel that it does not matter that none of the various stories of Manuel's miraculous exploits was true. The redeemer myth served a need, just as did the myth of the Confederacy.

Three of Cabell's novels carry the imaginative quests of the Manuel series into contemporary Virginia. *The Cords of Vanity* describes the efforts of Robert Etheridge Townsend to live gallantly in the Old Dominion; *The Cream of the Jest* presents the artistic quest through the writer, Felix Kennaston; *The Rivet in Grandfather's Neck* depicts the aristocratic Rudolph Musgrave's attempt to live according to the chivalric ideal. Of these three novels, *The Rivet in Grandfather's Neck* is most germane to the study of the Cavalier figure because the notion of chivalry embodied in the principal character of this novel most closely approximates the qualities which Virginia's romantic writers traditionally ascribed to their aristocratic heroes. An analysis of Rudolph Musgrave indicates just how far Cabell had moved away from the simple adulatory treatment of the Cavalier, but it also suggests the ambivalence with which he regarded a character type that had become by the twentieth century increasingly outmoded and irrelevant.

The Rivet in Grandfather's Neck is subtitled *A Comedy of Limitations*. The title of the novel comes from Hans Christian Andersen's tale about the china chimney-sweep and shepherdess who elope from their

17. James Branch Cabell, "General Lee of Virginia," in his *Let Me Lie*, 178.

parlor table and climb high up the chimney but, frightened by the vastness of the world outside, creep silently back to their original home. To Rudolph Musgrave every man, like a china figurine, has a rivet or two in his neck. In this novel the rivet comes to stand for everything that is inflexible in the human spirit; it carries both positive and negative connotations. Thus, it prevents "too frequent nodding and too cowardly a compromise with baseness," but it also prevents a man from doing something because that something is contrary to his nature.[18]

Cabell's novel, however, is not only a comedy of limitations. As the writer pointed out in *Preface to the Past*, it is also "a comedy of words which serve as fetishes, as anodynes, and as intoxicants, in the while that reality is resolutely not faced."[19] In Rudolph Musgrave, Cabell presents a character who consistently defies reality in both word and deed. Musgrave, lineal head of the Musgraves of Matoctin, represents one of Lichfield's (Richmond's) oldest and most respected families. He supports himself and his sister through his job as librarian and corresponding secretary of the Lichfield Historical Association, and he supplements this income, as Cabell did himself for a number of years, by conducting genealogical research "directed mostly toward the rehabilitation of ambiguous pedigrees" (19–20). Trim and handsome for his years, affable and polished in social converse, he lives his life in strict adherence to the Cavalier code of his ancestors.

For Rudolph, life properly consists of a series of noble gestures, and in the course of his life he succeeds in making two great sacrifices. First, he allows Lichfield society to believe that he is the third party in the Pendomer divorce case. He assumes the blame for Jack Charteris, novelist, gallant, philanderer, and blackguard, who is married to Anne, Rudolph's ideal woman—the only woman, he tells himself, that he has ever loved. He sacrifices his reputation so that Anne will not be hurt by the knowledge of her husband's infidelity. His second great sacrifice comes after he has won the heart of his beautiful young cousin, Patricia, from an English nobleman. On the eve of the announcement of their

18. James Branch Cabell, *The Rivet in Grandfather's Neck: A Comedy of Limitations* (New York, 1915), 51–52, hereinafter cited in the text by page number only.

19. James Branch Cabell, *Preface to the Past* (New York, 1936), 192.

engagement, Patricia's former childhood sweetheart, Joe Parkinson, returns to Lichfield and for the moment recaptures the girl's fickle affections. Rudolph, believing that Patricia loves the younger man, seizes the occasion of his own engagement supper to toast the marriage of Patricia and Joe. The nobility of this gesture is somewhat diminished when Patricia changes her mind again and marries Rudolph.

Although there is an undeniable quality of nobility in Musgrave's actions, Cabell cannot resist taking some swipes at his major character. These sacrifices, Cabell tells us, are distinctly pleasing to Rudolph. The grander the gesture, the greater the sacrifice, the greater the pleasure he derives from performing it. Rudolph cherishes his nobility and his selflessness, just as he cherishes his hopeless passion for the ideal Anne. With delightful irony Cabell slowly removes the obstacles between Rudolph and his ideal until finally, with Patricia and John dead and with Anne's own illusions of the faithfulness of her husband shattered, he must face the fact that he really does not want to marry her. "I belong to Patricia," he finally confesses to Anne. "Upon the whole, I am glad that I belong to Patricia; for Patricia and what Patricia meant to me was the one vital thing in a certain person's rather hand-to-mouth existence" (351). Musgrave seems instinctively to realize that to embrace the ideal would be disastrous for him. Wisely and prudently he retreats to the imperfect, earthly, but comfortable memory of Patricia. His action recalls that of Manuel in *Figures of Earth*, who, upon the possession of each fair and seemingly unattainable princess, turns away from his object of worship and eventually chooses his ugly, prosaic, hectoring wife, Niafer. For Musgrave, as for the Wizard, Miramon, "He is wiser that knows the shadow makes lovely the substance."[20]

Musgrave's life is completely dominated by illusions of one sort or another, and he resolutely ignores anything in life that conflicts with these illusions. He refuses to face the fact that his sister is an alcoholic; he will not believe that his Negro maid, Virginia, is anything less than a loyal and loving family servant; and he cannot accept any publicly voiced criticism of his society. The cynic Jack Charteris tellingly labels life in

20. James Branch Cabell, *Figures of Earth: A Comedy of Appearances* (1921; rpr. New York, 1926), 22–23.

Lichfield tragic because "the most pathetic tragedy in life is to get nothing in particular out of it." To this observation Musgrave stoutly replies, "For my part, I don't see what you are driving at" (162).

Rudolph's folly is partly qualified by an inner awareness of the futility of his life and the impotency of the code to which he so strictly adheres. At one point he confesses to Patricia the uselessness of gentlemen of his type: "Ah, we may prate of our superiority to the rest of the world,—and God knows we do!—but, at bottom, we are worthless. We are worn out, I tell you! We are effete and stunted in brain and will power, and the very desire of life is gone out of us! We are contented simply to exist in Lichfield" (57). At the end of the novel Musgrave surveys his life from his deathbed and delivers this final judgment: "Rudolph Musgrave's life on earth was ending now—the only life that he would ever have on earth—and it had never risen to the plane of seeming even to Rudolph Musgrave a really important transaction on Rudolph Musgrave's part" (366).

In Rudolph Musgrave, Cabell presents a portrait of human limitations—a man who is a prey to stupidity, blindness, and folly, who is partially aware of his faults but is unable to rectify them. Yet Musgrave embodies as well those characteristics which Cabell finds most admirable in human nature—courage, fortitude, and the ability to endure. As imperfect as he may be, he comes off better in the end than Jack Charteris, a cynic who uses his gallant creed as a justification for his own selfish whims. Jack succeeds in persuading Patricia to leave her husband. Rudolph realizes that Jack does not really love Patricia, and he tries to dissuade him from committing a thoughtless act that will hurt other people. But Jack is characteristically immune to all moral considerations. Finally it is Musgrave's simple physical strength, founded on the moral certainty that Jack is committing an immoral act, that puts an end to the planned elopement.

Musgrave adheres with unswerving faith to illusions that are usually impractical and often stupid. Yet these illusions are at least a means of structuring his life. Rudolph's rivet does indeed make him an inflexible character, but at the same time it prevents him from falling into the selfishness and cowardice which characterize the life of Jack Charteris. Unlike Charteris, Musgrave can offer a limited justification for his life and his society: "We have been gentlefolk in spite of all, we have been true even in our iniquities to the traditions of our race. No, I cannot assert that these traditions always square with ethics or even with the Decalogue, for we have added a very complex Eleventh Commandment concerning honor. And for the rest, we have defiantly embroidered life, and indomitably we have converted the commonest happening of life into a comely thing. We have been artists if not artisans" (111). Given the limited and imperfect nature of man, the accomplishments of Rudolph Musgrave and of his race, though perhaps not praiseworthy, are hardly deserving of contempt.

Cabell's cosmic irony enables him both to satirize man's folly and to admire him for his incessant, though imperfect attempts to structure his life, to create order out of chaos. It is this complex point of view, compounded of irony and humor, sarcasm and pity, that enables him to analyze his modern-day Cavalier with a good degree of insight. Cabell's comment on Ellen Glasgow's aristocratic characters could equally be applied to Rudolph Musgrave: "Nor . . . can any known power take away, from the well-born Virginian, that ever-sustaining sense of moral uplift which he gets out of being chivalrous at no matter what costs to himself, or to other persons either. He thus lives, it may be, in a fool's paradise; yet I do not know that this earth of ours affords any other sort of paradise; and for this reason I adjudge a Virginian of the old school to be uncommonly lucky."[21]

The idea of chivalry that Cabell embodies in the character of Rudolph Musgrave is basically the same as that of his medieval knights of Poictesme. There is, however, one fundamental difference. Cabell's contemporary Cavalier is strictly limited in his actions by his contemporary milieu. Manuel is certainly no less flawed a human being than Rudolph. In fact, with the murder, the philandering, and the casual abandonment of women attributed to Manuel in *Figures of Earth*, it can be persuasively argued that he is a considerably less high-minded person than Musgrave. Yet Manuel is given the freedom to pursue his vision, and it

---

21. James Branch Cabell, "Miss Glasgow of Virginia," in his *Let Me Lie*, 250.

is this determined chivalric quest that in the end defines his character. In contrast, Musgrave and all of Cabell's contemporary Virginia aristocrats seem victims of an irresistible deterioration of personal strength. Arvin Wells gives a perceptive explanation for this decline. "The contemporary characters of the Biography," he writes, "live in a scientifically oriented world which allows little scope for the play of the imagination and which is destructive of the larger, bolder, illusions; consequently, not only have their lives not been subjected to the myth-making imagination, but they themselves have lost the power of believing in any but relatively mundane illusions. If Rudolph Musgrave's chivalry is timid and stiff-necked, it is because the roots of faith which once nourished the chivalric attitude have been cut away."[22] Cabell's aristocratic Virginian has degenerated into a modern-day Cavalier without a quest, a Cavalier *manqué*.

Cabell's emotional affinity drew him toward the chivalric gestures and the idealized concept of character embodied in the Cavalier, but his sense of reality told him that chivalric gestures in the twentieth century were antique leftovers from a bygone era. Thus in his characterization of Rudolph Musgrave he recognizes the strength and decency as well as the absurdity of his main character. His ambivalent feelings toward Musgrave are nicely counterpoised, but the weakness and uncertainty which mar Musgrave's chivalric stance suggest why Cabell preferred a medieval setting for most of his romances. He understood clearly enough what the modern age had done to the Cavalier, but he was not at all happy with the process. And so, rather than belabor the present, he made a strategic retreat into the past.

One might wonder why Cabell did not follow the example of Cooke and Page and retreat into Virginia's past. The answer to this question lies in the fact that he was not a mere sentimentalist. At the heart of his vision is an irony both comic and cosmic. As Cabell admitted in his essay on Lee, he was not completely free of the spell of Virginia's legendary past. Cabell's artistic instincts must have warned him away from Virginia toward an era which he could create entirely and which he

22. Wells, *Jesting Moses*, 20.

could control. Poictesme freed Cabell so that he could examine man, the mythmaker and creator of beautiful illusions, with both sympathy and bemused detachment. Such a finely balanced tone might have been impossible for him had he chosen to work with Virginia's flesh-and-blood heroes.

Looking over the whole of James Branch Cabell's work one would have to disagree with those who judge him a trivial concocter of shallow fantasies. He did write too much; but the best of his novels—*Figures of Earth, The Silver Stallion, Jurgen, The High Place, The Cream of the Jest, The Rivet in Grandfather's Neck*—are perceptive analyses of the confrontation of man's illusions with reality that can still be read today with considerable enjoyment. Cabell was also a superior essayist who wrote definitive essays on Virginia as a state of mind. However, one cannot avoid the conclusion that, for all the subtlety of his comic irony, Cabell falls short of being a writer of the first rank. In spite of the excessive severity of his detractors, there is an element of truth in their accusation that he is an escapist. *The Rivet in Grandfather's Neck* suggests Cabell's fundamental uneasiness with a modern age which denies heroic possibilities to would-be Cavaliers such as Rudolph Musgrave.

Of course Cabell was scarcely alone in casting a vote of no confidence against the present. Richard Ellman and Charles Feidelson have observed that "a sense of loss, alienation, and despair" is one of the distinguishing characteristics of the modern literary consciousness. But combined with this sense of alienation in the greatest contemporary literature is a concomitant sense of freedom, of "liberation from inherited patterns," which has made possible the brilliant formal innovations of modern poetry and fiction.[23] Cabell obviously expressed in his writing the contemporary sense of alienation from the present, but he was unable to completely achieve a corresponding emotional liberation from the past. Joseph Daniel Singal, in a recent assessment of Cabell, perceptively describes him as a post-Victorian skeptic who, despite his skepticism, found it impossible to embrace modernism. "What ultimately distinguishes Cabell from the Modernist writers," he observes,

23. Richard Ellman and Charles Feidelson, Jr. (eds.), *The Modern Tradition: Backgrounds of Modern Literature* (New York, 1965), vi.

"is his refusal to confront experience directly. His is a contrived allegorical world filled with masks, ambiguities, and incessant word play, highly reminiscent of that created by Oscar Wilde and other British post-Victorians in the 1890's."[24]

Cabell's rejection of the present is absolute; his flight into the past is determined and contrived. Probably, as Edmund Wilson has observed, this determined rejection of reality is born of bitterness, "the bitterness of the South at having had its dream proved a fiction, and then somehow having had still to live on it."[25] Wilson's insight suggests the strong link between the ambivalence at the core of Cabell's writing and the postbellum Virginia milieu out of which he came. In the characterization of Rudolph Musgrave, Virginia Cavalier *manqué*, one can see the carefully poised tone, the combination of ironic detachment and empathetic identification which might have reflected a profound artistic vision but which instead was qualified by a fundamental authorial evasiveness masked by erudition and preciosity.

ELLEN GLASGOW

In 1900 Ellen Glasgow published *The Voice of the People*, a novel that she believed to be the first authentic expression of realism in southern literature. She was no doubt aware of the significance of the publication date, and critics in the following decades also recognized the appearance of this novel at the threshold of the twentieth century as an important event in the literary history of the South. Stuart Sherman asserted in 1925 that with the advent of *The Voice of the People*, realism had "crossed the Potomac . . . going North."[26] *The Voice of the People* became the first of thirteen novels which Miss Glasgow would later call her Chronicle of Virginia. Dividing these works into "novels of the Commonwealth," "novels of the country," and "novels of the city," she

24. Daniel Joseph Singal, *The War Within: From Victorian to Modernist Thought in the South, 1919–1945* (Chapel Hill, 1982), 91.

25. Edmund Wilson, *The Bit Between My Teeth: A Literary Chronicle of 1950–1965* (New York, 1965), 325.

26. Stuart Sherman, "The Fighting Edge of Romance," *New York Herald-Tribune Books*, April 19, 1925, pp. 1–3.

sought to provide an extensive, realistic examination of the history and social changes within Virginia from the Civil War to the eve of the Second World War.

Ellen Glasgow asserted in the opening chapter of *A Certain Measure* that the major theme of her chronicle was "the rise of the middle class as the dominant force in Southern democracy" (4), and indeed, on the surface this would appear to be the dominant motif. The central characters of many of her novels, including *The Voice of the People*, *The Miller of Old Church*, and *Barren Ground*, are not aristocrats but men and women of the lower or middle classes who rise in society through their own strength and integrity. Some critics, focusing on these middle-class characterizations, have located the source of Glasgow's artistic energy in her identification with this social change, in her expressions of restrained optimism about the South's future, and in her welcoming of the growing urban influence in southern culture which accompanied the growth of the middle class. Nancy McCollum believes that Glasgow's realistic critique of the myth of the Old Dominion and her willingness to accept change mark a distinctive point of departure from the writings of her fellow Richmonder, James Branch Cabell. Cabell, she contends, satirizes, teases, and at the same time upholds the myth. But Glasgow never justifies "the prolonged adherence of Southerners to suffocating traditions."[27]

It is doubtful, however, that a convincing case can be made for Glasgow as a fictional spokeswoman for the rising middle class in the South. Such an interpretation presumes a consistently realistic examination of the social changes within Virginia, but not all of her novels are written from such a perspective. For example, one finds little realistic analysis of the myth of Virginia's antebellum golden age in *The Battle-ground* (1902), a novel which deals with the immolation of the old plantation aristocracy in the fires of war and which Glasgow placed first in her series in order of chronology. In spite of her insistence in *A Certain Measure* that *The Battle-ground* is not a romance, it is impossible for a reader today to categorize it in any other way.

27. Nancy M. McCollum, "Glasgow's and Cabell's Comedies of Virginia," *Georgia Review*, XVIII (1964), 238.

This novel focuses on the aristocratic Lightfoot and Ambler families and contains most of the familiar trappings of nineteenth-century plantation fiction. Major Lightfoot has a "Roman nose" inherited from a wellborn grandfather who lived in England. Governor Ambler possesses a "classic face." His wife is appropriately "frail and gentle" with a profile like "delicate porcelain." These finely chiseled members of this FFV regularly dine on Sally Lunn and "majestic home-cured ham fresh from a bath of Madeira." They are served by house servants with whom they live on a level of warm and easy familiarity. The women minister conscientiously and cheerfully to the inhabitants of the slave quarters. The Lightfoot manor is built with brick brought to the Valley of Virginia all the way from England. In a library stocked with portraits of distinguished ancestors, Major Lightfoot drinks brandy and reads Latin and the essays of Joseph Addison every day. And so on.

Of course, *The Battle-ground* is an early example of Miss Glasgow's fiction, an expression of what she called "romantic youth," which she would later look back on like some "long-departed spirit." Yet it is equally significant that this novel was published two years after *The Voice of the People*, her novel of pioneering realism, and that years later in *A Certain Measure* she would look back on her Civil War novel and detect "no flaw in the verisimilitude of the picture" (5–6). Certainly *The Battle-ground* reveals a division in Glasgow's early works between a realistic scrutiny of the Old Dominion and a tendency to evoke its past splendors romantically. And it is interesting that during the later years of her career, she seems to have failed to recognize the conventionally romantic tone of her early novel.

Even in the novels which are structured around the theme of the rise of the middle class, Glasgow betrays a marked ambivalence toward her humbly born heroes. This ambivalence is most strikingly revealed in *The Voice of the People*. In this novel Nicholas Burr, the ugly, red-haired son of a poor farmer, rises through hard work and self-education to the pinnacle of political power in the state—the governor's mansion. Burr is probably Glasgow's most interesting and successful middle-class characterization, and she emphasizes his social significance by pitting him against the state political machine whose candidate is an aristocrat of impeccable pedigree named Dudley. Dudley, a childhood acquaintance of Burr's, is used throughout the novel as an aristocratic foil to Burr's middle-class virtues.

But in spite of its proletarian hero, the theme of middle-class ascendency is heavily qualified in *The Voice of the People*. Burr would seem to represent those positive and progressive alterations in Virginia's social structure which Glasgow presumably applauds. Yet she seems far from assured of the desirability of change and progress at a number of points in her novel. Her description of late nineteenth-century Richmond, for example, is full of sad nostalgia for the gracious old city that has been largely obliterated by progress. Surveying the area around Capitol Square the author remarks that the "grave old" Capitol building remains "the one distinctive feature of a city where Iconoclasm has walked with destroying feet." Less than a generation ago, she reflects, the streets leading from the Capitol "were the streets of a Southern town—bordered by hospitable Southern houses set in gardens where old-fashioned flowers bloomed." Now all this loveliness is gone. "Progress has passed, and in its wake there have sprung up obvious structures of red brick with brownstone trimmings. The young trees leading off into avenues of shade soften the harshness of an architecture which would become New York, and which belongs as much to Massachusetts as to Virginia."[28] In the midst of a novel whose central theme is the transformation of Virginia society, this elegiac lament for the passing of a gracious, aristocratic, and distinctly southern way of life seems curiously discordant.

Glasgow's conflicting feelings about progress and the rise of the middle class inevitably extend to her protagonist. Nick Burr is made an appealing middle-class character because he combines an ambitious go-getting spirit with an old-fashioned Jeffersonian faith in the goodness and wisdom of the common man. But he lives in an age when Jeffersonian virtues are no longer in vogue. The political machine he opposes is commanded by the *nouveau riche* Rann, a character who embodies all the worst qualities of the upwardly mobile. Rann's attempt to destroy

---

28. Ellen Glasgow, *The Voice of the People* (1900; rpr. New York, 1902), 321.

Burr through vicious personal innuendo is voided by the honorable refusal of the aristocratic Dudley, the candidate Rann is scheming to have
elected to the United States Senate, to employ such vulgar tactics. On
the eve of the senatorial election, Burr is killed trying to prevent a lynch
mob from seizing its intended victim. Burr, a man of the people, is destroyed by the very people he represents. A close reading of *The Voice of
the People* indicates that, even in a novel which claims to celebrate the
increasing power of the middle class, Ellen Glasgow cannot accept such
social transformation with complete sanguinity.

In spite of Glasgow's professed social aims, at the end of the novel
her yeoman protagonist has been destroyed and Dudley, Burr's FFV
adversary, has survived. Dudley has also won the hand of Eugenia
Battle, an aristocratic flower for whose possession the two men had
struggled earlier in the novel. Burr's loss to his well-bred foe is thus
both political and personal. In his analysis of *The Voice of the People*,
Julius Raper asserts that, within the context of the novel, one cannot
determine whether Burr's failure to win Eugenia "results entirely from
psychological and social forces portrayed in the novel or is caused in
part by a residual class arrogance in Miss Glasgow herself."[29] Indeed, it
appears that, at least at this point in her career, Ellen Glasgow could
have no more allowed herself to join Eugenia and Burr in wedlock than
John Pendleton Kennedy could have allowed one of his Virginia belles
to marry Horse-Shoe Robinson.[30] For Glasgow, as for Virginia writers
before her, the Jeffersonian yeoman was a fine enough character—in his
place.

After reading Glasgow's early novels one is inclined to agree with
James Branch Cabell's observations concerning her embracing of the
present and her supposed repudiation of the past: "A little too much
had been made, I think, of Ellen Glasgow's revolt against the lofty traditions of the Old South. Beyond question, as a writer, she has received
these traditions with polite disrespect. Yet, as a person, she very sensi-

29. Julius Rowan Raper, *Without Shelter: The Early Career of Ellen Glasgow* (Baton
Rouge, 1971), 142.

30. Glasgow would later develop this yeoman-aristocrat romantic relationship much
more successfully in *The Sheltered Life* in the characters of Joseph Crocker and Isabella
Archbald.

bly has fallen in with that formalized and amiably luxurious manner of living to which, virtually, she was born."[31] Cabell understood that his friend was inherently aristocratic in her tastes and predilections, and like most aristocratic spirits Glasgow occasionally voiced an anxiety concerning the future direction of society and a yearning for the order and stability of the old regime. In a letter written to Signe Torsvig near the end of her life she lamented: "We are living without adjustments, in a broken world. The pattern has changed so utterly that we have almost forgotten it. But what I regret most will always be the lost harmonies of spirit. . . . Will the people who set the tone and dictate the manners of today ever prefer the greater harmonies, or ever . . . ever like all the little lost graces that made life so much easier?"[32] The tone of this private lament echoes the tone of the passage written more than forty years earlier describing the destruction of old Richmond.

If Glasgow's identification with progress and with the middle class in her fiction is, in fact, heavily qualified, where do her essential sympathies lie? Louis D. Rubin believes that her best novels deal with the Virginia aristocracy, and a survey of her thirteen-volume social history provides solid support for this judgment. Except for *Barren Ground*—which is certainly one of her strongest novels but which seems to have been generated more from the complex feminine emotions described in *The Woman Within* than from an understanding of the rural, yeoman-class origins of her heroine—Glasgow's best novels are those which have dealt with Virginians of aristocratic backgrounds—*Virginia*, *The Romantic Comedians*, *They Stooped to Folly*, and *The Sheltered Life*. "The true social history," Rubin believes, "is observable not only in what Miss Glasgow succeeded in doing, but in what she could not do. She could not give a meaning to twentieth-century democracy in Virginia. As a novelist all she knew—and she knew that so well—was the failure of the old order."[33] The major theme of Ellen Glasgow's social

31. Cabell, "Miss Glasgow of Virginia," 250.

32. Blair Rouse (ed.), *Letters of Ellen Glasgow* (New York, 1958), 343.

33. Louis D. Rubin, "Two in Richmond: Ellen Glasgow and James Branch Cabell," in Louis D. Rubin and Robert D. Jacobs (eds.), *South: Modern Southern Literature in Its Cultural Setting* (Garden City, N.Y., 1961), 129.

history of Virginia is not, as she believed, the rise of the middle class but the fall of the old aristocracy.

The passing away of the old order is thoroughly examined in three of Glasgow's Queenborough (Richmond) novels, published between 1926 and 1932, which can best be described as novels of manners— *The Romantic Comedians*, *They Stooped to Folly*, and *The Sheltered Life*. In each of these novels aging Virginia gentlemen play major roles. These aristocratic characters reveal much about Glasgow's ambivalent attitudes toward the once vigorous but now decayed social system which these elderly Cavaliers represent. In *The Sheltered Life*, the most serious of these studies of upper-class Queenborough society, can be found her most engaging and subtle portrayal of the old-school Virginia aristocrat.

The Sheltered Life is a story about people who seek unsuccessfully to protect themselves and their loved ones from brutal realities. The plot records the movement of Jenny Blair Archbald from innocence to experience. At the end of the novel Jenny Blair's romantic illusions are shattered by the tragic conclusion of a flirtation with George Birdsong. The point of view is divided between Jenny Blair and her grandfather, General Archbald. General Archbald is a courtly old Virginia aristocrat, a relic of the postwar Victorian era; his thoughts are directed primarily toward the past and his wisdom consists of an ironic acceptance of the bitterness and frustration which are an inevitable part of life. Through the effective juxtaposition of these two points of view, Glasgow suggests that the wisdom of old age is incapable of preventing the tragic fall of youth from innocence. Jenny Blair, by a bitter process of trial and error, must learn about life on her own.

General Archbald is the most interesting and completely developed character in the novel. As Glasgow wrote in *A Certain Measure*, his life represents the tragedy "of the civilized man in a world that is not civilized" (204). Archbald has sacrificed his life to the code of his ancestors and has received little compensation in return. All of his actions seem to him to have been taken in order to save his own or some other person's appearance. To save appearances he married a woman he did not love because after a country dance from which they had stolen away alone they had been stranded in a sleigh until the end of a snowstorm. After the death of his wife, he draws back from a second marriage with a much younger woman because he does not wish to wound the sensibilities of his daughters and of his widowed daughter-in-law, Jenny Blair's mother. As he surveys his life it seems to him that "for thirty years he had sacrificed youth, his middle age, his dreams, his imagination, all the vital instincts that make a man, to the moral earnestness of tradition." Toward the end of his life General Archbald has sunk into a state of spiritual exhaustion. He realizes that thinking about things cannot change them in the least. "Though thought may have created life in the beginning," he muses, "though the whole visible world may hang suspended in an invisible web of mind, one could not by taking heed mend the smallest break, not the tiniest loosened thread in the pattern."[34] Now in his old age, after forty years of bestowing "perfunctory caresses," all he desires are companionships that make no demands.

In a well-conceived scene entitled "The Deep Past," Glasgow places the general on a park bench in the warm April sunshine and allows his thoughts to wander. Slowly his past begins to appear before him again, and the external world, "this world of brick and asphalt, of men and women and machines moving, [breaks] apart and [dissolves] from blown dust into thought" (147). He vividly remembers scenes from his unhappy childhood spent at his family's ancestral country estate, Stillwater. From his earliest years General Archbald has lived in a society hostile or indifferent to his sensitive nature, a society which affirms that "hunting [has] given greater pleasure to a greater number of human beings than all the poetry since Homer," and that pity is "a woman's virtue" (138). He recalls a youthful love affair with a married English gentlewoman, the only woman he had ever deeply loved. She had possessed a sensitive temperament similar to his own, and like him, she had been lonely and afraid. Yet she had lacked the courage to break away from her husband and children and, despairing in her love for Archbald, had taken her life. With the tragic termination of the affair, the only intensely joyful part of Archbald's life dies. Time deposits over his

---

34. Ellen Glasgow, *The Sheltered Life* (Garden City, N.Y., 1932), 33, 129, hereinafter cited in the text by page number only.

wound a thick "crust of despair." Slowly the joy of living drains from him. Now, sitting on a park bench warming his venerable bones in the sun, General Archbald makes the only kind of affirmation of life that his depleted spirit will allow: "There was much to be said in favour of living if only one were careful not to probe deeply, not to touch life on the nerve. If only one were careful, tried not to shatter the hardened crust of despair" (162).

In her portrait of General Archbald, Glasgow presents a man whose search for happiness is frustrated by life, who sacrifices himself to a system that thwarts the expression of his sensitive temperament. However, she does not present the general as a complete failure. Glasgow's ironic distance from her character is constantly modified by the sympathy and pity she feels for a representative of a dying age. Significantly, she seems to value most highly those qualities in Archbald which Cabell admires in Rudolph Musgrave. Archbald, like Musgrave, is in the deepest sense defeated by life, but he has not been destroyed by it. Through the years he has compromised himself with his wife, his daughters, and his society. He has not fulfilled the demands of his nature, but in spite of his disappointments he has structured his life with an indomitability which Glasgow undeniably intends for the reader to admire. He has taken his place in society, for better or worse, and maintained the code of that society to the best of his ability. Above all, the spiritual lassitude of his final years is counterbalanced by a humaneness, an ironic self-knowledge of his faults, and a stubborn fortitude which forces the reader to feel respect as well as pity for him. Archbald has that final quality of endurance that survives disappointment and defeat. "After all," he affirms, "character may survive failure. Fortitude may be the last thing to go" (394).

In *From the Sunken Garden* Julius Raper deftly argues that in stressing Glasgow's sympathy for Archbald critics have overlooked the subtle and deep ironies which are contained in his characterization. Drawing on W. K. Wimsatt and Wayne Booth, Raper describes Archbald as a "capacitating character" through whom Glasgow speaks without herself intruding into her narrative. He believes that Glasgow is willing to ironically undercut that portion of herself which sentimentally identifies with the general. For example, Raper sees irony in the fact that Archbald persists in viewing his English affair "as the lost love of his life, rather than as adultery," comparable to the lusts of George Birdsong.[35] But though Raper's thesis is imaginatively presented, it seems more than a little contrived, an attempt to invest Glasgow with more ironic depth than her narrative can sustain by conveniently divorcing her central character from what Glasgow herself said about him. Though there is certainly a significant degree of irony inherent in the development of Archbald's character, it is balanced firmly by the strong and unqualified sympathy the author feels for both him and the aristocratic ethos he embodies.

The full measure of Glasgow's sympathy for General Archbald is revealed in her treatment of the younger generation. John Walsh is a young doctor who represents in his thinking all of the most modern and advanced attitudes. Confident, analytical, a worshiper of facts, he is effectively juxtaposed with General Archbald in a manner that suggests Cabell's opposition of Jack Charteris to Rudolph Musgrave. John disapproves of the general's "disorderly" romantic mind. He ridicules the illusions with which the older generation fends off reality. "All emotion, even a love of beauty, seemed disorderly to him, and his ideal world had all the clean bareness of a laboratory or a tiled bathroom" (206). Yet when his aunt, Eva Birdsong, once the pride of Queenborough society and now a middle-aged invalid, finds her husband in the arms of Jenny Blair and shoots him, John is no better able to cope with the tragic situation than General Archbald. He is drawn into the very world of illusion which he has consistently criticized. "It was an accident," he declares. "But how could it have happened? How was it possible?" the general questions. "Then John's answer, low, intense, determined, 'It did happen. It was an accident'" (394).

General Archbald shares a number of characteristics with the elderly aristocratic protagonists of Glasgow's other Queenborough nov-

35. Julius Rowan Raper, *From the Sunken Garden: The Fiction of Ellen Glasgow, 1916–1945* (Baton Rouge, 1980), 147.

els. Judge Gamaliel Bland Honeywell of *The Romantic Comedians* tries vainly, humorously, and pathetically to capture the ecstasy which escaped him in his youth by marrying a girl young enough to be his daughter who eventually abandons him for a younger lover. Virginius Littlepage of *They Stooped to Folly* is brushed tantalizingly by the wings of passion before he turns away from the tempting Amy Dalrymple to the faithful worship of a dead wife he never understood.

Glasgow treats the fates of her aging Virginia gentlemen with varying degrees of seriousness, but beyond individual differences of treatment, all of them represent a creaking Victorian high-mindedness and prudery that in the roaring twenties wears its obsolescence rather forlornly. All of them fail to attain the elusive state of self-fulfillment. All of them live by a code that places the highest premiums on prudent conduct and on the denial of any desire that might be judged by society as eccentric. All of them find themselves helplessly without their moorings in a modern sea of hedonism and moral relativity. But all of them cling stubbornly to their system of values, even though they no longer possess the certainty that these values are meaningful.

In spite of their disparate fictional modes, the close similarity between Cabell's and Glasgow's modern Cavaliers is striking. The aristocratic gentlemen of both writers are of middle or advanced age. They are world-weary survivors of a dead era who are denied vigorous strength and the potential for heroic action, and they are saddled with creeds in which they can no longer implicitly believe but to which they stoically adhere in the face of moral chaos. More than a little absurd and foolish, these Cavaliers *manqué* are nevertheless treated by both Cabell and Glasgow with sympathy, affection, and even respect. Both writers combine ironic detachment with sympathetic identification in developing their aristocratic gentlemen, and both writers reveal in their characterizations the complexity and ambiguity of their own response to Virginia's past.

C. Hugh Holman has described the Queenborough novels as "a triptych of Virginia aristocratic life and manners that treats them with knowing affection and yet submits them to the gently corrosive irony of a great comic wit. They succeed admirably in that difficult and rare genre, the American comedy of manners."[36] Most critics would agree that these comedies of manners represent the most assured expression of Ellen Glasgow's talent, but some would not agree with Holman's assertion that the comic wit exhibited in them is a "great one."

Essentially, the critical disagreement over Glasgow's achievement as a writer centers on the degree of sentimentality one judges to be present in her fiction. On one hand, Julius Raper argues that the tone of Glasgow's work is deeply and pervasively ironic and that those aspects of her novels which seem conventionally romantic do not, in fact, reflect authorial attitudes, but rather subtly mask them. On the other hand, Daniel Joseph Singal encounters in Glasgow's work, not ironic control, but intellectual confusion which results in lapses into clichéd sentimentality. He sees Glasgow as a halfhearted disciple of Darwin who, in mid-career, turned her back on modernism and took refuge in late Victorian stoic attitudes, attitudes that were inherently compatible with her Calvinistically molded conscience. In Singal's opinion it is not surprising "that, in her struggle to become modern, she often lost out, allowing her novels to degenerate into what one critic has called 'soap opera,' clinging persistently to the outward symbols of the Tidewater tradition, and, at the end of her career, turning her back on the very revolution in southern letters she had once helped to launch."[37]

An analysis of the aristocratic protagonists of the Queenborough novels leads to an assessment of Glasgow's fictional achievement that lies somewhere between the judgments of Raper and Singal. Raper makes excessive claims for Glasgow as a mistress of irony and capacitating character. Yet her creation of characters such as General Archbald is clearly the work of a writer who does more than simply cling "persistently to the outward symbols of the Tidewater tradition." Glasgow's Cavalier characters, like those of James Branch Cabell, reveal a fundamental ambivalence toward Virginia's heritage and tradition that

36. C. Hugh Holman, "The Comedies of Manners," in M. Thomas Inge (ed.), *Ellen Glasgow Centennial Essays* (Charlottesville, 1976), 128.

37. Raper, *From the Sunken Garden*, 147; Singal, *The War Within*, 93.

produces both finely textured irony and, occasionally, damaging softness of tone.

Significantly, Ellen Glasgow's authorial ambivalence is not limited
to her Virginia gentlemen; it extends to her characterizations of Virginia ladies as well, as a recent assessment of her work by Anne Goodwyn Jones makes clear. Jones argues that Glasgow never closely determined her attitude toward the southern lady either in her fiction or in
her life. "Ellen Glasgow started out to define and to embalm the southern lady of the 1880's," she observes. "She ended up almost enshrining
her." Jones's emphasis on the unresolved tensions within Glasgow's
own nature echoes the judgments of other critics. Stanley Godbold, her
biographer, views her as being torn between the desire to be Glasgow
the southern lady and Glasgow the emancipated woman. "In all of her
life," he believes, "she was not able to shed either role, nor was she able
to reconcile them." Monique Parent Frazee has described Glasgow as a
would-be liberated woman, lacking the resolve of a writer like George
Sand to accept fully the implications of her revolt from a repressive, dis-
approving society.[38] As these critics have perceived, Glasgow the rebel
was always held rather firmly in check by Glasgow the Virginia lady,
and the occasionally ambiguous fictional tone which is a product of this
unresolved internal tension is apparent even in her best novels.

Ellen Glasgow strove determinedly to bring realism—blood and
irony she called it—to her treatment of Virginia life. The Queenborough novels demonstrate that she could describe aristocratic Virginians
with a skillful blending of irony and sympathy. But they also show that
she could not render a definitive judgment on her modern-day Cavaliers because she was too authentically a product of the refined and
rigidly orthodox social system which she sought to submit to rigorously
realistic scrutiny. For all her self-proclaimed pioneering of realism,
Glasgow was no more able than Cabell to free herself completely from

38. Anne Goodwyn Jones, *Tomorrow Is Another Day: The Woman Writer in the
South, 1859–1936* (Baton Rouge, 1981), 253; E. Stanley Godbold, Jr., *Ellen Glasgow
and the Woman Within* (Baton Rouge, 1972), 99; Monique Parent Frazee, "Ellen
Glasgow as Feminist," in M. Thomas Inge (ed)., *Ellen Glasgow Centennial Essays*
(Charlottesville, 1976), 167–87.

the bondage of her past. In her characterizations of elderly Virginia aristocrats one can perceive the fundamental tension—the ironic dissection of an outmoded way of life playing against the sympathetic authorial association with that way of life—which is the source for both her fictional achievement and her artistic limitations.

SEVEN

The Cavalier Tradition and the Contemporary Milieu

STYRON AND EPPS

THE NEW DOMINION

In 1926 Harry Flood Byrd, the Old Dominion's newly inaugurated governor, asserted unequivocally, "The prosperity of Virginia depends primarily upon agriculture." Nearly twenty years later this traditional view of Virginia as an essentially agrarian state was echoed by Governor William Tuck, who warned his fellow citizens that it was "important for Virginia to remain an agricultural state."[1] What neither Byrd nor Tuck nor many other Virginians seemed willing to recognize was that the Old Dominion was becoming less and less agrarian in its economic composition.

1. J. Harvie Wilkinson, *Harry Byrd and the Changing Face of Virginia Politics, 1945–1966* (Charlottesville, 1968), 157.

247

The movement of wealth from plantation and farm to city, which had progressed slowly but steadily in the last decades of the nineteenth century and the opening decades of the twentieth, accelerated sharply after 1920. The urbanization of the Old Dominion became especially pronounced in the years which preceded and followed the Second World War. After 1930 economic growth in Virginia, which had been relatively slow, surged well ahead of the national average. While most other states languished in the midst of the Great Depression, Virginia enjoyed an early economic upturn. Between 1935 and 1940, 510 new manufacturing concerns began operating in the state, and Richmond became the fastest growing industrial center in the country.[2] Thanks in large part to the mushrooming of federal activities in Washington, northern Virginia was the setting for an explosion of suburban growth, increasing in population from fewer than 150,000 in 1940 to well over 500,000 by 1960. In the Tidewater area the enormous expansion of military and naval installations that occurred immediately before and during World War II turned the rather sleepy collection of towns along the shores of Hampton Roads into a substantial metropolitan area. By 1960 agriculture claimed just 10 percent of Virginia's workers, only half the total number of workers employed in industry.[3]

Yet despite the rapid industrialization and urbanization of the Old Dominion, Virginia continued to labor under myths which had lodged themselves in the minds of most of her citizens since Reconstruction days. In 1950 V. O. Key described the state as dominated by a political machine—the creation of Harry Flood Byrd—which constituted what Key termed "an oligarchy," thoroughly "Cavalier and aristocratic" in its outlook. Key concluded that Virginia possessed "characteristics more akin to those of England at about the time of the Reform Bill of 1832 than to those of any other state of the present-day South." The state was, he concluded, "a political museum piece."[4] Rooted firmly in county courthouses across the state, the Byrd machine employed the poll tax

2. Dabney, *Virginia, the New Dominion*, 502.
3. Wilkinson, *Harry Byrd and the Changing Face of Virginia Politics*, 15, 163.
4. V. O. Key, *Southern Politics in State and Nation* (New York, 1949), 19, 20.

and complex residency requirements to restrict the electorate. In addition to discouraging white voters from the lower end of the economic spectrum, Virginia's voting laws effectively excluded the great majority of the state's black voters; so that on the average only about 10 percent of Virginians over the age of twenty-one voted. With the support of only 5 to 7 percent of the adult population the machine regularly swept its handpicked, extremely conservative candidates into office. Even as late as the early 1960s the Old Dominion was ruled, though with increasing difficulty, by a man who, in the words of J. Harvie Wilkinson, represented "the quintessence of the Virginia gentleman, with blue-blood ancestry, impeccable integrity, refined manners, and an almost mystic identification with Virginia's past."[5]

Though Virginia as a physical entity might be described at mid-century by statistics and indices, Virginia as a state of mind was consummately incarnated by Harry Flood Byrd. The aristocratic planter ideal stalked the state in the person of the courtly apple grower from Winchester. Byrd was living proof that the gulf between myth and reality lay nearly as deep in the Old Dominion in 1950 as it had in 1900.

Those Virginia writers who came after Ellen Glasgow and James Branch Cabell thus resided in a state which was still struggling to harmonize its glorious past with its complex and challenging present. Indeed, the contradiction between the traditional bucolic ideal which the state's leaders continued to invoke in the maintenance of a social and political status quo and the reality of the expanding suburban sprawl of Tidewater, northern Virginia, and Richmond produced among a new generation of writers a sense of incongruity which was at least as powerful as that which had impressed their predecessors several decades earlier.

The best Virginia fiction of the post–World War II period reflects an intense awareness of the discrepancy between myth and reality in the Old Dominion. In *Lie Down in Darkness* and *The Confessions of Nat Turner* William Styron subjects both his native state's present and its

5. Wilkinson, *Harry Byrd and the Changing Face of Virginia Politics*, 173.

past to a sustained and sometimes brutally realistic analysis. Influenced by the achievements of those writers of the middle and lower South who came after Cabell and Glasgow, writers such as William Faulkner and Robert Penn Warren, Styron carries forth the dialectical mode of discourse which Allen Tate describes in "A Southern Mode of the Imagination" and which Cabell and Glasgow had pioneered fifty years earlier.

The Virginia gentleman plays an important part in the dialectical discourse of Styron's Virginia novels, as it does in a more recent novel by Garrett Epps entitled *The Shad Treatment*. The Old Dominion's novelists remain acutely conscious of the genteel character ideal. Though they have cast aside the cultural piety of earlier writers, they continue to ponder the paradoxical relation between their state's aristocratic mythic heritage and the socially fluid and ever more insistently egalitarian national culture of which Virginia is a part.

WILLIAM STYRON

William Styron's novels would appear to possess little in common with the novels of his Virginia predecessors, not even with the work of Glasgow and Cabell. His fiction is explicitly, sometimes savagely realistic, and in his concern for stream-of-consciousness technique, complex point of view, and Freudian psychology, he seems poles removed from the comparatively sedate realism of Glasgow or from the fanciful quasi allegories of Cabell. But Virginia as place and presence is nearly as central to his fiction as it was to the fiction of these earlier writers, and like his predecessors, Styron focuses effectively on Virginia gentlemen in all of his novels, raising through these characterizations important questions about the relationship between present and past and between myth and reality, as Cabell and Glasgow did before him.

Aristocratic Virginia and the Cavalier stereotype are central elements in Styron's first novel, *Lie Down in Darkness*. John Aldridge's early judgment that the work is "primarily a novel of place and must be judged in terms of its successful evocation of place" remains substantially accurate.[6] Much of the novel's power does indeed come from Styron's ability to invest his Virginia setting with immediacy and with an intense sense of reality. Styron knows what he describes. He captures the ambiance of suburban Tidewater country-club living in precise vignettes—from Sunday coffee on an awninged terrace that overlooks a sloping lawn and the wide expanse of the tidal James to a wedding reception where guests buzz like flies over a pink tablecloth "soaked with champagne" and overflow the dining room onto the porches, where they are served by "colored boys in white jackets." No one who has ever attended the University of Virginia could fail to recognize this lush, Fitzgerald-like description of a prehomecoming game fraternity party:

> It was not quite one o'clock yet, but the mood had already become one of celebration, as if the game, a formality at most, were already won: at least no contest could be lost, encouraged as this one was by such dizzy rejoicing. Outside it was getting grayer and colder, but here, warmed by the nearness of other faces and the fraternal glow of alcohol, it seemed that every cheek was lit by a beautiful flame. The phonograph played louder and louder, the piano kept rattling in a persistent off-beat, and the half-dozen boys now dancing led their partners in ever-widening, ever more precarious circles around the room. Through a haze of smoke, wide-eyed girls with pennants and cowbells wandered, to pet, and be petted by, the greying alumni, and they cornered people in doorways and chattered breezily of *party-party-party*—in Richmond last year, or last month, or they couldn't remember. The boys in the meantime had begun to gather up their football trappings—blankets, raincoats, a flask to keep them warm—but the music went on, now a sad love ballad, dropping guitar notes on the air like silver dimes.[7]

One is even inclined to agree with Aldridge that the Virginia setting

6. John W. Aldridge, "In a Place Where Love Is a Stranger," *New York Times Book Review*, September 9, 1951, p. 5.
7. William Styron, *Lie Down in Darkness* (Indianapolis, 1951), 198.

itself is the most successfully realized character in *Lie Down in Dark-ness*. But the regional quality of the novel extends beyond its evocative setting. Styron's major characters—Milton, Helen, and Peyton Loftis—exert a strong imaginative pull on the reader, not only because they are convincingly drawn, but also because, in drawing them, Styron con-sciously works against stereotypic qualities which the reader naturally tends to associate with people of their background. On the surface Helen Loftis is a typical upper-class Virginia lady—calm, poised, well-mannered, a bit rigid. Milton Loftis seems to be a pleasant and attrac-tive, if rather undistinguished, Virginia gentleman; and Peyton Loftis is as captivating a contemporary Virginia belle as one could hope to find. In fact we know these characters are emotional cripples, twisted and distorted and driven to acts that are both vindictive and self-destructive. Part of the fascination of the novel comes from the striking discrepancy we quickly perceive between the conventional roles the Loftis family plays in the seductively pleasant external world of the urban Tidewater aristocracy and the horror of their inner lives. Styron taps the tradi-tional sources of Virginia fiction and uses the familiar character stereo-types of Virginia lady, Virginia gentleman, and Virginia belle, but he works against and ironically inverts the meaning of these stereotypes with devastating effectiveness.

Styron manipulates social stereotype most effectively in his charac-terization of Milton Loftis, a modern-day Virginia gentleman. Milton represents the last of a line of Cavalier ancestors. His father, an aristo-cratic lawyer, "descended from a long line of lawyers," brings to mind the elderly, emotionally exhausted gentlemen of Cabell's and Glas-gow's, as well as Faulkner's novels. Sporting stiff wing collars and an Edwardian mustache until his death in 1920, he passes on to his son a legacy of inane clichés, the expressions of a spiritually bankrupt tradi-tion. "My son, paradoxically enough . . . being a Southerner and a Vir-ginian and of course a Democrat you will find yourself in the unique position of choosing between (a) those ideals implanted as right and proper in every man since Jesus Christ and no doubt before and espe-cially in Virginians and (b) ideals inherent in you through a socio-economic culture over which you have no power to prevail; consequently I strongly urge you my son always to be a good Democrat but to be a good man too if you possibly can."[8]

Unlike Faulkner, Styron does not give primary emphasis in his novel to the failure of meaningful cultural transmission; nevertheless, the presence of the elderly Loftis points to a progressive deterioration of the gentlemanly ideal, from the absurd sententiousness of the father to the self-indulgent, self-pitying mental flabbiness of the son. Yet the implication of those passages in which Milton remembers his father is that the father, whatever his inadequacies, at least conducted his life with a modicum of decency and discipline. With Milton the last restraints of the gentlemanly ideal are broken. Milton fulfills on paper all the criteria of a Virginia gentleman—education at Charlottesville, service in the army, law school, a respectable practice, memberships in the country club and the Episcopal Church. Yet at the end of the novel's disturbing sequence of events we see a pathetic middle-aged man, wasted by alcohol and mothered by a rather tacky and plebeian mistress. He is a man who is barely able to go through the motions of seeing his beloved daughter decently buried, who in a fit of rage after his daughter's funeral comes close to strangling to death the wife he both needs and hates.

Milton Loftis goes beyond the spiritual lassitude of Cabell and Glasgow's Cavalier *manqué*. He represents an inversion of all the qualities of character that the ideal of the Virginia gentleman has traditionally implied. In him selflessness is replaced by selfishness. Self-control gives way to self-indulgence. Discipline and honor are subverted by alcoholic binges and shabby love affairs. The worship of a beautiful lady is distorted into a scarcely concealed incestuous longing for a beautiful, youthful daughter. Our understanding of Milton's personal tragedy is heightened by our recognition of the discrepancy between the ideal of the Virginia gentleman and the grotesque imitation of that gentleman that he has become.

In a reassessment of *Lie Down in Darkness* John Aldridge has savagely attacked Styron for his intensely middlebrow and unoriginal view

8. *Ibid.*, 47–48.

of life. He argues that the novel cannot support its Faulknerian elements of doom and of cultural and moral derangement, and he describes the book as a "provincial tragedy, the issue of emotions overly confined by, and perversely conditioned by, the restraints of dogma and community."[9] Though one may feel that Aldridge is more disposed to analyze the novel's weaknesses than to recognize its considerable strengths, his description of *Lie Down in Darkness* as a "provincial tragedy" seems apt. Whatever the failures of Styron's larger thematic design, the novel does succeed on a more limited level as an examination of personal corruption masked by the deceptively appealing, decorous facade of upper-middle-class Tidewater society. *Lie Down in Darkness* is strongest, not when it strives for a type of Faulknerian grandeur, but when it is describing with knowing eye this Tidewater society.

Though *Lie Down in Darkness* is not a masterpiece, it is a good first novel whose strengths derive in large part from Styron's understanding of his Virginia setting, especially from his recognition of the strong influence that the traditional concepts of Virginia lady and Virginia gentleman continue to exert over contemporary residents of the Old Dominion. Although the tragedy of the Loftis family transcends state boundaries, it is difficult to imagine Helen, Peyton, or Milton Loftis in a context other than Virginia. Milton's failure could not have been the same had he been a product of Peoria, Illinois, or Billings, Montana. Essential to our understanding of him is an understanding of the tradition of the Virginia gentleman from which he descends. But Styron works with this tradition like no other Virginia writer before him, using it to create a convincing portrait of weakness, failure, and despair and subjecting his gentleman to an exacting and uncompromising examination.

Styron shifted this setting from Virginia to Italy in *Set This House on Fire* (1959), a novel that received a decidedly less favorable critical response than *Lie Down in Darkness*. But in 1967 he triumphantly returned to the fictional terrain he knew best in *The Confessions of Nat*

9. John W. Aldridge, "William Styron and the Derivative Imagination," in his *The Devil in the Fire: Retrospective Essays on American Literature and Culture, 1951–1971* (New York, 1972), 209.

Turner (1967). In his third novel Styron journeyed into Virginia's past to examine Nat Turner's bloody slave uprising in Southampton County in 1831. His approach to his material was daring and risky, for he chose to tell the story through the point of view of Nat Turner, thereby committing himself to the extensive analysis of a tormented and highly complex black psyche. Although some critics, particularly black critics, were outraged that a white writer should presume to interpret the inner feelings of a black slave, the general critical reception was overwhelmingly favorable, and *The Confessions of Nat Turner* was awarded the Pulitzer Prize for fiction in 1968. Today the novel seems destined to secure a reputation as one of the best American novels of the post–World War II period.

By virtue of its point of view, *The Confessions of Nat Turner* obviously falls outside the romantic plantation genre that in Virginia fiction extends back to the works of Thomas Nelson Page and John Esten Cooke. Yet because Nat is raised on a plantation and because his plantation experiences are the foundation of his hatred of the white man, the Virginia plantation system and the gentlemen who operate it become an important part of the novel's analysis of slavery. Almost a third of Nat's narrative is given to describing his experiences at Turner's Mills Plantation. In this section of the novel Styron accomplishes what had never before been successfully achieved by the Old Dominion's novelists. Through the eyes of an intelligent and unusually gifted young house slave he draws a portrait of a Virginia plantation, including white masters, house servants, and field hands, that rings with authenticity.

Styron's description of plantation life is convincing because he has created a character whose assessment of Turner's Mills impresses us as honest and inclusive. In spite of the murderous passion which precipitated his bloody revolt, Nat is able to look back on his past with a strange detachment after he is apprehended and condemned to die. The life he describes at Turner's Mills is essentially an easy one, for the Turners encourage Nat's precosity and treat him fondly, like a pet. Turner's Mills is not a vale of horrors like Simon Legree's Red River plantation, but neither is it the bucolic Eden that Thomas Nelson Page celebrates in his fiction.

Turner's Mills, a medium-sized plantation that includes fields, wood-lands, and a large sawmill, is owned by a civilized and moderately culti-vated family. The Turners treat their slaves with neither horrendous brutality nor philanthropic generosity. Slaves work hard on their plan-tation, but they are provided with plenty of coarse food, such as salt pork and corn meal, and adequate clothing and shelter.

Being a house slave, Nat is in a good position to record a wide vari-ety of plantation experiences. Through his eyes we see nearly every-thing, from the rambling wood plantation house with its polished floors, gilded hall mirror, and modest library, to the ten-hole slave privy shared by house servants and field hands and located two hundred yards be-hind the big house. Nat describes the privy with the same precision as he describes the plantation house.

> The earth around the entrance to the men's side (which I have used since I was five) is bare of vegetation, black hard clay worn glossy smooth by the trample of numberless bare or broganed feet, imprinted daily with a shifting pattern of booted heels and naked toes. Designed to prevent either malingering or seclu-sion—like the doors to all places frequented by Negroes—the privy door too is lockless, latchless, swinging outward easily on leather hinges to reveal the closet within drowned in shadows, almost completely dark save for slivers of light stealing in through the cracks between the timbers. I am used to the odor, which is ripe, pungent, immediate, smothering my nose and mouth like a warm green hand, the excremental stench partly stifled by quick-lime, so that the smell is not so much repellent to me as endur-able, faintly sweetish like stagnant swampwater. [10]

Armed with Nat's vision we vicariously experience the sensuous reali-ties of plantation life in all their forms.

George Core, in his favorable analysis of Styron's novel, variously describes its setting as "Tidewater" and "upcountry Tidewater." [11] In

---

10. William Styron, *The Confessions of Nat Turner* (New York, 1967), 136–37, hereinafter cited in the text by page number only.

11. George Core, "*The Confessions of Nat Turner* and the Burden of the Past," in

fact those who are familiar with the Old Dominion's geography will recognize its Southampton County locale as Southside Virginia—a broad area lying south of the James and Appomattox rivers, extending from the sandy flatlands around Franklin and Emporia west to the gently rolling clay hills of Halifax and Pittsylvania counties. This area has historically been a peanut- and tobacco-growing region of small- to medium-sized farms. It has always been different in its social complexion from Tidewater Virginia, an area dominated by large plantations, with impressive manor houses dotting the banks of the James, York, Rappahannock, and Potomac rivers.

The Confessions of Nat Turner hews closely and convincingly to its Southside Virginia setting, which Styron clearly recognizes as a more rustic modification of the original Tidewater social pattern. Though Turner's Mills lies only about fifty miles south of James River plantations such as Carter's Grove and Westover, it is much further removed in its social ambiance from these courtly mansions. Part of the achievement of Styron's novel is its accurate presentation of this Southside Virginia background.

The precision with which Nat describes plantation life extends to his description of the gentlemen who own the plantation. The novel provides an immensely effective exposition of the nineteenth-century plantation aristocrat. Never has a Virginia writer invested the Virginia planter with such a sense of flesh-and-blood substance. Styron's aristocrats are neither monsters nor angels, and they approach the question of slavery with the same variety of feelings one would expect of any privileged class dealing with a hideous and immoral institution which is also the foundation of its prosperity.

Styron summarizes the divided views of the Virginia aristocracy toward slavery during the first quarter of the nineteenth century in a brilliant scene which takes place on the plantation house veranda after a dinner which has been graced by a traveling Episcopal minister. Soliciting their general views on slavery, the minister is told by the younger

---

Robert K. Morris and Irving Malin (eds.), *The Achievement of William Styron* (Rev. ed.; Athens, Ga., 1981), 210, 214, 220, 221.

brother, Samuel Turner, that slavery "is the greatest curse a supposedly free and enlightened society has been saddled with in modern times" and that he prays "nightly for the miracle, for the divine guidance which will somehow 'show us the way out of this terrible condition" (159–60). At this point the elder brother, Benjamin, who is a heavy drinker, lurches from his chair, walks to the edge of the veranda, and commences to urinate on a nearby rosebush while he expatiates on the tribulation of living with such a saintly brother. The agitated minister forces himself to listen with respectful attention as the plantation's titled owner buttons his fly and gives succinct expression to the more conservative views of the planter aristocracy: "If you wish my belief to take back to the Bishop, you can tell him that my belief is that a darky is an animal with the brain of a human child and his only value is the work you can get out of him by intimidation, cajolery, and threat" (161).

Benjamin Turner is a hearty gentleman who, Nat observes, is accustomed to relieving himself while drinking with other men. This habit makes him, if anything, a more believable plantation master. His view of slavery is an insensitive one, but it is no more insensitive than the view of a large number of planters of his day, and it does not perforce turn him into a monster. He treats his slaves with stern but not inhumane discipline, and when he dies and the plantation passes to his more enlightened younger brother, Nat tells us that the slaves are somewhat relieved, but not overjoyed. One of the ironies of the novel is that it is the more enlightened Samuel, not Benjamin, who is eventually forced to liquidate the family slaves to pay off debts. Samuel earnestly believes that the Negro can be raised by education, but it is he who leaves Virginia for Alabama, abandoning Nat, the esteemed object of his good intentions, and neglecting to fulfill his promise of freedom. Samuel Turner is no more monstrous than his brother. He is simply a human being who trips over his own good intentions. The value of Styron's depiction of his Virginia gentlemen in *The Confessions of Nat Turner* is that he treats them neither as villains nor as paragons of virtue, but rather as men bound by the condition of their age and of their class just as straitly as their slaves.

Styron never capitulates to the romantic appeal of his Virginia gentlemen. He treats them humanely, but he recognizes the fundamental irony that, though they are not individually depraved, the system that they control is. Nat Turner embodies the savage violence which serves as a bloody expiation of this social depravity, an expiation which must exact its toll on the innocent and good as well as on the evil. Significantly Nat's first intense feelings of hatred for the white man are directed, not toward the poor whites who treat him like an animal, but toward the kindly aristocratic master who gave him the false hope that he could be a man. In Nat's first vision of violent retribution he strangles his once-beloved Marse Samuel and banishes his memory "as one banishes the memory of any disgraced and downfallen prince" (247). An understanding of the misguided paternalism of the Virginia aristocrat is essential to understanding the source of Nat's murderous vengefulness.

Because Styron retains his sense of objectivity about Virginia's past, he is able to use that past as an important part of a fascinating analysis of black rage. To enlist Virginia's hallowed traditions fully in the service of art required an unflinching honesty. Styron displayed such honesty in *The Confessions of Nat Turner*. In *Nat Turner* Styron was obligated to do violence to his native state's romantic past, violence as cruel as the scene that Nat comes upon at the "pillaged ruin of a manor house" on the second day of his campaign. "I watched a young Negro I had never seen before, outlandishly garbed in feathers and the uniform of an army colonel, so drunk that he could barely stand, laughing wildly, pissing into the hollow mouth of a dead, glassy-eyed white-haired old grandmother still clutching a child as they lay sprawled amid a bed of zinnias, and I said not a word to him, merely turned my horse about and thought: It was because of you, old woman, that we did not learn to fight nobly" (397). The voice is Nat Turner's, but the artistic consciousness is William Styron's—well-bred son of Newport News, Virginia. For such a man the creation of Nat Turner could not have been easy; it required artistic commitment of a high order.

The recent publication of Styron's *Sophie's Choice* invites immediate comparison with *Set This House on Fire* in the sense that both novels are set primarily outside the South. Indeed, on the surface *Sophie's Choice* seems to be Styron's least regional novel. Unlike *Set This House on Fire*, there are no detailed presentations of Virginia locales. The novel's action takes place in New York, in war-ravaged Warsaw, and in Auschwitz; and only one of the major characters, the narrator, Stingo, is a southerner.

Yet, in spite of the absence of southern local order, Styron's choice of Stingo as first-person narrator confirms the regional orientation of his fiction. As critics have noted, Stingo is a close approximation of William Styron. But he is also remarkably similar to Peter Leverett, the "white, Protestant, Anglo-Saxon, Virginia-bred" young gentleman narrator of *Set This House on Fire*. Both Stingo and Leverett are personally modest and prudent in their dealings with life. They display an inbred sense of courtesy and a natural attitude of justice and liberality when dealing with the mentally tormented characters who surround them.[12] Most of all, they both possess a solid sense of who they are and where they are from. Though both have wandered far beyond the boundaries of the Old Dominion, they carry with them a sense of *locus* which marks them in vivid contrast to the rootless characters whose agonies they describe. Thus the action of *Sophie's Choice*—the horrors of Auschwitz and of a fatally destructive relationship between a Polish concentration camp survivor and her brilliant but insane Jewish lover—is filtered, like the action of *Set This House on Fire*, through an authorial perspective that is intensely southern and that is defined in part by the code of the gentleman.

Peter Leverett and Stingo radically depart from the characterization of Milton Loftis, the dissipated Virginia gentleman of *Lie Down in Darkness*. Styron does not grotesquely invert the traditional associations of the Cavalier figure in *Set This House on Fire* and in *Sophie's*

12. For an opposing view of Peter Leverett, see Jane Flanders, "William Styron's Southern Myth," in Robert K. Morris and Irving Malin (eds.), *The Achievement of William Styron* (Rev. ed.; Athens, Ga., 1981). Flanders views Leverett as representing a desiccated southern aristocracy and locates its moral center in Cass Kinsolving, the humbly born southern white who, in committing murder, precipitates the climax of the novel.

Choice. The narrators of these novels are contemporary gentlemen who embody some of the best qualities of their ancestors. It is as if, having created a seedy parody of a Virginia gentleman, Styron sought to rehabilitate the type by developing men whose strengths are drawn to a significant degree from the Renaissance code which defined the original Cavalier figure.

Uncertain though the final critical verdict on Styron may be, one feels safe in asserting that his strongest novels to date have been those set in Virginia, *Lie Down in Darkness* and *The Confessions of Nat Turner*. It is also apparent that characters formed by the genteel southern tradition play important roles in all of his novels, including those set outside the Old Dominion. Though he deftly inverts their romantic associations, the traditional staples of the Virginia novel—the plantation, the Cavalier figure, and the idea of gentility—occupy an important place in Styron's fiction, as they have for the generations of Virginia novelists who have preceded him.

THE VIRGINIA GENTLEMAN IN THE SEVENTIES

The significant alterations in Virginia's social and political composition that have occurred in this century as a result of rapid economic development continue to reshape life in the Old Dominion profoundly. In 1975 Virginia boasted a diversified industrial output valued at more than $5 billion a year, and it had registered a 64.7 percent increase over 1950 totals in the number of workers employed in manufacturing. Such impressive advances have led to what Neal Peirce describes in *The Border South States* as "the emergence of two very different Virginias in our time—a metropolitan Virginia, sharing fully in the affluence of the United States in the post–World War II period, and an 'old' Old Dominion, still chiefly of the land, a rural backwater in its time." [13]

Though a more traditional rural Virginia still survives, recent decades have witnessed the triumph of a new economic and political or-

13. Neal R. Peirce, *The Border South States: People, Politics, and Power in the Five Border South States* (New York, 1975), 84, 87.

der. Power today resides, not in the rural county courthouses, but in the banking and brokerage houses of Main Street Richmond and in the far-flung suburbs of Tidewater and northern Virginia. Long established natives of the Old Dominion will ultimately have to face the unsettling fact that their state is becoming less and less recognizably southern, at least in its political texture. "Although the characteristics of Virginia politics remain distinctive as always," Ralph Eisenberg writes, "they now produce outcomes more similar to those that occur in states outside the South rather than within." [14] The accuracy of Eisenberg's observation seems to have been confirmed in the presidential election of 1976, in which Virginia was the only southern state to spurn Georgia Democrat Jimmy Carter for Republican Gerald Ford.

Progress has, of course, exacted its price from the Old Dominion. One of the results of fast economic development has been urban sprawl. Neal Peirce characterizes northern Virginia as "a suburban nightmare, an example of pell-mell development gone wrong, devastating a region of great natural beauty." [15] The same observations might be made about Tidewater. The specter of pollution has also accompanied industrialization. The recent disastrous contamination of the James River and of the lower Chesapeake Bay by deadly Kepone residue rudely awakened Virginians to the reality that their lovely tidal rivers, as well as their magnificent bay, were in danger of being destroyed by unrestricted industrial and urban growth. Today the majestic river that flows past some of Virginia's oldest and most beautiful plantations is closed to specific types of commercial fishing because of the high concentrations of carcinogenic insecticide that lethally lace its muddy bottom.

And how has the Cavalier fared in Virginia fiction during this most recent period of economic expansion and social flux? Like the generations which immediately precede them, contemporary Virginia writers have found it impossible to ignore the ugly urban realities which have obtruded and marred the pastoral perfection of the old plantation ideal. It seems that every Virginia writer with serious pretensions to author-

14. Ralph Eisenberg, "Virginia: The Emergence of Two-Party Politics," in William C. Havard (ed.), *The Changing Politics of the South* (Baton Rouge, 1972), 39.
15. Peirce, *The Border South States*, 100–101.

ship now accepts the charge of subjecting his state's myths to rigorous critical examination.

Perhaps the most interesting of the recent generation of Virginia writers is Richmonder Garrett Epps. His *The Shad Treatment* (1977) is the best new work to come from a Virginia writer since William Styron's *Lie Down in Darkness*. Although the novel is strong enough to stand alone, it will inevitably possess a unique interest for Virignia readers, for *The Shad Treatment* as a political *roman à clef*, Old Dominion style. The narrative's protagonist, Mac (MacIlwain Kuykendall) Evans, is a young member of a prominent Richmond family who works in the campaign organization of populist Tom Jeff Shadwell during his spirited though ultimately unsuccessful crusade for the governor's mansion. Very quickly, however, Virginia readers will realize that Epps's fictional characters are modeled closely after some of the state's real politicians. For example, Mac's brother, Lester, whose promising political career is cut short by a brain tumor, is obviously based on the life and untimely death of J. Sargeant Reynolds. The titanic struggle between Shadwell and his conservative adversary, Miles Brock, mirrors the 1973 election campaign between liberal Democrat Henry Howell and former governor Mills Godwin, who left the Democratic party and ran against Howell as a Republican to save the state from Howell's liberal menace. The Howell candidacy, though it was barely defeated by the coalition of Republicans and Byrd Democrats who united behind Godwin, marked the most serious liberal challenge to the state's conservative political establishment in recent Virginia history.

Like William Styron, Garrett Epps adopts a refreshingly cynical attitude toward life in the Old Dominion, especially toward the conservative political shibboleths that collectively constitute what Virginians often refer to admiringly as "the Virginia way." In *The Shad Treatment* Tom Jeff Shadwell confronts an organization that fondly justifies its serving of established business interests with the axiom that the machine has "kept the state honest." Through Shadwell's campaign manager, Knocko Cheatham, Epps unleashes a withering barrage of invective against such conservative self-righteousness. "You explain to me, then," he explodes, how honest it was to have all that state money in the interest-free accounts, and how honest were all those hundred-dollar bills from the power company and the truckers floating around come election time, and how honest it was when, if you got out of line, your wife or your father-in-law or your brother-in-law lost his job with the county. Merciful suffering Jesus! . . . I believe on my soul the people of this state have been starved, swindled, hood-winked, and led by the nose so long they don't know what a real honest man is anymore! Honest! An honest man in this state means somebody who believes stealing is beneath his dignity, that's all![16]

Though Mac Evans is the novel's protagonist, the novel's hero is the Henry Howell–like political crusader, Tom Jeff Shadwell. Shadwell combines political flimflammery with sheer good-natured exuberance, descending on unsuspecting voters in his Winnebago, blasting them with his microphone—"A PERSONAL HOWDY-DO TO ALL THE FOLKS IN CAR NUMBER ATS-479 FROM TOM JEFF SHADWELL! ISN'T IT A GREAT DAY TO FIGHT THE TAX ON FOOD?"—and leaving them behind, dazed, as he passes "raucously along the narrow mountain roads" (69). Shadwell combines shrewdness, intelligence, and the oratorical skills of a charismatic evangelist with a genuine sense of political and moral principles as he leads the fight to "turn the government back to the people." In the end, however, his skillful opponent, Miles Brock, evokes the specter of forced busing and judiciously dispenses "contributions" to certain black political leaders, narrowly turning back Shadwell's challenge.

Employing a limited omniscient point of view Garrett Epps presents his story through the eyes of Mac Evans. Evans is a well-born young Virginian who seems to have inherited the maverick personality of his father, a liberal who has been destroyed by the machine and sent into exile in South America. From his brother Lester he inherits a healthy disrespect for the conventional pieties of Virginia politics. Four years at Harvard complete his education and help him to look at his

---

16. Garrett Epps, *The Shad Treatment* (New York, 1977), 22, hereinafter cited in the text by page number only.

state with an admirable degree of detachment. By the time he joins Shadwell's campaign he has acquired an ironic awareness of the limitations of the gentlemanly tradition in which he has been schooled at his select Richmond academy:

> From their first day in kindergarten until graduation, however, St. Cyprian's did teach its students to be gentlemen, as that term was defined in Virginia: special creatures for whom there may once have been a place in the universe, nineteenth-century petty squires who lived close to the land without living off it, gentlemen farmers, hunters, horsemen, fishermen who made their livings by dabbling in law or medicine or finance or real estate, rejoicing in their station in nature and society; the middle class of the great chain of being. The St. Cyprian's gentleman would never lie to, steal from, or cheat his social equal, was unfailingly polite to ladies and helpful to idiots, maintained a proper uncomprehending reverence for the Episcopal Church, a suspicious but unshakable allegiance to the national government of the United States, a judicious fealty to the Apple-Farmer and his political organization, and a moist-eyed worship for the memory of General Robert E. Lee. (214)

Mac understands not only that the Cavalier tradition in which he has been steeped is "long gone" but also that it probably never really existed. His own investigation of the Evans pedigree reveals the tortuous path which finally leads a Virginia family to the social plateau of the FFV. Arriving in the New World with no past worthy of remembering, "as blank and empty as blue sky after a rainy morning," Mac's Welsh ancestors take root unspectacularly around the little trading post that eventually becomes Richmond. Four generations of "carpenters, coopers, wheelwrights" yield a man who finally establishes the Evans line on a firm base, Stephen R. Evans (1813–1871). Stephen Evans uses his engineering skills, acquired at West Point, to establish the profitable Kanawha Iron Works. Though his factory is destroyed with the burning of Richmond in 1865, he bestows on his son the fabulous fortune of nearly two hundred thousand English pounds. This sum has been accumulated in London banks from the sale of "vitally needed supplies" from the family's blockade-runner, supplies such as "corsets, cigars, silk dresses, French wines, opera hats—vitally needed by those few in the Confederacy who still had hard cash to pay for them, hard cash which had ended up in London, in Stephen Evans' personal account, as insurance against the awful prospect of defeat" (160). With these not-so-decently acquired spoils of war, future generations of Evanses are able to ply the traditional trades that are respectable in the Old Dominion, becoming bankers, Episcopal bishops, and lawyers.

Mac realizes that his Cavalier inheritance is founded on a largely fraudulent view of history. In addition, he realizes that it is a tradition shorn of its legendary grandeur by progress. Virginia's modern-day squires find "less and less room to live their gentlemen's lives." The land for their estates is being "bought up for housing tracts and giant corporate farms" and "the rivers for their crabbing and catfishing" are "choking in filth" produced by the nearby "skyscraper-and-freeway metropolis" (214). During the Shadwell campaign Mac observes this bogus Cavalier tradition being employed to mask the narrow economic interests of an urban upper middle class.

In *The Shad Treatment*, inflexibility, intolerance, and downright ugliness are inherent in the grotesque distortions of the gentlemanly ideal which pass in contemporary Virginia for the genuine article. This degeneration from the traditional ideal is epitomized by E. K. Jarvis, Jr., of Omega, Virginia. Overhearing an intoxicated Mac in Richmond's elite Confederate Club holding forth blasphemously with his theory that Robert E. Lee was a traitor to the southern cause, Jarvis ambushes him in the club's basement and leads him to the parking lot at the point of a gun. Here he instructs the security guard to beat him until he apologizes for "talking dirty about Robert E. Lee." Jarvis transforms the gentleman's traditional concern for honor into a nasty expression of reactionary paranoia.

Yet in spite of spiritually barren replicas of Virginia gentlemen that one encounters in *The Shad Treatment*, the Cavalier ideal is manifested in a more positive way in several of the novel's characters. Mac's father, the defeated and disgraced liberal, and his father's old friend, Judge

Kenlow Anderson, a conservative member of the Virginia political establishment, are both gentlemen of the old school. Each of them possesses a sense of honor and integrity that joins smoothly with their good manners and their good breeding. Ultimately, the reader realizes that Mac himself is partially defined by the gentlemanly code of his father. Though he approaches his native state with irony and irreverence, he is to a significant degree a product of the traditional Virginia upbringing which he judges as deceptive and outmoded.

Mac Evans, in fact, shares a number of qualities with Peter Leverette and Stingo, the young Virginia gentlemen who narrate William Styron's *Set This House on Fire* and *Sophie's Choice*. Like them he is intelligent and well bred. He has none of the snobbishness and arrogance that one might associate with an FFV. He is discreet and self-effacing in the best sense of these terms. He is not boastful or neurotically self-assertive. He has learned to respect the virtues of kindness and tolerance, and his southern exposure makes him naturally uncomfortable in the presence of the dogmatism which passes among his northern friends at Harvard for idealism. His ingrained respect for the virtue of ladies and his inability to divorce sex from a puritanical moral inheritance render him a virtual celibate. Finally and most importantly, he possesses a gentleman's sense of honor. When a Virginia politician is angered by a bribe that has been offered him by Shadwell's campaign manager in return for his support, Mac must convince him that Shadwell never knew of the offer. Finally he gives the only proof that one gentleman needs to give another. "I give you my sworn word that this offer did not come from Tom Jeff. . . . I swear to you before heaven, as a gentleman, a Democrat, and a human being. Isn't that enough for you?" (381). One suspects that the oath of a human being or a Democrat would not be enough for the outraged politician, but the word of a gentleman is.

Mac Evans' Virginia heritage is in many ways a burden which needs to be understood and cast off. Paradoxically, it is also an inheritance that gives him, like Styron's young protagonists, a sense of *locus*, or place, and a sense of identity. Mac knows who he is and where he comes from. Though one can interpret his departure from Virginia at the conclusion of the novel as a repudiation or casting aside of his past, it seems more likely that Mac has simply learned to come to terms with his heritage. Henceforth he will see the world anew and "work out his salvation" away from Virginia, "northbound, away from home." But his salvation will be achieved by means of the positive and vital aspects of his heritage which he has wisely conserved and which he will carry with him wherever he goes.

CONCLUSION

ALL of Virginia's writers have recognized at least dimly that there is something inadequate and insufficient in the Cavalier ideal. They have shared a common pessimism that the Cavalier can prevail in a land whose dominant myths are profoundly egalitarian in nature and whose national mission is so firmly founded on the democratic ideal. The inadequacy of the Cavalier type is, of course, not hard to detect in modern Virginia fiction. We see it clearly displayed, from the Cavalier *manqué* we find in Cabell and Glasgow's novels to the grotesque distortions of the gentlemanly ideal we encounter in Styron's *Lie Down in Darkness* and Epps's *The Shad Treatment*. But it must not be forgotten that even the most romantic of the Old Dominion's nineteenth-century writers also acknowledge, if only implicitly, the insufficiency of their heroes' aristocratic ethos. The Cavaliers of George Tucker and John Pendleton Kennedy, for all their emotional appeal, are clearly impractical men doomed by the progressive forces of history. And the more swashbuckling creations of William Alexander Caruthers and John Esten Cooke are compromised by the robust yeoman figures who occupy the scenic background but who suggest, nevertheless, the eventual triumph of the common man in America. The elegiac tone of many antebellum treatments of the Cavalier is revived with greater force after the Civil War. Thomas Nelson Page, for example, both apotheosizes the Cavalier and mourns the destruction of his way of life in the cataclysm of civil war. Thus, in spite of enormously different fictional approaches, over the past two centuries all of Virginia's writers have invested their Cavaliers to some degree with a sense of futility and failure.

Yet, having made the point that the Old Dominions' writers share a collective intuition of the Cavalier's limitations, one must also observe that these same writers share a common conviction that the code of the Virginia gentleman ought to have, indeed *must* have, some positive connection with our national experience. Paradoxically, the state's novelists seem always to have hoped that the Cavalier ideal, though estranged from many of America's cultural values, might still positively affect the national character. It is easy to distinguish those aristocratic qualities which Virginia's nineteenth-century creators of the Cavalier judge worthy of preserving. From Tucker to Page, the Old Dominion's novelists routinely suggest that though the exalted standards of conduct embodied by their planter aristocrats may ultimately be swept away in a flood of Yankee materialism, Virginia and the entire nation will be the worse for having lost them. It is more difficult to recognize the positive aspects of the Cavalier code in modern Virginia fiction because the twentieth-century Virginia gentleman is less glorified than his nineteenth-century ancestor and is commonly depicted as being depleted by life. Still, most of these recent novels, from *The Rivet in Grandfather's Neck* to *The Shad Treatment*, contain sympathetically drawn aristocratic characters who discipline their lives in a positive way by drawing on the best elements of their Cavalier inheritance. Novelists as diverse as Cabell and Styron seem to believe that, used wisely, the code of the gentleman can still be a source of personal strength for their characters. Writers of the Old Dominion have been composing the Cavalier's obituary since the days of George Tucker, but not even the state's most iconoclastic contemporary novelists have been willing to dismiss all the ideals associated with the tradition as being completely irrelevant or completely moribund.

There are thus specific attitudes toward the Virginia gentleman which are broadly shared by the state's nineteenth- and twentieth-century writers. It is obvious, however, that the writers of the present century have been much more successful in dealing with the moral and social implications of the Cavalier tradition than their nineteenth-century predecessors. From the very beginning the Virginia writer has confronted a dilemma in developing his Virginia gentleman: how to translate an aristocratic ideal that is the product of a unique local culture into a character capable of living in harmony with the nation's fundamental political and social ideals. As we have seen, antebellum Virginia novelists such as John Pendleton Kennedy, in *Horse-Shoe Robinson*, and William Alexander Caruthers, in *Knights of the Golden*

Horse-shoe, sought to make the Cavalier an organic part of American mythology—Kennedy by attempting to create an amalgam of Cavalier and yeoman and Caruthers by making his aristocratic Virginians instruments of the nation's manifest destiny. But these attempts failed to convincingly demonstrate how a tradition profoundly aristocratic in spirit could be made to coexist peacefully with the frontier yeoman ideal.

Ironically, the only Virginian of the nineteenth century who clearly saw a way of uniting the aristocratic ideal with America's commitment to democracy was not a novelist but a politician. That man was Thomas Jefferson. In a letter to John Adams written in 1813 Jefferson proposed the concept of a "natural aristocracy" of "virtue and talents" and contrasted this positive social principle with the "artificial aristocracy" of "wealth and birth" which he believed Adams as well as many Americans in both the South and the North sought to maintain. The sage of Monticello believed that the challenge confronting the new nation was to create forms of government and educational systems which would provide "the most effectively for a pure selection of these natural aristoi into the offices of government." Unlike Adams, who believed that some sort of privileged class must dominate any society, Jefferson optimistically asserted that systems could be devised so that "rank, and birth, and tinsel-aristocracy [would] finally shrink into insignificance."[1]

Jefferson's ideal state was, of course, an agrarian society dominated by independent yeoman farmers, and the great democrat was unable to imagine how his meritocracy might work in a modern industrial society. Still his concept of an agrarian republic ruled by a democratically elected natural aristocracy was one which the antebellum South might have embraced with positive social consequences. Unfortunately, after a period during which Dixie awkwardly sought to profess both yeoman and Cavalier ideals, the South ultimately pledged its primary allegiance to the aristocratic plantation myth, using it to defend the enslavement of black Americans and carrying it hysterically into battle. The triumph of the Cavalier ideal was nowhere more thoroughly dem-

1. Lester J. Cappon (ed.), *The Adams-Jefferson Letters: The Complete Correspondence Between Thomas Jefferson and Abigail and John Adams* (Chapel Hill, 1959), II, 388, 391.

onstrated than in Virginia fiction of both the antebellum and postbellum periods. After George Tucker every Virginia writer almost completely shunned Jefferson's noble yeoman and the attendant ideal of a natural aristocracy. Rather than critically analyzing their society, the Old Dominion's nineteenth-century writers chose to defend a morally reprehensible institution and a historically anachronistic way of life by evoking a myth and a character ideal which had little relevance to the lives of the vast majority of Virginians.

The course of nineteenth-century Virginia fiction reflected the larger failure of the South's writers during this period to fashion a Cavalier who could evoke the most positive elements of southern culture and relate in an affirmative way to a broader national context. Lamentably, the conventionally romantic aristocratic figure these writers did create has remained to haunt the region in this century. As late as the 1960s the distinguished southern historian, Francis Butler Simkins, boasted that the aristocratic concept was still the unifying principle of southern culture, opposing the "money concept," which dominated in the North. "The Southerner," Simkins contended, "whatever he may say in his formal moments, does not wish the type of democracy envisaged by the Declaration of Independence and expressed in the Fourteenth and Fifteenth Amendments. Actually he wishes to maintain a caste system more rigid than any which has ever existed in Europe."[2]

Reading Simkins' essay, one experiences a disturbing sense of déjà vu. In 1860 many southerners of substance had violently turned against their Jeffersonian heritage; government by the people had been twisted into "demon democracy." As Kenneth Stampp observes, "no other group was so solidly dedicated, by interest and necessity, to the proposition that men were created unequal as were the slaveholders of the Old South. No other group was so firmly rooted in a dying past, so fearful of change, so alienated from the spirit of the age."[3] The leaders of the antebellum South used the Cavalier concept to vindicate their reactionism

2. Francis Butler Simkins, "The South's Democratic Pose," in his *The Everlasting South* (Baton Rouge, 1963), 30.

3. Kenneth Stampp, *The Peculiar Institution: Slavery in the Antebellum South* (New York, 1968), 419–20.

and their alienation. One hundred years later many influential southerners of intelligence and learning, such as Simkins, continued to in-
veigh against the threat posed by the "meddlesome Yankee."[4] They
were again using the aristocratic myth to preserve what they believed to
be the southern way of life, though the foundation of this way of life was
now seen as resting on segregation rather than slavery. Defensive and
reactionary thinking was once again intimately linked to the South's
vision of its aristocratic heritage.

As the Old Dominion epitomized the triumph of the Cavalier ideal
in the nineteenth-century South, modern Virginia has epitomized the
stubborn survival of the aristocratic myth in Dixie into the twentieth
century. The romantic Cavalier ideal is still intimately linked to what
Raymond Pulley has described as the "Virginia mystique," an ambiance
which has sustained the state's "unmistakably aristocratic and undemo-
cratic flavor."[5] It has made Virginia the most politically and socially
conservative state of the modern South. This aristocratic ethos helped
to sustain until the 1960s the nation's most reactionary political machine, a machine that in the words of J. Harvie Wilkinson "reflected a
pleasant provincialism which maintained that the genteel life exempted
the Old Dominion from statistical scrutiny and the tyranny of fact."[6]

Given this social and political context, Virginia's modern writers
have admirably striven to free themselves from the stultifying bondage
of their past. Their more analytical scrutiny of their native state's history and heritage has resulted in especially penetrating characterizations of contemporary Cavaliers. As I have observed earlier, James
Branch Cabell and Ellen Glasgow succeeded partially, but only partially,
in attaining ironic distance from their fictional Virginia gentlemen. So
thoroughly were their lives molded by the "Virginia mystique" and
so thoroughly were they themselves a part of that genteel tradition,
that, although they were burdened with relatively few illusions about
the Old Dominion's past, neither of them could assay her present or an-

---

4. Simkins, "The South's Democratic Pose," 31.
5. Raymond H. Pulley, *Old Virginia Restored: An Interpretation of the Progressive Impulse, 1870–1930* (Charlottesville, 1968), 2.
6. Wilkinson, *Harry Byrd and the Changing Face of Virginia Politics*, 343.

ticipate her future with genuine confidence. They were pulled strongly toward the antique Cavalier characters whom they sought to dissect. One feels that they would desperately have liked to find a place in the modern world for their Virginia gentlemen, but they could not.

It is far from certain that the fictional achievement of William Styron and Garrett Epps will match that of James Branch Cabell and Ellen Glasgow. Yet these recent Virginia writers have moved beyond their predecessors in the depiction of the Virginia gentleman. Their novels look with thorough honesty at the perversion of the genteel ideal and and at the proliferation of sham gentility in the state. Styron and Epps are Virginia's first writers to treat the Old Dominion's myths and its social and political pieties with an attitude of consistent and uncompromising realism. Unlike Cabell and Glasgow, who continually qualify their irreverence for Virginia with reverence, they convey in their novels a vigorous—and, in Epps's case a zestful—iconoclasm which, after 150 years of varying degrees of fictional Shintoism, can most simply be termed refreshing.

Because Styron and Epps have no illusions about Virginia's Cavalier tradition, they are free to imagine a positive role for the character ideal in contemporary America. Having completely dismantled the myth, they can expose and discard the limiting, false, and life-denying aspects of the aristocratic ethos while validating the positive and affirmative aspects. The gentlemanly narrators of *Set This House on Fire* and *Sophie's Choice* and the protagonist of *The Shad Treatment* present the reader with a new type of Virginia gentleman. This new type embodies the politeness, the modesty, and the sense of personal integrity of the older model. Perhaps most significantly, he retains the sense of place and being, the sense of soundly knowing who he is and where he is from, that the Cavalier tradition has always vouchsafed. Yet this sense of *locus* is not, as it has so often been in the past, a limitation. Styron's and Epps's gentlemen are free of the snobbery, condescension, and class consciousness that has historically been part and parcel of the Cavalier ideal. They are also free of the intolerance, the reactionism, and the xenophobia that the benign figure of the Virginia gentleman has all too often masked and implicitly validated. The modern-day gentlemen of

Styron and Epps live in a chaotic world which we have come to recognize as the world of modern fiction. One feels, however, that, carrying the vital elements of their heritage with them into such a world, these contemporary Cavaliers are as well equipped to make their way as any men could be.

In "Education for the Uncommon Man" Ronald Howell presents perhaps the most inclusive modern definition of what a southern gentleman ideally should be. Howell describes the type as "tolerant, kindly, broad-minded, non-puritan, moderate, hospitable, and courteous. . . . Laying claim to what the Renaissance called *virtu*, he is a man of parts, catholic interests, and large compassion. A totally integrated personality, he is also supremely gregarious and sees himself as rightly assimilated into an organic familial and social order that has a sense of purpose and continuity. More concerned with *being* and *thinking* than *doing*, he has a critical though genial view of life. The southern gentleman boasts the spiritual lineage of the English Cavalier transplanted to these shores centuries ago." One notes that Howell is careful to define the southern gentleman's Cavalier heritage as a "spiritual" one; it is not a physical or genealogical heritage. Indeed he goes on to stress that a true southern gentleman embraces the Jeffersonian political tradition. "Translating 'aristocracy' literally as the 'rule of the best' and understanding by 'conservatism' the philosophy of 'preserving the best,'" this tradition "restricts the highest offices not to the 'rich and well born' but to the most qualified and deserving, wherever they are found."[7]

Howell's precarious fusion of an English Renaissance social ideal with the Jeffersonian political ideal suggests the unique situation of the Cavalier ideal in America. A survey of Virginia fiction reveals that few fictional Cavaliers have approached this felicitous blending of European with New World traditions. The Old Dominion's writers have usually been content merely to emphasize the physical Cavalier lineage of their fictional aristocrats, and they have typically used the Cavalier to justify

7. Ronald F. Howell, "Education for the Uncommon Man," in Louis D. Rubin and James J. Kilpatrick (eds.), *The Lasting South: Fourteen Southerners Look at Their Home* (Chicago, 1957), 147.

attitudes which were anything but tolerant and broad-minded. Indeed, the fictional evolution of the Cavalier in Virginia fiction and the influence of the stereotype on life in the Old Dominion and in the South illustrates David Halberstam's cautionary observation that though "dreams are fine both for people and for nations," they can be "dangerous as well, for they may turn into myth, diverting us from what we are and what we might be into what we think we are."[8]

It is possible that the Cavalier ideal which Virginians and southerners have historically carried before them may yet be redeemed and may yet be linked in a positive way to the fundamental ideals of our nation. Certainly the South's writers will play an important role in such an evolution of the character type. William Styron's and Garrett Epps's novels suggest that the redemption of the gentlemanly tradition may have begun and that Virginia, as it has done in the past, will make an important contribution to future transformation of the Cavalier figure.

8. David Halberstam, "A Letter to My Daughter," *Parade*, May 2, 1982, p. 5.

BIBLIOGRAPHY

Abernethy, Thomas P. *The South in the New Nation, 1789–1819*. Baton Rouge, 1961.

Adams, Henry. *History of the United States of America During the Administrations of Jefferson and Madison*. Abridged and edited by Ernest Samuels. Chicago, 1967.

Aldridge, John W. *The American Novel and the Way We Live Now*. New York, 1983.

———. "In a Place Where Love Is a Stranger." Review of *Lie Down in Darkness*, by William Styron. *New York Times Book Review*, September 9, 1951, p. 5.

———. "William Styron and the Derivative Imagination." In his *The Devil in the Fire: Retrospective Essays on American Literature and Culture, 1951–1971*. New York, 1972.

Appleby, Joyce, "Reconciliation and the Northern Novelist, 1865–1880." *Civil War History*, X (1964), 117–29.

Bagby, George William. "Editorial." *Southern Literary Messenger*, XXXII (January, 1861), 71–79.

———. *The Old Virginia Gentleman and Other Sketches*. Edited by Thomas Nelson Page. New York, 1910.

———. "The Virginia Editor." *Harper's Monthly Magazine*, XIV (December, 1856), 66–69.

Bailyn, Bernard. "Politics and Social Structure in Virginia." In *Seventeenth-Century America: Essays in Colonial History*, edited by James Morton Smith. Chapel Hill, 1959.

Baldwin, Joseph Glover. *The Flush Times of Alabama and Mississippi: A Series of Sketches*. Americus, Ga., 1853.

Bass, Jack, and Walter DeVries. *The Transformation of Southern Politics: Social Change and Political Consequence Since 1945*. New York, 1976.

Beatty, Richmond Croom. *William Byrd of Westover*. New York, 1932.

Beaty, John Owen. *John Esten Cooke, Virginian*. New York, 1922.

Berger, Yves. *The Garden*. New York, 1963.

Berkeley, Sir William. *A Discourse and View of Virginia*. 1663; rpr. Norwalk, Conn., 1914.

Beverley, Robert. *The History and Present State of Virginia*. Edited by Louis B. Wright. 1705; rpr. Chapel Hill, 1947.

Billings, Warren M., ed. *The Old Dominion in the Seventeenth Century: A Documentary History of Virginia, 1606–1689*. Chapel Hill, 1975.

Bohner, Charles H. *John Pendleton Kennedy, Gentleman from Baltimore*. Baltimore, 1961.

Bontemps, Arna. *Black Thunder*. New York, 1936.

Bridenbaugh, Carl. *Myths and Realities: Societies of the Colonial South*. Baton Rouge, 1952.

Brissot de Warville, Jacques Pierre. *New Travels in the United States of America, Performed in 1788*. London, 1792.

Brooks, Cleanth. "The Crisis in Culture as Reflected in Southern Literature." In *The American South: Portrait of a Culture*, edited by Louis D. Rubin, Jr. Baton Rouge, 1980.

————. *William Faulkner: Toward Yoknapatawpha and Beyond*. New Haven, 1978.

Brown, Robert E., and B. Katherine Brown. *Virginia, 1705–1786: Democracy or Aristocracy*. East Lansing, 1964.

Bruce, Philip Alexander. *History of the University of Virginia, 1819–1919: The Lengthened Shadow of One Man*. 5 vols. New York, 1920–22.

————. *Social Life of Virginia in the Seventeenth Century*. 1907; rpr. New York, 1964.

————. *The Virginia Plutarch*. 2 vols. Chapel Hill, 1929.

Bruner, Jerome S. "Myth and Identity." In *Myth and Mythmaking*, edited by Henry A. Murray. New York, 1960.

Buck, Paul H. *The Road to Reunion, 1865–1900*. Boston, 1937.

Buckley, William F., Jr. "Introduction: Did You Ever See a Dream Walking?" In *Did You Ever See a Dream Walking? American Conservative Thought in the Twentieth Century*, edited by William F. Buckley, Jr. Indianapolis, 1970.

Bullock, William. *Virginia Impartially Examined*. London, 1649.

Burt, Nathaniel. *First Families: The Making of an American Aristocracy*. Boston, 1970.

Cabell, James Branch. *Beyond Life: Dizain des Demiurges*. New York, 1919.

————. *The Cords of Vanity*. New York, 1909.

————. *The Cream of the Jest: A Comedy of Evasions*. New York, 1917.

————. *Figures of Earth: A Comedy of Appearances*. 1921; rpr. New York, 1926.

————. *Jurgen: A Comedy of Justice*. New York, 1919.

————. *Let Me Lie: Being in the Main an Ethnological Account of the Remarkable Commonwealth of Virginia and the Making of Its History*. New York, 1947.

————. *Preface to the Past*. New York, 1936.

————. *The Rivet in Grandfather's Neck: A Comedy of Limitations*. New York, 1915.

————. *The Silver Stallion: A Comedy of Redemption*. New York, 1926.

————. *Smirt: An Urbane Nightmare*. New York, 1934.

Cady, Edwin Harrison. *The Gentleman in America: A Literary Study in American Culture.* Syracuse, 1949.

Campbell, Mildred. "Social Origins of Some Early Americans." In *Seventeenth-Century America*, edited by James Morton Smith. Chapel Hill, 1959.

Cappon, Lester J., ed. *The Adams-Jefferson Letters: The Complete Correspondence Between Thomas Jefferson and Abigail and John Adams.* Vol. II of 2 vols. Chapel Hill, 1959.

Cargill, Oscar. *Intellectual America: Ideas on the March.* New York, 1941.

[Carter, St. Leger Landon?]. "Interesting Ruins on the Rappahannock." *Southern Literary Messenger*, I (August, 1834), 9–10.

Caruthers, William Alexander. *The Cavaliers of Virginia; or, The Recluse of Jamestown: An Historical Romance of the Old Dominion.* 2 vols. 1834; rpr. Ridgewood, N.J., 1968.

————. *The Kentuckian in New-York; or, The Adventures of Three Southerns, by a Virginian.* 1834; rpr. Ridgewood, N.J., 1968.

————. *The Knights of the Golden Horse-shoe: A Traditionary Tale of the Cocked Hat Gentry in the Old Dominion.* 1845; rpr. Chapel Hill, 1970.

Cash, Wilbur Joseph. *The Mind of the South.* New York, 1941.

Cason, Clarence E. "Middle Class and Bourbon." In *Culture in the South*, edited by W. T. Couch. Chapel Hill, 1935.

Chastellux, Marquis de. *Travels in North America in the Years 1780, 1781, and 1782.* Translated by Howard C. Rice, Jr. 2 vols. Chapel Hill, 1963.

Chesson, Michael B. *Richmond After the War, 1865–1890.* Richmond, 1981.

Clemens, Samuel. *Life on the Mississippi.* New York, 1927.

Coleman, Charles W. "The Recent Movement in Southern Literature." *Harper's New Monthly Magazine*, LXXIV (1887), 837–55.

Cooke, John Esten. *Hammer and Rapier.* New York, 1870.

————. *Henry St. John, Gentleman, of "Flower of Hundreds," in the County of Prince George, Virginia: A Tale of 1774–75.* New York, 1859.

————. *A Life of General Robert E. Lee.* New York, 1871.

————. *Mohun, a Novel.* 1868; rpr. New York, 1896.

————. *Surry of Eagle's Nest; or, The Memoirs of a Staff Officer Serving in Virginia.* 1866; rpr. New York, 1894.

————. *Virginia: A History of the People.* 1883; rpr. Boston, 1894.

————. *The Virginia Comedians; or, Old Days in the Old Dominion.* 2 vols. 1854; rpr. Ridgewood, N.J., 1968.

————. "Virginia Girls and Gallants Four Score Years Ago." *Southern Literary Messenger*, XXIII (July, 1856), 333–46.

Cooper, James Fenimore. *Notions of the Americans.* 1828; rpr. New York, 1963.

Core, George. "*The Confessions of Nat Turner* and the Burden of the Past." In *The Achievement of William Styron*, edited by Robert K. Morris and Irving Malin. Rev. ed. Athens, Ga., 1981.

Cowie, Alexander. *The Rise of the American Novel*. New York, 1948.

Cowley, Malcolm. "The Faulkner Pattern." *New Republic*, October 8, 1951, pp. 19–20.

Craven, Avery. *Edmund Ruffin, Southerner: A Study in Secession*. New York, 1932.

———. *The Growth of Southern Nationalism, 1848–1861*. Baton Rouge, 1953.

Craven, Wesley Frank. *The Southern Colonies in the Seventeenth Century, 1607–1689*. Baton Rouge, 1949.

———. *White, Red, and Black: The Seventeenth Century Virginian*. Charlottesville, 1971.

Dabney, Virginius. "An Approach to Virginia." Review of *Virginia Is a State of Mind*, by Virginia Moore. *Saturday Review of Literature*, January 23, 1942, pp. 18–19.

———. *Virginia, the New Dominion*. Garden City, N.Y., 1971.

Davenport, F. Garvin, Jr. *The Myth of Southern History: Historical Consciousness in Twentieth Century Southern Literature*. Nashville, 1970.

Davis, Curtis Carroll. *Chronicler of the Cavaliers: A Life of the Virginia Novelist Dr. William A. Caruthers*. Richmond, 1953.

———. Introduction to *The Knights of the Horse-shoe: A Traditionary Tale of the Cocked Hat Gentry in the Old Dominion* by William Alexander Caruthers. Chapel Hill, 1970.

Davis, David B. "Ten-Gallon Hero." *American Quarterly*, VI (1954), 111–125.

Davis, John. *Captain Smith and Princess Pocahontas: An Indian Tale*. Philadelphia, 1805.

———. *The First Settlers of Virginia: An Historical Novel*. New York, 1806.

———. *Travels of Four Years and a Half in the United States of America During 1798, 1799, 1800, 1801, and 1802*. 1803; rpr. New York, 1909.

Davis, Richard Beale. *A Colonial Southern Bookshelf: Reading in the Eighteenth Century*. Athens, 1979.

———. "The Intellectual Golden Age in the Colonial Chesapeake Bay Country." In his *Literature and Society in Early Virginia, 1608–1840*. Baton Rouge, 1973.

———. *Intellectual Life in Jefferson's Virginia, 1790–1830*. Chapel Hill, 1964.

———. *Intellectual Life in the Colonial South, 1585–1763*. 3 vols. Knoxville, 1978.

———. "Literary Tastes in Virginia Before Poe." *William and Mary Quarterly*, n.s., XIX (1939), 55–68.

———. "The Virginia Novel Before *Swallow Barn*." In his *Literature and Society in Early Virginia, 1608–1840*. Baton Rouge, 1973.

———, ed. *William Fitzhugh and His Chesapeake World, 1676–1701: The Fitzhugh Letters and Other Documents*. Chapel Hill, 1963.

"The Difference of Race Between the Northern and Southern People." *Southern Literary Messenger*, XXX (June, 1860), 401–409.

Dowdey, Clifford. *The Virginia Dynasties: The Emergence of "King" Carter and the Golden Age.* Boston, 1969.

Eaton, Clement. *Freedom of Thought in the Old South.* Durham, 1940.

———. *The Growth of Southern Civilization, 1790–1860.* New York, 1961.

———. *A History of the Old South.* 2nd ed. New York, 1966.

———. *The Mind of the Old South.* Baton Rouge, 1964.

Eggleston, George Cary. "The Old Regime in the Old Dominion." *Atlantic Monthly,* XXXVI (1875), 603–16.

Eisenberg, Ralph. "Virginia: The Emergence of Two-Party Politics." In *The Changing Politics of the South,* edited by William C. Havard. Baton Rouge, 1972.

Eliot. T. S. *After Strange Gods: A Primer of Modern Heresy.* London, 1934.

Elkins, Stanley M. *Slavery: A Problem in American Institutional and Intellectual Life.* Chicago, 1959.

Ellmann, Richard, and Charles Feidelson, Jr., eds. *The Modern Tradition: Backgrounds of Modern Literature.* New York, 1965.

Epps, Garrett. *The Shad Treatment.* New York, 1977.

"Essay on Honour." *The Virginia Gazette.* Edited by William Parks. No. 157, July 27–August 3, 1739, p. 1.

Farish, Hunter Dickinson, ed. *Journal and Letters of Philip Vickers Fithian, 1773–1774: A Plantation Tutor of the Old Dominion.* Charlottesville, 1957.

Faulkner, William. *Absalom, Absalom!* New York, 1936.

———. *The Unvanquished.* New York, 1938.

Faust, Drew Gilpin, ed. *The Ideology of Slavery: Proslavery Thought in the Antebellum South, 1830–1860.* Baton Rouge, 1981.

Fishwick, Marshall W. "Civil War II." *Texas Quarterly,* II (1959), 109–18.

———. *The Hero, American Style.* New York, 1969.

———. *Virginia: A New Look at the Old Dominion.* New York, 1959.

———. *The Virginia Tradition.* Washington, 1956.

Fitzgerald, F. Scott. "The Ice Palace." In *The Stories of F. Scott Fitzgerald,* edited by Malcolm Cowley. 1921; rpr. New York, 1951.

———. *Tender Is the Night.* New York, 1933.

Fitzhugh, George. *Cannibals All! or, Slaves Without Masters.* Richmond, 1857.

Flanders, Jane. "William Styron's Southern Myth." In *The Achievement of William Styron,* edited by Robert K. Morris and Irving Malin. Athens, 1981.

Floan, Howard R. *The South in Northern Eyes, 1831–1861.* New York, 1958.

Franklin, John Hope. "The Great Confrontation: The South and the Problem of Change." *Journal of Southern History,* XXXVIII (1972), 3–20.

Fraser, John. *America and the Patterns of Chivalry.* New Rochelle, N.Y., 1982.

Frazee, Monique Parent. "Ellen Glasgow as Feminist." In *Ellen Glasgow Centennial Essays,* edited by M. Thomas Inge. Charlottesville, 1976.

Freeman, Douglas Southall. *The South to Posterity: An Introduction to the Writings of Confederate History.* New York, 1951.

————. "Virginia: A Gentle Dominion." In *The United States: A Symposium*, edited by Ernest Gruening. New York, 1924.

Friddell, Guy. *We Began at Jamestown*. Richmond, 1968.

————. *What Is It About Virginia?* Richmond, 1966.

Frye, Northrop. "New Directions from Old." In *Myth and Mythmaking*, edited by Henry A. Murray. New York, 1960.

Gaines, Francis Pendleton. *The Southern Plantation: A Study in the Development and the Accuracy of a Tradition*. New York, 1924.

Gaston, Paul M. *The New South Creed: A Study in Southern Mythmaking*. New York, 1970.

Genovese, Eugene. *The World the Slaveholders Made: Two Essays in Interpretation*. New York, 1969.

Gerster, Patrick, and Nicholas Cords. *Myth in American History*. Encino, Calif., 1977.

————, eds. *Myth and Southern History*. Chicago, 1974.

Girouard, Mark. *The Return to Camelot: Chivalry and the English Gentleman*. New Haven, 1981.

Glasgow, Ellen. *Barren Ground*. Garden City, N.Y., 1925.

————. *The Battle-ground*. 1902; rpr. New York, 1936.

————. *A Certain Measure: An Interpretation of Prose Fiction*. New York, 1943.

————. *The Deliverance: A Romance of the Virginia Tobacco Fields*. 1904; rpr. New York, 1929.

————. *The Miller of Old Church*. New York, 1911.

————. *The Romantic Comedians*. Garden City, N.Y., 1926.

————. *The Sheltered Life*. Garden City, N.Y., 1932.

————. *They Stooped to Folly: A Comedy of Morals*. Garden City, N.Y., 1929.

————. *The Voice of the People*. 1900; rpr. New York, 1902.

Godbold, E. Stanley, Jr. *Ellen Glasgow and the Woman Within*. Baton Rouge, 1972.

Gottmann, Jean. *Virginia at Mid-century*. New York, 1955.

————. *Virginia in Our Century*. Charlottesville, 1969.

Govan, Thomas P. "Americans Below the Potomac." In *The Southerner as American*, edited by Charles Grier Sellers. Chapel Hill, 1960.

Gray, Richard L. *The Literature of Memory: Modern Writers of the American South*. Baltimore, 1977.

Grayson, William John. "The Character of a Gentleman." *Southern Quarterly Review*, n.s., VIII (January, 1853), 58.

Green, Fletcher M. "Democracy in the Old South." *Journal of Southern History*, XII (1946), 3–23.

Greene, Jack P., ed. *The Diary of Colonel Landon Carter of Sabine Hall, 1759–1778*. 2 vols. Charlottesville, 1965.

Gross, Theodore L. *Thomas Nelson Page*. New York, 1967.

————. "Thomas Nelson Page: Creator of a Virginia Classic." *Georgia Review*, XX (1966), 338–51.

Gwathmey, Edward M. *John Pendleton Kennedy*. New York, 1931.

Gwynn, Frederick L., and Joseph L. Blotner, eds. *Faulkner in the University: Class Conferences at the University of Virginia, 1957–1958*. Charlottesville, 1959.

Halberstam, David. "A Letter to My Daughter." *Parade*, May 2, 1982, pp. 4–7.

Hall, Francis. *Travels in Canada and the United States in 1816 and 1817*. London, 1818.

Hammond, John. *Leah and Rachel; or, The Two Fruitful Sisters Virginia and Maryland: Their Present Condition, Impartially Stated and Related. Narratives of Early Maryland, 1633–1684*. Edited by Clayton Colman Hall. 1656; rpr. New York, 1910.

Harrison, Constance Cary. *Flower de Hundred: The Story of a Virginia Plantation*. New York, 1890.

———. *A Son of the Old Dominion*. Boston, 1897.

Hartwell, Henry, James Blair, and Edward Chilton. *The Present State of Virginia, and the College*. Edited by Hunter Dickinson Farish. 1727; rpr. Williamsburg, 1940.

Harwell, Richard B. "The Stream of Self-Consciousness." In *The Idea of the South: Pursuit of a Central Theme*, edited by Frank E. Vandiver. Chicago, 1964.

Heath, James Ewell. *Edge-Hill; or, The Family of the Fitzroyals*. Richmond, 1828.

Henneman, John Bell. "The National Element in Southern Literature." *Sewanee Review*, XI (1903), 345–66.

Hergesheimer, Joseph. *Balisand*. New York, 1924.

———. *Swords and Roses*. New York, 1929.

Hesseltine, William Best. "Four American Traditions." *Journal of Southern History*, XXVII (1961), 3–32.

Higginson, Thomas Wentworth. "The Case of the Carpet-baggers." *Nation*, March 2, 1899, pp. 162–63.

Holman, C. Hugh. "The Comedies of Manners." In *Ellen Glasgow Centennial Essays*, edited by M. Thomas Inge. Charlottesville, 1976.

———. "Ellen Glasgow and the Southern Literary Tradition." In *Southern Writers: Appraisals in Our Time*, edited by Rinaldo C. Simonini, Jr. Charlottesville, 1964.

———. "The Southerner as American Writer." In *The Southerner as American*, edited by Charles Grier Sellers, Jr. Chapel Hill, 1960.

———. *Three Modes of Southern Fiction: Ellen Glasgow, William Faulkner, Thomas Wolfe*. Athens, 1966.

Holman, Harriet R. "The Literary Career of Thomas Nelson Page, 1884–1910." Ph.D. dissertation, Duke University, 1947.

Howell, Ronald F. "Education for the Uncommon Man." In *The Lasting South: Fourteen Southerners Look at Their Home*, edited by Louis D. Rubin, Jr. and James J. Kilpatrick. Chicago, 1957.

Hubbell, Jay Broadus. "Cavalier and Indentured Servant in Virginia Fiction." *South Atlantic Quarterly*, XXVI (1927), 22–39.

———. Introduction to *Swallow Barn; or A Sojourn in the Old Dominion*, by John Pendleton Kennedy. New York, 1929.

———. "Literary Nationalism in the Old South." In *American Studies in Honor of William Kenneth Boyd*, edited by David Kelley Jackson. Durham, 1940.

———. *Southern Life in Fiction.* Athens, 1960.

———. *The South in American Literature, 1607–1900.* Durham, 1954.

———. "Thackeray and Virginia." *Virginia Quarterly Review*, III (1927), 76–86.

———. *Virginia Life in Fiction.* Dallas, 1922.

Hundley, Daniel R. *Social Relations in Our Southern States.* New York, 1860.

Hunter, Thomas Lomax. *Columns from the Cavalier.* Richmond, 1935.

Isaac, Rhys. *The Transformation of Virginia, 1740–1790.* Chapel Hill, 1982.

Jackson, David Kelley. *The Contributors and Contributions to the Southern Literary Messenger (1834–1864).* Charlottesville, 1936.

James, G[eorge] P[aine] R[ainsford]. *The Old Dominion; or, The Southampton Massacre.* New York, 1856.

Jefferson, Thomas. *Notes on the State of Virginia.* Edited by William Peden. Chapel Hill, 1955.

Jenkins, William Sumner. *Pro-slavery Thought in the Old South.* Chapel Hill, 1935.

Johnson, Gerald W. "To Live and Die in Dixie." *Atlantic*, CCVI (July, 1960), 29–34.

Johnston, Mary. *Cease Firing.* Boston, 1912.

———. *The Great Valley.* Boston, 1926.

———. *Hagar.* Boston, 1913.

———. *The Long Roll.* New York, 1911.

———. *Prisoners of Hope: A Tale of Colonial Virginia.* 1898; rpr. Boston, 1926.

———. *To Have and to Hold.* New York, 1900.

Jones, Anne Goodwyn. *Tomorrow Is Another Day: The Woman Writer in the South, 1859–1936.* Baton Rouge, 1981.

Jones, Hugh. *Present State of Virginia: From Whence Is Inferred a Short View of Maryland and North Carolina.* Edited by Richard L. Morton. 1753; rpr. Chapel Hill, 1956.

Kellogg, Thelma Louise. *The Life and Works of John Davis, 1774–1853.* University of Maine Studies, second series, no. 1. Orono, 1924.

Kennedy, John Pendleton. *At Home and Abroad: A Series of Essays: With a Journal in Europe in 1867–68.* New York, 1872.

———. "Hoppergallop House." In *Swallow Barn; or, A Sojourn in the Old Dominion.* 1832; rpr. New York, 1962.

———. *Horse-Shoe Robinson: A Tale of the Tory Ascendency in South Carolina, in 1780.* 1835; rpr. New York, 1928.

———. *Rob of the Bowl: A Legend of St. Inigoe's.* Edited by William S. Osborne. 1838; rpr. New Haven, 1965.

———. *Swallow Barn: A Sojourn in the Old Dominion.* Rev. ed. Philadelphia, 1861.

Key, V. O. *Southern Politics in State and Nation.* New York, 1949.

King, Joseph Leonard. *Dr. George William Bagby: A Study of Virginia Literature, 1850–1880.* New York, 1927.

King, Kimball. Introduction to *In Ole Virginia: or, Marse Chan and Other Stories,* by Thomas Nelson Page. Chapel Hill, 1969.

Kirby, Jack Temple. *Media-Made Dixie: The South in the American Imagination.* Baton Rouge, 1978.

Kirk, Russell. *John Randolph of Roanoke: A Study in American Politics.* 1951; rpr. Indianapolis, 1978.

Kluckhohn, Clyde. "Recurrent Themes in Myths and Mythmaking." In *Myth and Mythmaking,* edited by Henry A. Murray. New York, 1960.

La Rochefoucault Liancourt, François Alexandre. *Travels Through the United States of North America.* 4 vols. London, 1799.

Lehmann, Karl. *Thomas Jefferson, American Humanist.* 1947; rpr. Chicago, 1965.

Levin, Harry. "Some Meanings of Myth." In *Myth and Mythmaking,* edited by Henry A. Murray. New York, 1960.

Lewis, C. S. "Addison." In *Eighteenth-Century English Literature: Modern Essays in Criticism,* edited by James L. Clifford. New York, 1959.

Lindsay, Nicholas Vachel. "The Virginians Are Coming Again." In *The New Poetry,* edited by Harriet Monroe and Alice Corbin Henderson. Rev. ed. New York, 1932.

Lively, Robert Alexander. *Fiction Fights the Civil War: An Unfinished Chapter in the Literary History of the American People.* Chapel Hill, 1957.

"London." *Virginia Gazette.* Edited by William Hunter. No. 14, April 4, 1751, p. 2.

Lukács, Georg. *The Historical Novel.* Translated by Hannah and Stanley Mitchell. Boston, 1962.

Luraghi, Raimondo. *The Rise and Fall of the Plantation South.* New York, 1978.

Lynn, Kenneth A. "William Byrd: The Style of a Gentleman." In *Critical Approaches to American Literature,* edited by Ray B. Browne and Martin Light. Vol. I of 2 vols. New York, 1965.

McCardell, John. *The Idea of a Southern Nation: Southern Nationalists and Southern Nationalism, 1830–1860.* New York, 1979.

McClelland, Mary Greenway. *Broadoaks.* St. Paul, 1893.

McCollum, Nancy M. "Glasgow's and Cabell's Comedies of Virginia." *Georgia Review,* XVIII (1964), 236–41.

McLean, Robert Colin. *George Tucker: Moral Philosopher and Man of Letters.* Chapel Hill, 1961.

McWhiney, Grady. *Southerners and Other Americans*. New York, 1973.

Maddex, Jack P., Jr. *The Virginia Conservatives, 1867–1879: A Study in Reconstruction Politics*. Chapel Hill, 1970.

Magill, Mary Tucker. *The Holcombes: A Story of Virginia Home Life*. Philadelphia, 1871.

———. *Women; or, Chronicles of the Late War*. Baltimore, 1871.

Magruder, Julia. *Miss Ayr of Virginia and Other Stories*. 1896; rpr. Freeport, N.Y., 1970.

Marquand, John P. "Dispatch Box No. 3." *Saturday Evening Post*, November 5, 1932, pp. 12–13.

———. "Far Away." *Saturday Evening Post*, August 13, 1932, pp. 10–11.

———. "High Tide." *Saturday Evening Post*, October 8, 1932, pp. 12–13.

———. "Jack Still." *Saturday Evening Post*, June 11, 1932, pp. 10–11.

———. "Jine the Cavalry." *Saturday Evening Post*, April 16, 1932, pp. 10–11.

———. "Solid South." *Saturday Evening Post*, March 12, 1932, pp. 6–7.

Martin, Jay Herbert. *Harvests of Change: American Literature, 1865–1914*. Englewood Cliffs, N.J., 1967.

Mays, David John, ed. *The Letters and Papers of Edmund Pendleton, 1734–1803*. 2 vols. Charlottesville, 1967.

Meade, Julian R. *I Live in Virginia*. New York, 1935.

Meehan, James. "The Solitary Horseman in Virginia: Novelist G. P. R. James as British Consul, 1852–1858." *Virginia Cavalcade*, XXVII (Autumn, 1977), 58–67.

Mesick, Jane Louise. *The English Traveller in America, 1785–1835*. New York, 1922.

Michener, James A. *Chesapeake*. New York, 1978.

Miller, John C. *The First Frontier: Life in Colonial America*. New York, 1966.

Minor, Benjamin Blake. *The Southern Literary Messenger, 1834–1864*. New York, 1905.

Mixon, Wayne. *Southern Writers and the New South Movement, 1865–1913*. Chapel Hill, 1980.

Moger, Allen W. *Virginia: Bourbonism to Byrd, 1870–1925*. Charlottesville, 1968.

Moore, Virginia. *Virginia Is a State of Mind*. New York, 1942.

Mordecai, Samuel. *Richmond in By-Gone Days*. 1860; rpr. Richmond, 1946.

Morgan, Edmund S. *American Slavery, American Freedom: The Ordeal of Colonial Virginia*. New York, 1975.

Morton, Richard Lee. *Colonial Virginia*. 2 vols. Chapel Hill, 1960.

Myrdal, Gunnar. *An American Dilemma: The Negro Problem and Modern Democracy*. New York, 1962.

Nelson, Lawrence G. "Mary Johnston and the Historical Imagination." In *Southern Writers: Appraisals in Our Time*, edited by Rinaldo Simonini, Jr. Charlottesville, 1964.

Nicholls, William H. *Southern Tradition and Regional Progress*. Chapel Hill, 1960.

Noble, Donald R. Introduction to *The Valley of Shenandoah; or, The Memoirs of the Graysons*, by George Tucker. Chapel Hill, 1970.

Oakeshott, Michael. "The Masses in Representative Democracy." In *Did You Ever See a Dream Walking? American Conservative Thought in the Twentieth Century*, edited by William F. Buckley, Jr. Indianapolis, 1970.

O'Brien, Michael. *The Idea of the American South*. Baltimore, 1979.

Oldmixon, John. *British Empire in America: Containing the History of the Discovery, Settlement, Progress and Present State of All the British Colonies on the Continent and Islands of America*. 2 vols. London, 1708.

Oldschool, Oliver [James Mercer Garnett]. "Social Classification." *Southern Literary Messenger*, VII (March, 1841), 191–98.

Olmsted, Frederick Law. *A Journey in the Seaboard Slave States in the Years 1853–1854 with Remarks on their Economy*. Introduction by William P. Trent. 2 vols. New York, 1904.

Ormond, John Raper. "Some Recent Products of the New School of Southern Fiction." *South Atlantic Quarterly*, III (1904), 285–89.

Osborne, William S. Introduction to *Swallow Barn; or, A Sojourn in the Old Dominion*, by John Pendleton Kennedy. New York, 1962.

Osterweis, Rollin G. *The Myth of the Lost Cause, 1865–1900*. Hamden, Conn., 1973.

———. *Romanticism and Nationalism in the Old South*. New Haven, 1949.

Owsley, Frank Lawrence. *Plain Folk of the Old South*. Baton Rouge, 1949.

Page, Rosewell. *Thomas Nelson Page: A Memoir of a Virginia Gentleman*. New York, 1923.

Page, Thomas Nelson. *Address at the Three Hundredth Anniversary of the Settlement of Jamestown*. Richmond, 1919.

———. *Gordon Keith*. New York, 1903.

———. *In Ole Virginia; or, Marse Chan and Other Stories*. 1887; rpr. Chapel Hill, 1969.

———. Introduction to the Plantation Edition. *In Ole Virginia*. New York, 1908. Vol. I of *The Novels, Stories, Sketches, and Poems of Thomas Nelson Page*. 18 vols.

———. *John Marvel, Assistant*. New York, 1909. Vols. XV–XVI of *The Novels, Stories, Sketches, and Poems of Thomas Nelson Page*. 18 vols.

———. *The Negro: The Southerner's Problem*. New York, 1904.

———. *The Old Dominion: Her Making and Her Manners*. New York, 1910, Vol. XIII of *The Novels, Stories, Sketches, and Poems of Thomas Nelson Page*. 18 vols.

———. *The Old South: Essays Social and Political*. New York, 1892.

———. *The Old South: Essays Social and Political*. New York, 1906. Vol. XII of *The Novels, Stories, Sketches and Poems of Thomas Nelson Page*. 18 vols.

———. *Red Rock: A Chronicle of Reconstruction*. New York, 1899.

Parrington, Vernon L. *The Romantic Revolution in America, 1800–1860.* New York, 1927. Vol. II of his *The Main Currents of American Thought: An Interpretation of American Literature from the Beginnings to 1920.* 3 vols.

Paulding, James Kirke. *Letters from the South, Written During an Excursion in the Summer of 1816.* 2 vols. New York, 1817.

Peirce, Neal R. *The Border South States: People, Politics, and Power in the Five Border South States.* New York, 1975.

Pollard, Edward Alfred. *The Lost Cause: A New Southern History of the War of the Confederates.* New York, 1866.

Pulley, Raymond H. *Old Virginia Restored: An Interpretation of the Progressive Impulse, 1870–1930.* Charlottesville, 1968.

Randolph, Edmund. *History of Virginia.* Edited by Arthur H. Shaffer. Charlottesville, 1970.

Raper, Julius Rowan. *From the Sunken Garden: The Fiction of Ellen Glasgow, 1916–1945.* Baton Rouge, 1980.

———. *Without Shelter: The Early Career of Ellen Glasgow.* Baton Rouge, 1971.

Reid, James. "The Religion of the Bible and the Religion of K[ing] W[illiam] County Compared." In *The Colonial Virginia Satirist: Mid–Eighteenth Century Commentaries on Politics, Religion, and Society,* edited by Richard Beale Davis. Philadelphia, 1967.

Review of *Red Rock,* by Thomas Nelson Page. *Atlantic Monthly,* LXXXIII (1899), 519–21.

Review of *Red Rock,* by Thomas Nelson Page. *Nation,* March 2, 1899, p. 167.

Ridgely, Joseph V. *John Pendleton Kennedy.* New York, 1966.

———. *Nineteenth Century Southern Literature.* Lexington, Ky., 1980.

Riley, Edward Miles, ed. *The Journal of John Hanover: An Indentured Servant in the Colony of Virginia, 1773–1776.* Williamsburg, 1963.

Rouse, Blair, ed. *Letters of Ellen Glasgow.* New York, 1958.

Rouse, Parke. *James Blair of Virginia.* Chapel Hill, 1971.

Rubin, Louis D., Jr. *The Faraway Country: Writers of the Modern South.* Seattle, 1963.

———. "The Image of an Army: The Civil War in Southern Fiction." In *Southern Writers: Appraisals in Our Time,* edited by R. C. Simonini, Jr. Charlottesville, 1964.

———. *No Place on Earth: Ellen Glasgow, James Branch Cabell, and Richmond-in-Virginia.* Austin, 1973.

———. "Notes on a Rear-Guard Action." In *The Idea of the South: Pursuit of a Central Theme,* edited by Frank E. Vandiver. Chicago, 1964.

———. "Two in Richmond: Ellen Glasgow and James Branch Cabell." In *South: Modern Southern Literature in Its Cultural Setting,* edited by Louis D. Rubin, Jr., and Robert D. Jacobs. Garden City, N.Y., 1961.

———. *Virginia: A Bicentennial History.* New York, 1977.

Russell, William Howard. *My Diary North and South*. Edited by Fletcher Pratt. 1863; rpr. New York, 1954.

Savage, Henry. *Seeds of Time: The Background of Southern Thinking*. New York, 1959.

Schorer, Mark. "The Necessity of Myth." In *Myth and Mythmaking*, edited by Henry A. Murray. New York, 1960.

Scott, Anne Firor. *The Southern Lady: From Pedestal to Politics, 1830–1930*. Chicago, 1970.

Sealts, Merton M., Jr., ed. *The Journals and Miscellaneous Notebooks of Ralph Waldo Emerson*. Vol V of 12 vols. Cambridge, Mass., 1965.

Sedgwick, Henry Dwight. *In Praise of Gentlemen*. Boston, 1935.

Sherman, Stuart. "The Fighting Edge of Romance." Review of *Barren Ground*, by Ellen Glasgow. *New York Herald Tribune Books*, April 19, 1925, pp. 1–3.

Simkins, Francis Butler. *The Everlasting South*. Baton Rouge, 1963.

———. "Tolerating the South's Past." In *Myth and Southern History*, edited by Patrick Gerster and Nicholas Cords. Chicago, 1974.

Simpson, Lewis P. *The Dispossessed Garden: Pastoral and History in Southern Literature*. Athens, 1975.

Singal, Daniel Joseph. *The War Within: From Victorian to Modernist Thought in the South, 1919–1945*. Chapel Hill, 1982.

Singleton, Arthur. *Letters from the South and West*. Boston, 1824.

Smith, Francis Hopkinson. *Colonel Carter of Cartersville*. 1891; rpr. Saddle River, N.J., 1970.

Smith, Henry Nash. "The South and the Myth of the Garden." In *Myth and Southern History*, edited by Patrick Gerster and Nicholas Cords. Chicago, 1974.

———. *Virgin Land: The American West as Symbol and Myth*. Cambridge, 1950.

"Southern Literature." *Scribner's Monthly*, XXII (1881), 785–86.

Stampp, Kenneth M. *The Peculiar Institution: Slavery in the Antebellum South*. New York, 1968.

Stith, William. *The History of the First Discovery and Settlement of Virginia*. 1747; rpr. New York, 1865.

Styron, William. *The Confessions of Nat Turner*. New York, 1967.

———. *Lie Down in Darkness*. Indianapolis, 1951.

———. *Set This House on Fire*. New York, 1960.

———. *Sophie's Choice*. New York, 1979.

Sydnor, Charles S. *The Development of Southern Sectionalism, 1819–1848*. Baton Rouge, 1948.

———. *Gentlemen Freeholders: Political Practices in Washington's Virginia*. Chapel Hill, 1952.

———. *Political Leadership in Eighteenth-Century Virginia*. Oxford, 1951.

Tales of an American Landlord; Containing Sketches of Life South of the Potomac. 2 vols. New York, 1824.

Tate, Allen. *The Fathers.* New York, 1938.

———. "A Southern Mode of the Imagination." In his *Collected Essays.* Denver, 1959.

Taylor, John. *Arator: Being a Series of Agricultural Essays Practical and Political.* 5th ed. Petersburg, Va., 1818.

Taylor, William R. *Cavalier and Yankee: The Old South and American National Character.* New York, 1961.

Thackeray, William Makepeace. *The Virginians: A Tale of the Eighteenth Century.* 1855–59; rpr. New York, 1923.

Tiernan, Charles B. *The Tiernan Family in Maryland.* Baltimore, 1898.

Tiernan, Mary Spear. *Homoselle.* Boston, 1881.

———. *Jack Horner.* Boston, 1890.

———. *Suzette: A Novel.* New York, 1885.

Tindall, George Brown. *The Emergence of the New South, 1913–1945.* Baton Rouge, 1967.

———. "Mythology: A New Frontier in Southern History." In *The Idea of the South: Pursuit of a Central Theme*, edited by Frank E. Vandiver. Chicago, 1964.

"To the Printer." *Virginia Gazette.* Edited by William Hunter. No. 28, July 11, 1751, p. 1.

Tourgée, Albion W. "The South as a Field for Fiction." *Forum*, VI (1888), 404–13.

Tragle, Henry Irving. *The Southampton Slave Revolt of 1831.* Amherst, Mass., 1971.

Trent, William Peterfield. *English Culture in Virginia.* Vols. 5–6 of Johns Hopkins University Studies in Historical and Political Science. 7th series. Edited by Herbert B. Adams. Baltimore, 1889.

———. "Tendencies of Higher Life in the South." *Atlantic Monthly*, LXXIX (1897), 766–78.

Tucker, George. *A Century Hence; or, A Romance of 1941.* Edited by Donald R. Noble. Charlottesville, 1977.

———. *Essays on Various Subjects of Taste, Morals, and National Policy, by a Citizen of Virginia.* Georgetown, D.C., 1822.

[Tucker, George?]. *Letters from Virginia, Translated from the French.* Baltimore, 1816.

———. *The Valley of Shenandoah; or, The Memoirs of the Graysons.* 1824; rpr. Chapel Hill, 1970.

Tucker, Nathaniel Beverley. *The Partisan Leader: A Tale of the Future.* 1836; rpr. Chapel Hill, 1971.

Turnbull, Andrew. *Scott Fitzgerald.* New York, 1962.

Van Auken, Sheldon. "The Southern Historical Novel in the Early Twentieth Century." *Journal of Southern History*, XIV (1948), 157–91.

Vandiver, Frank E. "The Confederate Myth." In *Myth and Southern History*, edited by Patrick Gerster and Nicholas Cords. Chicago, 1974.

Voegelin, Eric. "Gnosticism: The Nature of Modernity." In *Did You Ever See a Dream Walking? American Conservative Thought in the Twentieth Century*, edited by William F. Buckley, Jr. Indianapolis, 1970.

Wagenknecht, Edward. "The World and Mary Johnston." *Sewanee Review*, XLIV (1936), 188–206.

Wecter, Dixon. *The Hero in America: A Chronicle of Hero Worship*. New York, 1941.

Weld, Isaac. *Travels Through the State of North America and the Provinces of Upper and Lower Canada*. 2 vols. 1799; rpr. New York, 1970.

Wells, Arvin R. *Jesting Moses: A Study in Cabellian Comedy*. Gainesville, Fla., 1962.

Wertenbaker, Thomas Jefferson. *Patrician and Plebeian in Virginia; or, The Origin and Development of the Social Classes of the Old Dominion*. 1910; rpr. New York, 1959.

Wilkinson, J. Harvie. *Harry Byrd and the Changing Face of Virginia Politics, 1945–1966*. Charlottesville, 1968.

Williams, T. Harry. "Romance and Realism in Southern Politics." In *Myth and Southern History*, edited by Patrick Gerster and Nicholas Cords. Chicago, 1974.

Wilson, Edmund. "James Branch Cabell: 1879–1958." In his *The Bit Between My Teeth: A Literary Chronicle of 1950–1965*. New York, 1965.

———. "The James Branch Cabell Case Reopened." In his *The Bit Between My Teeth: A Literary Chronicle of 1950–1965*. New York, 1965.

———. *Patriotic Gore: Studies in the Literature of the American Civil War*. New York, 1962.

Wirt, William. *The Letters of a British Spy*. 1803; rpr. Chapel Hill, 1970.

Wister, Owen. *The Virginian: A Horseman of the Plains*. New York, 1904.

Woodward, C. Vann. *American Counterpoint: Slavery and Racism in the North-South Dialogue*. Boston, 1971.

———. *The Burden of Southern History*. Baton Rouge, 1960.

———. *Origins of the New South, 1877–1913*. Baton Rouge, 1951.

Wright, Louis B. *The Cultural Life of the American Colonies, 1607–1763*. New York, 1957.

———. *The First Gentlemen of Virginia: Intellectual Qualities of the Early Colonial Ruling Class*. San Marino, Calif., 1940.

———, ed. *Letters of Robert Carter, 1720–1727: The Commercial Interests of a Virginia Gentleman*. San Marino, Calif., 1940.

———, ed. *The Prose Works of William Byrd of Westover: Narratives of a Colonial Virginian*. Cambridge, Mass., 1966.

Wyatt-Brown, Bertram. *Southern Honor: Ethics and Behavior in the Old South*. New York, 1982.

Zinn, Howard. *The Southern Mystique*. New York, 1964.

INDEX

Abdy, Edward, 61
Abolitionists, 101, 146
Adams, Henry, 13, 30, 159
Adams, John, 271
Addison, Joseph, 86–87. See also
 Spectator
Adventures of Huckleberry Finn, The, 85,
 93. *See also* Twain, Mark

Bagby, George W., 37–40
Baldwin, Joseph Glover, 65–66
Berger, Yves, 30–31
Beverley, Robert, 35–36, 51
Black characterization, 75–76, 167–68,
 190, 191–93, 194, 201–202, 208,
 254–59. *See also* Slavery
Blair, James, 35
Bontemps, Arna, 193
Boone, Daniel, 129
Bridenbaugh, Carl, 6, 21, 43, 44, 46, 51
Brissot de Warville, Jacques, 60
Bruce, Philip Alexander, 40
Buckley, William F., 12
Bullock, William, 34–35
Bumppo, Natty, xii. *See also* Cooper,
 James Fenimore; Leatherstocking
Bunyan, Paul, xii
Bush, Ishmael, 93
Byrd, Harry Flood, 247, 248, 249
Byrd, William, 44, 47, 55–58

Cabell, James Branch, 222–33; as southern literary pioneer, 220–21; relation
 to Virginia's past, 221–22; critical reputation of, 223; fictional world view of,
 223–25; use of Confederate myth,
 225–26; rejection of present in, 232–
 33; compared with William Styron,
 250; and the "Virginia mystique,"
 273–74; mentioned, xi, 197, 237, 241,
 242, 243, 249, 250, 253, 269
—works of: *Beyond Life*, 220, 221; *The
 Biography of the Life of Manuel*, 223,
 226; *The Cords of Vanity*, 226; *The
 Cream of the Jest*, 224–25, 226, 232;

Figures of Earth, 228, 230, 232; *The
 High Place*, 232; *Jurgen*, 223, 232; *Let
 Me Lie*, 218–19, 225–26, 237–38;
 Preface to the Past, 227; *The Silver Stallion*, 226, 232; *Smirt*, 220. See also
 Rivet in Grandfather's Neck, The
Cable, George Washington, 162, 168
Carr, William, 44
Carter, Landon, 109–10
Carter, Robert "King," 53–55
Caruthers, William Alexander, 112–30;
 life of, 113; *A Kentuckian in New York*,
 113–14; and American nationalism,
 129; and southern sectionalism, 149–
 50; and limitations of the Cavalier,
 150–51; mentioned, x, 5, 33, 76, 102,
 144, 145, 146, 149, 164, 167, 199,
 204, 209, 269, 270, 271. See also *Cavaliers of Virginia, The; Knights of the
 Golden Horseshoe, The*
Cash, Wilbur J., 7, 24, 41
Cavalier ideal: migration of, 7, 14–15;
 contemporary appeal of, 9, 13; appeal
 to southerners, 10; appeal to northerners, 10–11; opposed to Yankee
 ideal, 12; and repudiation of modern
 culture, 12, 30–31; and nineteenth-
 century northern writers, 12–13; and
 modern northern writers, 17–24; influence on cowboy hero, 27; and European fiction, 27–31; as instrument of
 social criticism, 30; and modern historical scholarship, 41–47; and per-
 sistence of appeal, 58; and the doomed
 aristocrat, 99; and antebellum medieval
 revival, 103–106; and chivalric love,
 111; in contemporary Virginia, 112;
 and abolitionists, 146; and antebellum
 reactionism, 146–51; and postbellum
 romanticism, 154; and Lost Cause
 myth, 158; postbellum northern popularity of, 158–60; and postbellum
 women writers, 185–97; failure associated with, 269; relation to national culture, 269–70; and defense of slavery,

293